iPad® 2

FULLY LOADED

Alan Hess

WILEY

Wiley Publishing, Inc.

iPad® 2 Fully Loaded by Alan Hess

Published by
Wiley Publishing, Inc.
10475 Crosspoint Boulevard
Indianapolis, IN 46256
Copyright © 2011 by Wiley Publishing, Inc., Indianapolis, Indiana

Published simultaneously in Canada

ISBN: 978-1-118-09319-1

Manufactured in the United States of America

10 9 8 7 6 5 4 3 2 1

For general information on our other products and services or to obtain technical support, please contact our Customer Care Department within the U.S. at (800) 762-2974, outside the U.S. at (317) 572-3993 or fax (317) 572-4002.

Wiley also publishes its books in a variety of electronic formats and by print-on-demand. Some content that appears in standard print versions of this book may not be available in other formats. For more information about Wiley products, visit us at **www.wiley.com**.

Library of Congress Control Number: 2011924912

About the Author

ALAN HESS

Alan is a San Diego-based photographer and author, specializing in concert and event photography. He has also photographed everything from portraits to products. He is the author of the *iPad Fully Loaded* and four Digital Field Guides: *The Composition Digital Field Guide*, *The Exposure Digital Field Guide*, the *Sony A200 Digital Field Guide* and the *Sony A700 Digital Field Guide*. His concert and backstage images appear in numerous online and print publications, and they've been used for promotional purposes, including music packaging.

Alan has written for *Photoshop User Magazine* and teaches concert photography and the Basics of Exposure and Composition at Photoshop World.

He is a huge computer nut and tends to live on the bleeding edge of technology. A long-time Apple user, Alan eagerly awaits the announcement every year from Cupertino and has been an iPod, iPhone and iPad user from the day these devices were released.

Alan can be contacted through his website, **www.alanhessphotography.com**, where he publishes a regular blog, and you can follow Alan on Twitter, where he goes by **ShotLivephoto**.

Credits

Acquisitions Editor
Courtney Allen

Project Editor
Jenny Larner Brown

Technical Editor
Garth Murphy

Copy Editor
Jenny Larner Brown

Editorial Manager
Robyn Siesky

Business Manager
Amy Knies

Senior Marketing Manager
Sandy Smith

Vice President and Executive Group Publisher
Richard Swadley

Vice President and Publisher
Barry Pruett

Book Designer
Erik Powers

Acknowledgments

I first and foremost want to thank my wife, parents, brothers, sisters-in-law, nephews and nieces for their patience with me as I wrote this book. The schedule was really tight this time around, and I know I practically vanished into the world of iPads, Apple and Apps for the month of March.

To Courtney, Jenny and Erik, it was great working with you again. Thanks for keeping up with the crazy schedule I set and producing a book I'm very proud of. I want to thank Garth for joining the team on this edition and making sure that I got the technical stuff right. Any mistakes are mine, not his.

To all my really helpful followers on Twitter who came up with sug-gestions, answers and some interesting questions—I thank you for all of it. Special thanks to Moose, William, Michelle, Mike, RC, Ken and Josh for always seeming to have the right answer ... or at least the right question at the right time. Thanks again to all of you.

A very special thank you to Glyn Dewis and Dave Clayton. Both of these fine gentlemen have helped spread the word about my books and photography in the United Kingdom.

And as always, a very special thanks to my wife Nadra who no longer minds that I carry my iPad around with me everywhere, because she now does the same thing with the iPad 2.

Contents

 Contents

For Nadra

Introduction

I have used my iPad every day since it first came out. And it's been great. On a quick road trip with my brother in December 2010, I didn't even bother to take my laptop. I just used my iPad ... without regret. So when Apple announced a media event on March 2, 2011, to announce the iPad 2, I hoped to soon be using a newer, faster, thinner, lighter iPad. Dreams come true, my friends!

So Apple announced the iPad 2 ... along with a new version of the mobile Operating System iOS 4 that runs the iPad (and the iPhone, iPod Touch and Apple TV). The new iPad, unsurprisingly called the *iPad 2*, is a major upgrade over the original version of the device, and it comes with not one ... but two cameras!

The original iPad is considered one of the biggest success stories in the world of consumer electronics, and the iPad 2 looks to keep that trend going. The addition of the aforementioned two cameras, along with a faster processor and more memory, makes the second generation of iPad a big step up from the original.

But that doesn't mean this book is only for people who have the iPad 2. Although we cover some content that is only available on the iPad 2, most of the information in this book applies to both devices. The real differences relate to video and taking photographs, because the new iPad has two cameras and the original version has none. But don't worry, I point out these differences when they apply.

This is the second edition of this book, and it doesn't offer the same information as the first version. Instead, I wanted to update what I consider to be important apps and add information on a variety of specific applications for the iPad, including remote desktop access, travel, entertainment, social media, sports and education.

I talked to iPad users and asked what they wanted to see in a second edition. These are the subjects that they wanted to see. I also talked to folks about iPad uses while in line to buy the iPad 2. Yes, I buy my iPads at the Apple Store and don't get anything for free or from Apple. That allows me to tell you exactly what I think works well ... what apps I like ... without influence.For the record, my iPad 2 is the White, 32 GB version that has Wi-Fi + 3G on the AT&T network.

The basic premise of this book remains unchanged. It's a book about iPad content: music, videos, photos, eBooks, PDFs, word documents, Internet radio, and even Facebook and Twitter. All of this is part of your iPad experience.

And before we get started... the iPad 2 comes in eighteen versions. Yes, you read that right, there are *eighteen* different iPads. Actually, that's a little misleading. There are actually nine different iPads, but each can be purchased in either black or white. Those nine different models can be further broken down into two types of iPad: Those that are Wi-Fi-enabled only and those that are Wi-Fi- and 3G-enabled.

The Wi-Fi + 3G iPads come in two different versions: Those that run on the AT&T network and those that run on the Verizon network. It is important to pick the right iPad 2 up front, because you can't change the carrier later. Finally, each of the iPad models comes in three different memory sizes: 16GB, 32GB and 64GB.

As with the first generation iPad, the iPad 2 comes with a 9.7-inch diagonal touch screen display, weighs about 1.3 lbs and is roughly a third of an inch thick. The iPad 2 is actually thinner than the current iPhone 4. This book will cover both the Wi-Fi and the Wi-Fi+3G models along with the pros and cons of each.

THE WI-FI-ONLY VERSION

The Wi-Fi-only version of the iPad 2 has a built-in 802.11a/b/g/n chip. So you can connect it to the fastest Wi-Fi networks: the 802.11n networks.

The iPad 2 can function great without being on a network at all, but certain functions will not be available unless you are online. For example, I can easily read an iBook, watch a movie or TV show, take and edit video and photos, write a paper, create a spreadsheet, and even work on a presentation … all without being actively connected to the Internet.

The functions that require an Internet connection include using the Mail app; web browsing; accessing the iTunes Store, App Store and the iBooks Store; and operating many apps. All this means is that using the iPad away from a Wi-Fi network can take a little planning. You need to make sure that you load your iPad with all the content you'll need until you find a Wi-Fi access point.

WI-FI + 3G VERSION

The Wi-Fi + 3G version of the iPad costs more than the Wi-Fi-only model. This makes sense, because the Wi-Fi + 3G version does more. Primarily, it connects to 3G networks, which offers much more functionality.

Yet there is another cost, and this is the price of the data plan you have to buy to access the 3G network. With the original iPad, you were limited to the AT&T 3G network. But with the release of the iPad 2, you can know pick AT&T or Verizon as the cellular data provider. The only caveat is that you have to make that decision before purchasing the device. For the technical-minded folks out there, here are the specs for 3G iPad 2 versions:

AT&T: UMTS/HSDPA/HSUPA (850, 900, 1900, 2100 MHz); GSM/EDGE (850, 900, 1800, 1900 MHz)

Verizon: CDMA EV-DO Rev. A (800, 1900 MHz)

It's important to discuss the data plans needed to take advantage of the 3G cellular network. The good news is that you don't have to sign up for a long-term data plan. The bad news is that if you use the iPad 2 on the road a lot, the data plan can set you back a pretty penny … especially over the long term.

Wi-Fi Only	16 GB	32 GB	64 GB
	Black - $499.00	Black - $599.00	Black - $699.00
	White - $499.00	White - $599.00	White - $599.00

Wi-Fi + 3G	16 GB	32 GB	64 GB
AT&T	Black - $629.00	Black - $729.00	Black - $829.00
AT&T	White - $629.00	White - $729.00	White - $829.00
Verizon	Black - $629.00	Black - $729.00	Black - $829.00
Verizon	White - $629.00	White - $729.00	White - $829.00

These prices are for iPad 2 sold in the United States at product launch.

AT&T

There were originally only two options for data here in USA through AT&T. You could get either 250MB for 30 days for $14.99 or a 2GB plan for $25 per 30 days. If you chose the smaller data plan and exceeded it, you'd get an additional 250 MB for another $14.99. If you exceeded the bigger data plan, you'd purchase an additional 1GB for $10.

So, if you have the cheapest data plan and don't go over the 250 MB per 30 days, it'll cost you $179.88 per year. If you go with the bigger data plan and stick to the 2GB per 30 days, it totals about $300 a year.

AT&T has started to offer a different type of data plan. The pricing is the same for the basic plan; but instead of paying for the data separately on a credit card, the data plan is part of your wireless bill. This is the AT&T postpaid plan and it has a real bonus: You can add an extra 1GB to the data plan at $10 per GB.

Verizon

Verizon offers four different data plans for the iPad 2. And depending on how you use the device, these might offer you a better choice than the AT&T plans. I hope that the competition between the two carriers will lower the price of the data plans in the long run, but right now these are the Verizon plans. All plans are pay as you go for 30-day periods.

1GB for $25 | 3GB for $35

5GB for $50 | 10GB for $80

Total Cost of iPad Use

All this adds up. A 16GB iPad with Wi-Fi and 3G goes for $629.00. Add to that the big data plan, and you can spend more than $1200 in 24 months of using your iPad. Yeah, iPads aren't cheap.

One nice thing about the data plans is that they run for 30 days and not per the calendar month.

So if you need a data plan and sign up for one, then you have 30 days for data. Each country has its own plans and providers, so check in your area. But do the math first, so you're prepared for the hidden costs and understand the true overall price you're paying for data.

It's also important to know that the data plans are set to automatically renew. So unless you travel frequently in areas without Wi-Fi service, you might want to turn off the auto renew. Check with your data provider on how to do this.

Another thing you need to know about using the 3G data plan: It has a limit. You can't download more than 20MB at a time over the 3G network. This means it's not possible to download movies or TV shows on your iPad unless you're connected to a Wi-Fi network. There are also some apps that are too big to be downloaded via the 3G network and thus require Wi-Fi. Watch for notes about this.

TAP, TAP, TAP … READY YET?

One last thing: A term that's used over and over in this book is *Tap*. Since the iPad is controlled with your fingers, all you do is tap on menu choices or icons to select them. There is no mouse, so there's no way to click on anything on your iPad.

Also, when I refer to the device as *the iPad* in this book, it includes the original iPad and the new iPad 2. If I specifically call the device the iPad 2, then the information is for the updated version only.

Alright. Those are the basics.
Now, let's get started …

PART 1

Content Basics

Operating System and File Types

The Skim

When people talk about the difference between PCs and Apple computers, they are really discussing the differences in operating systems. Windows is an operating system; so is Mac OSX. Although Apple doesn't consider the iPad a computer—instead, the company calls it a post-PC device—the reality is that the iPad needs an operating system to run, and it's called iOS by Apple.

When the original iPad shipped, it came loaded with iOS 3.2, which was updated to iOS 3.2.1 in July of 2010 … and then up to 3.2.2 in August of 2010. The iPhone, iPod Touch and iPad finally got the same iOS when Apple released iOS 4.2.1 in November 2010. Now, they all come with iOS 4.3, which offers some key improvements.

iOS 4.3

Without an operating system, the iPad is just a fancy-looking piece of glass and metal. It's the operating system that gives the device its functionality. And the cool part is that as Apple updates the operating system, the company continues to add more features to the iPad. For

Figure 1-1
These are the preloaded apps on the iPad 2.

example, folders, multitasking and AirPrint were not part of the operating system when the first iPad came out, but these valuable features were added later in an operating system update.

Multi-Touch

The first thing to cover here is the Multi-Touch interface, because the only input device needed for the iPad is a finger moving around the screen. Your finger controls everything on the iPad. You tap on an app to open it; you can swipe your finger across the screen to move from one page to the next; and there's the very cool pinch-to-zoom feature—which refers to how users control the screen view. Moving your fingers closer together zooms out; moving them further apart zooms in.

Manage Apps

When you first turn on your iPad, you'll see that Apple has preloaded it with some apps:

- Calendar
- Contacts
- Notes
- Maps
- Videos
- YouTube
- iTunes
- App Store
- Game Center
- FaceTime
- Camera
- Photo Booth
- Settings
- Safari
- Mail
- Photos
- iPod

You may even notice that three of these iPad 2 apps—FaceTime, Camera and Photo Booth—don't appear on the original iPad.

While none of these preinstalled apps can be deleted from your iPad, they can be moved around. And any other app that you install can be deleted at any time. The method for moving and deleting apps is the same. Just hold your finger on top of any app until the apps start to wiggle. Once that happens, you can rearrange the apps by moving them to the place you want. To move an app from one page to the next, just hold your finger on the app you want to move and slide it to the left or right until it is at the edge of the screen. After a few seconds, the screen will change to the next or previous page, depending on which side of the screen you're touching.

Delete an app by clicking on the little x on the top left of the app. Notice that the pre-loaded apps don't have the x, because they can't be deleted.

It is also possible to move and delete the apps in iTunes.

1. Plug your iPad into your computer and launch iTunes.

2. Select the iPad from the Device list on the left.

3. Click on the Apps tab at the top of the screen. This will show the apps installed and will allow you to move them around.

4. When the mouse hovers over an app, a small x will appear on the top left. Click on the x to remove the app from your iPad.

Multitasking

The original iPad was enhanced with multi-tasking when the iOS was upgraded to 4.2. And this made a HUGE difference to the iPad's functionality. It allows for fast app switching.

Figure 1-2

The apps that can be deleted have an x at the top left of the icon, which becomes visible when you hold your finger on the app icon for a few seconds. Notice that the x appears on the Dropbox app but not on the preinstalled Settings app right next to it.

The multitask bar, accessed by double tapping the Home button, controls this feature on the iPad. When you double tap the Home button, the main screen slides up, revealing the multitask bar. This is where the iOS keeps a list of recently used apps.

You can easily switch between apps by tapping on the icon of the app you want to resume. When in portrait orientation, the iPad shows the six most recently used apps. When it's in landscape orientation, it shows seven apps. When viewing the multitask bar, you can also

Figure 1-3

Tapping the Home button twice brings up the multitasking dock. Swiping sideways scrolls through the recently used apps. You can lock the orientation on this dock as well. If the side switch is set to orientation lock, then this is where the Mute button will be.

swipe to the left, which will show the following controls instead of the most recently used apps:

• Orientation Lock

• Brightness Control

• iPod Play Controls (back, play/ pause and next)

• Volume Control

• iPod App Icon

When you double click on the Home button and switch apps, what's happening is that all the apps are suspended while those that need to operate in the background (like the music playing apps) will keep running ... as long as there is enough memory. The good news is that the iPad 2 has twice the memory of the original iPad, so these apps should run even better. When you pick an app to resume, it does so from where

it left off—assuming that the developer has enabled this type of fast switching.

Folders

A folder in iOS is just a way of grouping apps. The iPad screen can show 26 apps at one time. That is, it can show twenty on the screen and six in the dock at the bottom of the screen. That means, when you install app number 27, you'll have to use a second page. And trust me, apps add up fast. I try to keep the number of apps on my iPad at a minimum, and I still have about ten pages of them.

Folders allow you to group apps and access them by tapping on the folder icon that then opens to show the apps inside. You can create and populate the folders on the iPad or in iTunes when the iPad is connected to the computer. Up to 20 apps can be stored in a single folder. Creating a folder is simplicity itself. To create a folder on the iPad:

1. Turn on the iPad.

2. Place your finger on any app and hold it there until all the apps start to wiggle.

3. Place your finger on an app that you wish to group with another app and slide it so that the one app is on top of the second app.

4. As if by magic, the two apps will suddenly become a folder with a title that iPad creates, based on the category of the apps. Many times this title will be accurate, but you can edit it at any time.

5. You can now slide other apps into the folder by dragging them there.

6. When you want to run an app that's in a folder, tap on the folder and then tap on the app you want to run. It's that easy.

Figure 1-4
A folder full of productivity tools, including the iWork apps (Pages, Numbers, Keynote) and more helps me quickly find the programs I need.

To create a folder using the computer:

1. Connect the iPad to the computer and launch iTunes.

2. Select the iPad from the Device list on the left.

3. Click on the Apps section.

4. On the screens view, on the right side of the window, find the apps you want to group in the same folder.

5. Use the mouse to drag one app onto another to create a folder.

6. You can now edit or add a name for the folder, if needed.

Unlike apps, you can't just delete folders. Instead, you have to delete or remove the apps from the folder. Just hold your finger on an app in the folder until it starts to wiggle. Then either move it out of the folder or tap the x in the top corner. Once the folder is empty, it will automatically be removed.

Accessibility

Apple is really proud of the accessibility options in its devices, and the iPad is no different. These options include:

- VoiceOver
- Zoom
- Large Text
- White on Black Text
- Mono Audio
- Speak Auto-Text
- Easy activation of accessibility options by triple clicking the Home button.

Note that these options are turned off as a default setting.

To access the accessibility options, turn on your iPad and tap on Settings. Then tap on General. Finally, tap Accessibility.

- The **VoiceOver** tool speaks the items on the screen. When you turn on VoiceOver, it directs the iPad to read aloud whatever you tap on the screen. With VoiceOver activated, you need to double tap to open an app (instead of a single tap), and you use three fingers to scroll (instead of using a single finger). You can also turn on the Speak Hints option, which gives you voice directions for most situations. You can change the rate of the speech, use phonetics and even change the pitch of the voice. It's also possible to tell the voice to give you typing feedback. That is, it actually speaks out the characters and words as your type. This tool can also adapt to Braille devices and control the Web Rotor and Language Rotor.

- The **Zoom** function allows you to magnify the whole screen at any time. When the zoom function is turned on, a double tap with three fingers zooms in; a second

Figure 1-5

The Large Text option is great for people who need a little help seeing small text.

double tap will zoom back out. To move around the zoomed-in screen, just use three fingers to navigate. To change the amount of zoom, double tap the screen with three fingers, and drag up to zoom in or down to zoom out.

- The **Large Text** option makes the text appear larger in Mail and Notes. You can pick between 20pt, 24pt, 32pt, 40pt, 48pt and 56pt text. This is really great for those folks who find it tough to see the default size of text.

- **White on Black** Text changes the whole look of the iPad by reversing the colors. It makes the text white and background black. This high contrast is meant to help people with vision problems. But this can make the apps look really weird. Since it reverses all the colors, this makes everything look like an old film negative.

- **Mono Audio** changes the audio output from stereo to Mono.

- **Speak Auto-Text** is meant to automatically speak auto-corrections and auto-capitalizations. But in my tests, it didn't seem to do much of anything.

- **Triple-Click Home** allows you to decide what happens when you triple click the Home button. The options are:
  - Off
  - Toggle VoiceOver
  - Toggle White on Black
  - Ask

The Ask option allows you to pick between Turn VoiceOver On, Turn Zoom On, Turn White on Black On or Cancel … every time the Home button is triple clicked.

Figure 1-6

The Triple-Click Home button setting makes it easy to access VoiceOver, White on Black, and Zoom.

Figure 1-7
The AirPlay button shows that the Apple TV is present on the same network.

AirPlay

With AirPlay, you can stream music and video wirelessly from your iTunes or iPad to AirPlay-enabled speakers and receivers. AirPlay also allows you to stream content from your iPad (and iPhone and iPod Touch) to your HDTV using Apple TV. This means you can stream video footage from your iPad Photos app to your TV. And with the new built-in Camera on the iPad 2, you can shoot video and instantly share it.

I keep waiting for more AirPlay-enabled devices to show up, but right now the best is the $99 Apple TV. Once you have the Apple TV set up and on the same network as your iPad 2, you'll see an AirPlay button appear in apps that can use it.

Safari

Apple has updated Safari for iOS 4 by using a new Nitro JavaScript engine. According to Apple, this runs Safari twice as fast as previous versions. Find more on Safari in Chapter 11.

iTunes Home Sharing

This is a feature that I've been hoping for since the iPad was first released. Home Sharing allows you to play your entire iTunes library anywhere … as long as your devices are on the same network. So you can play your iTunes media that's stored on your Mac or PC on your iPad. You don't have to sync or download the info; it streams wirelessly from your computer to your iPad. There's much more on this in Chapter 6.

Side Switch

When the original iPad was released, the side switch was used to lock the screen orientation. Then Apple changed the side switch into a Mute button and moved the screen rotation lock to the multitasking menu. Now Apple has backtracked on this decision and is allowing the user to choose how the side switch is used.

For me, it will be used as a rotation lock, because that matches the way I use the iPad. But this is one of those cool little features that can make a big difference in how you use your iPad.

Change the function of the side switch in the Settings app under the General tab.

AirPrint

When the iPad was released, users talked about wanting to print right from the iPad. So Apple announced that this capability would be added with iOS 4.2; the new feature is called AirPrint.

This program allows you to print wirelessly from the iPad. But the part that is not so widely advertised is that AirPrint only works with a few printers—all 17 of them (listed on the Apple AirPrint website, **http://www.apple. com/ipad/features/airprint.html**) are HPs.

FILE TYPES

Any book about the iPad will obviously deal with many different apps, and this book is no different. But it also deals with the content on your iPad, and that means some coverage of file types. There are many different kinds of files used in this digital age. Many can be used on the iPad, but some can't. This holds true for both the original iPad and the iPad 2.

Image Files

The iPad is perfect for viewing images. These are the image file types that can be used on the iPad.

- The **JPEG** image type was created and named for the Joint Photographic Experts Group. It's a method of reducing the file size of an image while keeping the quality high. This image type is really common on the Internet, because it doesn't need any special software to be viewable. All web browsers and most e-mail programs will allow users to view JPEG images.

- The **TIFF** (Tagged Image File Format) is a method for saving images with no loss of image quality. This results in much larger file sizes than the same image as a JPEG; but because of its widespread acceptance, TIFF is supported natively on the iPad.

- The **GIF** (Graphics Interchange Format) is a bitmap image format and one of the default methods for presenting graphics on the Internet. The file quality can be very low, because the method used to create the small file size throws away a lot of the image's color information. GIF images are supported natively on the iPad.

- **RAW** image files are created by individual camera manufactures, so support for this type of file is hit or miss. RAW files for many cameras are supported. But keep in mind that RAW files can be rather large and therefore suck up the available memory on your iPad quickly.

PDF Files

PDF (Portable Document Format) files are used everywhere. PDFs are really useful, because they retain their formatting no matter what platform they're viewed on. Created originally in 1993 by Adobe Systems, the PDF format is independent of software and hardware ... and even operating systems. Better yet, in 2008 Adobe officially released the PDF as an open standard, meaning that there would be no proprietary software required to create or read this type of file.

You'll see a lot of uses for PDF files mentioned throughout this book. It can be used in many different apps, including iBooks and Mail. The business iWork applications on the iPad also use PDF files, and many of the document reader apps have PDF support built in. So if there is one file type that you should pay attention to, even at the expense of others, it is the PDF.

Business Files

These types of files are traditionally used in business, but they also apply to anyone who is in school or likes to/ needs to write or play with numbers ... or do presentations. Yes, they can used by nearly everyone at some point.

And before we dig into these files types, let me mention that the most basic type of file used for electronic text communication, whether it's personal or business, is a text file (.txt). This is the simplest file type and contains basic, clean text (no formatting) and no graphics. This is a good type of file to use when transferring text from one type of file to another using the cut-and-paste approach, because any code or program-specific formatting will be stripped away to help you avoid strange font and spacing issues.

The business files we'll cover here were created initially for use on either PCs or Macs. Yet the iPad can handle them all.

- **Word**
  There are actually two different types of Microsoft Word documents:

  - The first are files with the **.doc extension**, which represents older documents that go back all the way to Word for DOS and up to Word 97, 2000, 2003 and 2004 for Windows and Word 98, 2001X and 2004 for Mac.

  - The second type of Word file ends in the **.docx extension**. This is used by Word 2007 for the PC and Word 2008 for the Mac. It will be used by Microsoft going forward.

  The iPad supports both types of Word files natively and allows viewers to see these file types without any extra apps.

- **Excel**
  There are two Excel spreadsheet file types that the iPad can read and view without any extra help. These are the files that use the **.xls** and the **.xlsx extensions**. The older BIFF files need to be translated in Excel before they can be used on the iPad.

- **PowerPoint**
  As with Word and Excel, there are two different file PowerPoint file types that can be seen on the iPad. These are **.ppt** and the **.pptx** files.

- **RTF**
  Rich Text Documents (**.rtf**) is a file type created and owned by Microsoft that is used mainly inside Microsoft applications and when dealing with different operating systems, like Windows and Apple OS.

- **Pages**
  The iWork Pages application is Apple's version of a word processor. And since there is also a Pages app, it makes sense that all Pages documents can be seen natively on the iPad—even if you don't have the app installed.

- **Numbers**
  Numbers is the Apple iWork spreadsheet program, and all Numbers spreadsheets are viewable on the iPad. There is a Numbers app available on the iPad that allows iPad users to edit Numbers documents on the device.

- **Keynote**
  Along with Pages and Numbers, Keynote is part of the Apple iWork application. Presentations created in Keynote are viewable on the iPad in Mail without any extra software. There is a Keynote app that allows editing of Keynote files on the iPad, but it costs extra.

Book Files

The iPad makes a great electronic book reader; but to perform, it needs books. The format that the iBooks app uses for its electronic books is ePub. This is covered more in Chapter 5. But it's helpful to know that the iBooks app treats PDFs as books, so any PDF can be read inside of the iBooks app.

Newer versions of the Apple Pages app for the Mac allows you to export your documents as ePubs. This means you can create a file that will be treated as a book on the iPad. This comes in handy.

Audio Files

The iPad has built-in support for a ton of audio formats. This really isn't much of a surprise since the iPad is part of a long line of media players that began with the iPod—the most popular music player ever.

The following audio formats are supported on the iPad and can be played through the iTunes app.

- The Advanced Audio Coding (**AAC**) format (16 to 320 Kbps) is a standard lossy compression audio format that creates a smaller file by getting rid of some of the original's audio data.

- High-Efficiency Advanced Audio Coding (**HE-AAC V1**) is an extension of the AAC audio format. It's mainly used where every bit counts, such as situations in which small file sizes are better … as when streaming audio. Think *digital radio*.

- **Protected AAC** (from iTunes Store) is also a version of the AAC file. It's protected by a Digital Rights Management (DRM), so content bought through the iTunes Store can be played only on authorized devices.

- The **MP3** audio format uses a lossy data compression to make small audio files that still sound good. Many audiophiles claim that the loss of audio data harms the sound and that the tradeoff between size and quality just isn't worth it. But MP3 is still a very popular format … mainly because it's been around for a long time.

- **Audible** (formats 2, 3 and 4) is used for audio books.

- **Apple Lossless** is a lossless audio compression developed by Apple, usually with the extension of .m4a. This format has no DRM built in, but many think that this will

be added in the future. All Apple products, including the iPad, can play the Apple Lossless format with no problems.

- **AIFF** (Audio Interchange File Format) is an audio format developed in 1988 to store audio files on a personal computer. It was developed by Apple and is most used on Apple computers, so it's no surprise to see it supported here. The data in a standard AIFF file is uncompressed and therefore takes up more space than a compressed audio file.

- **WAV** (Waveform) is an audio format developed by Microsoft and IBM that's used for storing audio on PCs. The format is very similar to the AIFF format; it also stores audio in an uncompressed manner, resulting in retention of data as well as large file sizes.

Video Files

The iPad has a great screen and can be used to play back video in a variety of formats.

- **H.264** is a standard in video compression and it's used in a variety of applications, including YouTube videos and content purchased through the iTunes Store. The H.264 compression grew out of the need to provide good video quality at a much smaller file size than was available at the time of its creation. The H.264 standard encompasses a wide variety of video types. To get really technical for a moment, the actual limitations on playback on the iPad are: H.264 video up to 720p, 30 frames per second, Main Profile level 3.1. The files will be in the .m4v, .mp4, and .mov file formats.

- **MPEG-4** is a set of standards used for compressing video and audio that was agreed on by the Moving Pictures Experts

Group in 1998. The iPad can play MPEG-4 video up to 2.5 Mbps, 640 by 480 pixels, 30 frames per second with movies that use the following file extensions .m4v, .mp4 and .mov.

- **M-JPEG**, or Motion JPEG, is a video format in which the movie is compressed by consolidating each of the individual frames. It was originally developed for multimedia applications, but it's falling out of use as more advanced methods of compression replace it. On the iPad, M-JPEG movies can be up to 35 Mbps, 1280 by 720 pixels, 30 frames per second for files in the .avi format.

Contact Files

The Address Book on the iPad uses vCards (**.vcf**) to store contact information. These files allow you to send an individual contact's vCard by e-mail, and vCard files can then be viewed in Mail and added to your recipient's address book if wanted.

MOVING iPAD CONTENT

It's great to have content on your iPad or on your computer, but it's even better to be able to move that content from one device to another. And there are really only two methods of moving information. You can use the USB cable or a wireless transfer.

USB Cable

The iPad comes with a USB 2.0 cable that connects your iPad (or iPhone, iPod, …)—directly or through a dock—to your computer's USB port for syncing and charging. This is the fastest (and in some cases, the only) way to sync information between a computer and iPad.

SYNC VS TRANSFER

I know they sound the same, but there is a real difference between syncing your data and transferring info between a computer and iPad. *Syncing* is the process of transferring data from the computer to the iPad using iTunes. When you sync data, you install content on the iPad from the content that is in your iTunes library. This includes music, movies, TV shows, podcasts, audio books, iBooks and even photos. (Actually, the photos are transferred from iPhoto on the Mac or My Photos on the PC.)

When you *transfer* data from a computer to an iPad (or from an iPad to a computer), you move content that can be used on the iPad … but that isn't part of the iTunes library. This can include Word documents, PDFs, Excel spreadsheets, Comic files, image files and a host of other file types. These files can be transferred using the iPad's USB cable through iTunes as well as wirelessly over the network.

All the file transfers done with the USB cable are done through iTunes on the computer, and this can actually be quite difficult to find. The basic steps are below. Note: This is covered again later in the book, when we go through specific file transfers for specific programs, but it doesn't hurt to know where this is now.

1. Open iTunes on the computer.

2. Attach the USB cable to the computer and the iPad.

3. Select the iPad from the Device list on the left side of the iTunes window.

4. Select Apps from the tabs across the top of the screen.

5. Scroll down until you see the File Sharing window.

This is the area that allows you to transfer application-specific files on and off the iPad. The transfers happen without having to sync the device.

Wireless Transfer

There is no official method for syncing wirelessly between an iPad and a computer. What you *can* do wirelessly is transfer files to and from the iPad using a variety of third-party apps. Some of these work better than others, but all basically do the same thing. They allow file transfers to and from the iPad using a wireless connection.

My favorite app in this category is Dropbox, which allows users to access the same files whether they're working on their computer, the Internet or iPad. More on Dropbox in Chapter 3.

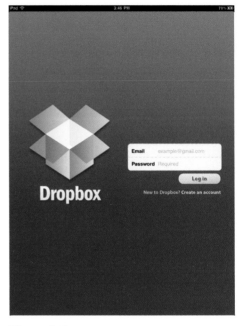

Figure 1-8
Here is the Dropbox login screen.

iTunes

The Skim

The ease of buying content for the iPad has really helped make this device successful. Being able to rent a movie, purchase a TV show or buy the latest music right from the iPad ... without having to attach the device to a computer ... is just fantastic.

It's true. There is a lot you can do with the iPad as a stand-alone device. But the iPad can't be used without first connecting it to a computer that's running iTunes. So you'll need to set up iTunes on your computer. Once that's done, you can get away with not using iTunes on your computer much.

This book is all about the iPad—not iTunes. (There are other books covering that.) But since the two are very closely related—there is an iTunes Store (on your computer) and an iTunes app (on the iPad)—both versions of iTunes need to be covered. I'll try to make it as short and sweet as possible.

THE BASICS

iTunes is a free application created by Apple for use on the Macs and PCs that store and play back your media. It's the all-in-one solution to playing music, movies, TV shows, audiobooks and podcasts on a

Figure 2-1
Download iTunes for free from the Apple iTunes website.

computer. Chances are, you already use iTunes and know a lot of the stuff I'm covering in this section. This information is here as a reminder.

The iTunes software that runs on your computer (Mac or PC) is a free program from Apple (**www.apple.com/itunes/**). This is basically a program that stores and organizes your media and allows it to be used on multiple devices (e.g., iPhone, iPod, iPad and Apple TV).

Part of the iTunes computer program is the iTunes Store, which is a retail site that's designed to sell media. It makes it very easy to get (in most cases, *purchase*) content in the form of music, movies, TV shows, audio books, apps and podcasts.

The iTunes Store makes it as simple as possible for you to spend money on content, but you don't actually have to buy anything from the iTunes Store, because there's plenty of free content available (e.g., podcasts and classes on iTunes University). Realistically though, at some point, you'll probably end up purchasing some content.

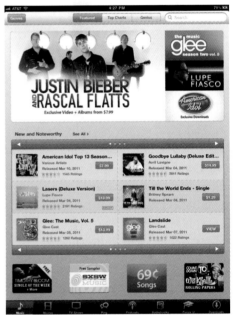

Figure 2-2
The Apple iTunes Store looks similar on the computer and on the iPad.

It's important to understand that there's a difference between the iTunes app on your computer that we've been talking about and the iTunes application on your iPad. On the iPad, the iTunes app *is* the iTunes Store; on the computer, the iTunes application, referenced as just iTunes, is used to play, organize, import

Figure 2-3
The separate App Store on the iPad looks like the App Store that's available in iTunes on the computer.

and control your media. Only a small part of iTunes on the computer is the iTunes Store.

Another big difference is that on the iPad, the App Store is not part of the iTunes Store; there is a separate App Store app and an electronic bookstore as part of the iBooks app. Neither is present on the computer at all. (See Chapter 5 for more information on the iBooks app.)

So, you may be asking, if there's an iTunes Store and an App Store on the iPad 2, why do you need iTunes on the computer?

Good question! There's a two-part answer. For starters, you need an easy way to get previously purchased content from your computer onto your iPad. iTunes provides this. The second part is that the iPad needs to be

synced to a single iTunes account to ensure that your purchased content is not shared among multiple accounts and/ or devices. This helps Apple keep the music, television and movie companies happy. Tying the iPad to a single iTunes account makes it easier to control content use.

ADD CONTENT TO iTUNES

There are different ways to add media to your iTunes library. The first and easiest is to buy the content directly from Apple through the iTunes Store (described a little later in this chapter). When you do, the media and all the information associated with it is loaded onto your computer and becomes accessible in iTunes. It's ready to go as soon as the transfer is complete.

NOTE

Just because the media file that you just loaded into iTunes will play in iTunes, don't assume it will play on your iPad. You may try to load a media file onto the iPad and iTunes will tell you that it couldn't transfer because the file isn't the right file type. There is help.

iTunes can convert most files, because it has access to Quick-Time and can use the code to create a compatible version. So if you get this messages, try clicking the Advanced tab to see what versions of the file iTunes can create. There will be a menu choice that reads: "Create iPad or Apple TV Version." Select this and be on your way. Apple will take care of the rest.

New Playlist	⌘N
New Playlist from Selection	⇧⌘N
New Playlist Folder	
New Smart Playlist...	⌥⌘N
Edit Smart Playlist	
Close Window	⌘W
Add to Library...	**⌘O**
Library	▶
Get Info	⌘I
Rating	▶
Show in Finder	⇧⌘R
Display Duplicates	
Sync "iPad 2"	

Figure 2-4
The iTunes File > Add to Library menu on your computer makes it easy to transfer files to your iTunes account.

to add a single media file or a whole folder of files. In the Windows version, you can either Add File or Add Folder.

3. Select the music or video file (or folder) you want to import into iTunes.

4. Click the Open button on the Mac. On a PC, it will be OK for a single file and Open if it's a whole folder.

There is one other way to add music into iTunes. It's to drag and drop the files right into iTunes. If you can see and grab a media file in the Apple Finder window or the Windows Explorer window, then you can drag the file and drop it into any of the following iTunes areas:

• iTunes desktop icon
• Title in the Windows taskbar
• Icon in the Mac dock

This will copy the media into iTunes, making it available for you to load onto the iPad.

You can also easily import your music CDs into iTunes by inserting them into the CD/DVD drive of your computer and importing (ripping) the music into iTunes. (Find more on this in Chapter 6.)

Or, you can use the Add to Library command to import media that is on your computer into iTunes. Here's how:

1. Go to File > Add to Library.

2. In the Mac version of iTunes, there is one Add to Library command that allows you

SET UP AND SYNC THE iPAD

The first time you plug your new iPad into your computer and launch iTunes, you'll need to give your iPad a name and decide how the device will deal with content when it's attached to iTunes. There are four actions to take at this point:

- Name your iPad.
- Decide if the iPad will automatically sync songs and videos to the computer when plugged in.
- Decide if the iPad will automatically add photos to the computer when plugged in.
- Decide if the iPad will automatically sync apps to the computer when connected.

My best advice is to name the iPad and uncheck the other three options. Instead of using the automatic settings, we'll add content ourselves … and not give iTunes too much power. Plus, if you're like me, then you probably have a good amount of media loaded in iTunes—way more media than available space on your iPad—so going the automatic route is probably just asking for trouble anyway.

I know that some of you may be thinking that you won't use iTunes, since you can buy content directly on the iPad. But there are some good reasons to sync your iPad with your computer-based iTunes account, even though you don't have to. They are:

- When you sync the iPad to the computer, the computer backs up all the data from your iPad; so if something happens, the data can be recovered.
- It's much easier to sort and arrange app icons using the iTunes interface on your computer than to do it on the iPad, especially if you have a lot of apps.
- Syncing is the fastest way to get data files on and off the iPad.
- The fastest way to get a large number of photos on your iPad is syncing.
- Syncing is the only way to move content that's purchased on the computer to your iPad.
- This is the only way to use your iPad to access the music, movies and TV shows that you have on your computer.
- Specifically, if you have a season pass to a TV show, syncing is the only way to get new episodes onto your iPad.

Set Up Your iPad

Name: iPad 2

☐ Automatically sync songs and videos to my iPad
iTunes can automatically sync your iPad to mirror its music library and playlists each time you connect it to this Mac.

☐ Automatically add photos to my iPad
iTunes will first sync all of your music to your iPad and then use the remaining space for photos.

☐ Automatically sync apps to my iPad

Done

Figure 2-5

You'll need to make some decisions when you see the Setup your iPad window. This appears when you first plug your iPad into a computer that's running iTunes.

So, when you plug your iPad into your computer and launch iTunes, you'll see that your iPad is now listed under Devices on the left. Go ahead and select it. This is where you set up how iTunes and the iPad play with each other. Make sure they play nice, because a good relationship between your two devices will make your life a lot easier.

The first screen that comes up is the Summary page, which gives basic info about your iPad. From here, you can use the tabs across the top of the window to control the media that you put on the iPad. But the first thing to do is set up the options on the front page, which is divided into three sections:

- The first section shows the info for the attached iPad, including the Capacity, Software Version and Serial Number.

- The second area is all about making sure you are running the latest version of the iPad software. It also offers an option to restore the iPad to its original settings if it starts acting up. (We'll get into this later.)

- The third window is the Options menu. This is where users set up preferences for files on the iPad. And these are important, because two of the options directly affect how much space you have available on your device. They are the *Convert Higher Bit Rate Songs to 128 kbps AAC* and the *Prefer Standard Definition Videos* options. If you select the latter, then your iPad will use the standard definition copy (if HD and SD are both available), because it takes up less space.

You can also set up iTunes to encrypt your iPad backup. This is useful if you frequently connect to a work machine or a computer that you share with other users.

Finally, here is where you can configure the Universal Access for the iPad, if needed. This Universal Access button allows you to enable VoiceOver and Zoom; (de)activate White-on-Black display and Speak Auto-Text; use Mono Audio; or Show Closed Captions (when available).

When it comes to loading content onto the iPad, I really like to be in control. So I open

each of the tabs on the iPad (described below and visible when the device is attached to the computer) and set up things manually through iTunes on my computer.

- **Info:** This is where you can sync the Address Book Contacts, iCal Calendars, Mail Accounts and Other, which includes Bookmarks and Notes. There is also an Advanced section where you can replace the content on your iPad. But since this actually happens continuously via wireless sync for me, I have none of these controls checked.

- **Apps:** This is where you can sync all those cool apps and data files for specific applications. This tab also allows you to decide where to position your apps on the iPad. Once an application is selected to be synced onto the iPad, you can move it around and place it wherever you want. You can sort the apps that you have purchased by name, category, date or size. This is much easier to do here than on the actual iPad. To add an app to the iPad, just select it from the list on the left.

Figure 2-6
On the Apps tab, add apps to the iPad and sort them on the screen.

- **Music:** Want music on you iPad? Well, this is the place to add it. I have the Sync Music button checked. But instead of trying to sync the entire music library, I have specific playlists, artists and genres selected for the sync. There are lots of options here, and they're covered in more detail in Chapter 6. Here, it's just important to know that this is where you can choose the playlists and smart playlists that sync to your iPad.

- **Movies:** Use this tab to add movies to the iPad. What's really nice is that you can see the size of each movie you want to move (next to its icon). This is important, because movie files are BIG, so they take up a lot of space on your iPad. For example, *Inception* is 2.05 GB and *Red* is 1.53 GB. With files this size, it's easy to fill the whole iPad with movies quickly.

- **TV Shows:** Apple sells a lot of TV shows, and this is where you can add shows to the iPad. You can even set your iPad to automatically sync a selection of shows based on rules. For instance, I have mine set to automatically transfer all unwatched episodes of my favorite shows. This means that iTunes will automatically add the episodes I download with my season pass. You can also add any episode or season using the Show menu. And if you keep scrolling down, you'll see a place to include episodes from Playlists. More on managing TV show content in Chapter 6.

- **Podcasts:** If you listen to or watch podcasts, you can add those to your iPad here. It's a shame that there's not a way to have smart playlists for Podcasts, but at least you can input a rule when syncing. I usually have mine set to automatically include all unplayed episodes of a selected podcast,

> **TIP**
>
> An interesting thing about eBooks is that there's no Books tab until you buy one on the iPad and transfer it to the computer. The files in this tab also include ePub and PDF files that you've imported to iTunes.

which ensures that I have all the unheard segments of the ones I listen to regularly.

- **iTunes U:** This is where you sync all the iTunes U material. This page has the same layout and rules as the podcasts section, which is because iTunes U material works like a podcast.

- **Books:** I use the iPad to read books, so I have the Sync Books checkbox selected. But I don't want to keep all my books on the iPad (taking space), so I also have the Selected Books radio button checked. I have my books sorted by author, because that's usually the way I buy books, but you can also sort by title. This is also the tab to use to sync Audiobooks. Again, I checked the Selected audiobooks, because I don't want all of my audiobooks on the iPad at the same time.

- **Photos:** If you're using a PC, you can select images from any folder that has images in it. On a Mac, there are many more choices for managing image files, especially if you use iPhoto. Find more on this in Chapter 3.

NOTE

If you print out the *iTunes Store Terms & Conditions* and *Apple's Privacy Policy*, it will run about 20 pages. Here are the main points:

- Don't sell the music you buy.
- If a third-party app crashes, don't blame Apple.
- There are a lot of ways to send Apple money, including checks, wire transfers and money orders along with credit cards and gift certificates.
- Don't let anyone use your account, because you are responsible for all charges.
- You can't burn ringtones or video products to a CD or DVD.

There's more, especially when it comes to renting movies, TV season passes and dealing with electronic books. So I suggest that you actually read this. It's boring but important.

iTUNES ACCOUNT/ APPLE ID

The first thing to know before you buy any content through the iTunes Store is that you need an iTunes account ... otherwise known as an *Apple ID*. Even if you never plan on buying anything—if you intend to download only free content, like podcasts and iTunes University media, and use free apps—you still need to set up an iTunes account.

You can set up the Apple ID on your computer or you can do it on the iPad. Let's first walk through signing up for an account on your computer.

Set Up an Apple ID: Computer

Keep in mind that it's possible to set up an account with or without a credit card. Here, we'll start with signing up *with* a payment (credit card) option. To do this:

1. Start iTunes on the computer.

2. Click on the iTunes Store in the list on the left side of the screen.

3. Click on the Sign In button at the top right side of the window. (If, instead of the Sign In button, you see a name there, then you or someone is already signed in.)

4. At this point, you can either sign in to an existing account or set up a new one.

5. If you don't have an account, click on Create New Account. This will take you to a welcome screen. Click on the Continue button to sign up for an account.

6. Now it's time for that legal mumbo jumbo that no one ever reads. It's the iTunes Store Terms & Conditions and Apple's Privacy Policy, and you have to check the "I have read and agree to the iTunes Terms and Conditions and Apple's Privacy Policy" before you are allowed to continue.

7. The next step is to enter the information used to create the Apple ID, along with your birthday, so that Apple's records show that you are older than 13, the minimum age to have a Apple ID.

8. The third and final screen is where your payment info goes. Apple wants this information so it's very easy for you to purchase content without having to enter your credit card number each time.

9. Once you've set up the account, you can sign in and begin using the iTunes Store.

It's a little more complicated to sign up for an Apple ID without a credit card, but it can be done. Just:

1. Open iTunes.
2. Click on iTunes Store, located on the left side of the window.
3. Click on App Store, located across the top of the screen.
4. Pick a free app to download.
5. Click Create New Account when the "Sign in to download from the iTunes Store" window appears.
6. Click Continue.
7. Read and agree to the iTunes Terms of Service.
8. Enter an e-mail address. (This will be your Apple ID.)
9. Enter a password.
10. Create a security question and answer it.
11. Enter your birthday.
12. Click Continue.
13. Select None as payment type.
14. Fill out the name and address fields.
15. There will be a Verify your Account screen. Click Done and check your e-mail.
16. Once you get a verification e-mail from Apple, open and click the link to activate your account.
17. Your account is now activated.

You can access your account information from inside of iTunes at any time. Open iTunes and place your mouse over the account name on the right side of the screen. Then, click on the down arrow to open the Account menu. You can now choose:

- **Account:** This shows your account information. (At times, iTunes might ask you to re-enter your password to keep your data safe.)
- **Redeem:** If you ever get an iTunes gift card, this is where you redeem it.
- **Wish List:** You can mark items in the iTunes Store to be put on your wish list. Here is where that list lives.
- **Sign Out:** If you share a computer with others, it is probably best to sign out when you're done, so your account doesn't get used without your permission.

If you need to change any of your account information—from the payment information to your recent purchases—this is the spot to do it.

Set Up an Apple ID: iPad

Here's how to set up your Apple ID on your iPad with a credit card, gift card or gift certificate:

1. Turn on your iPad.
2. Tap Settings.
3. Tap Store.
4. Now, tap Create New Account.
5. Choose a Country or Region that matches your billing address. Tap Next.
6. Read all 35 pages of the Terms and Conditions and then tap Agree. You can also have the Terms and Conditions e-mailed to you for later reading.
7. Once you have agreed to the Terms and Conditions, enter:
   - Your e-mail (This becomes your Apple ID.)

- Password
- Password verification
- A security question
- Security question answer
- Date of birth
- Opt to receive iTunes updates ... or not.
- Opt to receive News and Special offers from Apple ... or not.

8. Tap Next.

9. Enter your billing information. You can use a credit card or an iTunes gift card or gift certificate to open the account. Just scroll down to the proper area to enter the payment information.

10. Tap Next to complete the account.

11. Tap Done.

12. You can now use the iTunes Store, the App Store and the iBooks Store on your iPad.

If you want to set up an account but don't have a credit card or gift card, you can still do that on the iPad. It's just a little more complicated. But once it's set up, you're good to go. So, to set up an account on your iPad without payment information:

1. Open the App Store on your iPad.

2. Find a Free application. I suggest the iBooks app since you'll want that at some point anyway.

3. Tap Install App. A menu will pop up that asks you to Sign In using an Existing Account or to Create New Account.

4. Tap Create New Account.

5. Enter the Country or Region in which you live.

6. Tap Next.

7. Read and agree to the iTunes Terms of Service.

8. Enter an e-mail address. (This will be your Apple ID.)

9. Enter a password and verify it.

10. Create a security question and answer it.

11. Enter your birthday.

12. Opt to receive iTunes updates ... or not.

13. Opt to receive News and Special Offers from Apple ... or not.

14. Tap Next.

15. Select None as payment type.

16. Fill out the name and address fields.

17. When you see the Verify your Account screen, tap Done and check your e-mail.

18. When you get a verification e-mail from Apple, open and click the link to activate your account.

19. The App Store will open.

20. Enter your account information to sign in and start downloading apps!

Once you have an Apple ID, you can utilize the iTunes Store in all its glory.

iTUNES STORE PRODUCTS

The iTunes Store resides in the iTunes program that's accessible through your computer. It has grown tremendously since it opened in 2003. Today, there are seven distinct categories of media available through the iTunes Store, and each of these categories has a huge amount of content that can be consumed on a computer or iPad (or an iPhone, iPod, etc).

Remember, iTunes is a term that describes two different things. On the iPad, iTunes is the place to get music, movies, TV shows, audio-books, podcasts and iTunes U content. When referencing the program on a computer, iTunes is the application that plays and organizes your content, and it provides the portal for accessing the iTunes Store in order to sync content from your computer to the iPad.

Music

The Music Store is the one that started the iTunes Store, and it's still growing every day. The store has a ton of content, but it tries to make it easy for you to find what you're looking for … and even suggests new music to match your taste.

In the most current version, the audio tracks download at the highest level of quality (256 kbps AAC audio), which is twice the audio quality of the older DRM-enabled songs from the iTunes Store. And the tracks can be played everywhere. The DRM-free status means you can burn your music to a disc or play them on any computer anywhere, anytime. Nice …

One more thing you need to know about iTunes music is the iTunes LP, which is Apple's answer to the long-playing album. The iTunes LP tries to re-create the whole album experience by providing more artwork and bonus features like outtakes, extra liner notes and even video clips. These albums cost a little more. And while I don't think they've been as successful as Apple would have liked, the iTunes LPs are cool.

Here's the thing though: The iPad doesn't support the LP format. So while you can download the individual tracks of an iTunes LP to your iPad, and all the music will be available there, the interface will not have the cool LP features that you paid extra to get. It'll look and act the same as all your

TIP

iTunes is a term that describes two different things. On the iPad, iTunes is the place to get music, movies, TV shows, audio books, podcast and iTunes U content. When referencing the program on a computer, iTunes is the application that plays and organizes your content, and it provides the portal for accessing the iTunes Store in order to sync content from your computer to the iPad.

regular albums. This is true even if you buy the LP album on the iPad. But once you sync back over to the computer, iTunes will go back online and get any of the missing files, so you can enjoy the extras on your computer.

Movies

The iTunes Movie Store has changed the way I buy and rent movies. I used to actually buy movies … on VHS tapes! Remember those? And then I transitioned to the DVD format, and now I buy digital files.

Not all the movies released on DVD show up on the iTunes Store, but there are more and more movies there every day. The movies are protected by DRM, and they need to be played on devices that are either authorized to play your purchased movies (up to five computers) or on iPads that are under the same Apple ID. So if you buy a movie using an

Apple ID and transfer the movie to an iPad that has a different Apple ID, it won't play.

Many of the movies that you can purchase through iTunes now come with extra features like outtakes and content that was previously only available on the DVD. When it comes to the iTunes extras, it's important to understand that, like the music LPs, they are not compatible with the iPad. They'll show up on your computer but not on the iPad.

Renting movies from the iTunes Store is also a viable option, and rented movies can be transferred from a computer to the iPad. But rented movies, unlike purchased movies, can only live on a single device at a time. This means that you do not *copy* a movie to the iPad, but rather transfer it. And this is done in iTunes. So if you have a rented movie in your iTunes library, you can transfer it to the iPad using the following process:

1. Open iTunes on the computer.

2. Plug in your iPad using the USB cable.

3. Select the iPad from the Device list.

TIP

You do not need to be connected to the Internet to begin watching a rented movie that's loaded on your iPad. It works everywhere. Keep in mind that once you start to watch a rented movie, you have to finish within 24 hours.

4. Select Movies on the iPad menu.

5. Select the move arrow that corresponds to the direction you want to transfer the movie.

6. Click the Apply button.

7. The movie will transfer as directed.

You can now watch the movie on your iPad. You need to have an active Internet connection for this to work though, and the iTunes Store will check to make sure you are allowed to make the transfer before actually transferring the movie to the iPad.

TV Shows

I definitely use my iPad and computer to watch some of my favorite TV shows. You can buy individual episodes in both standard definition (SD) and in high definition (HD), and you can buy season passes, which are entire TV seasons, in SD or HD. You can buy the season pass before the season is even complete, and episodes will become available to subscribers within 24 hours of their broadcast.

To provide season pass holders access to a new episode, Apple will send an e-mail notification when new episodes becomes available to download. Just open this e-mail and tap the link in the message. iTunes will launch. The episode will download automatically.

There are some problems with season passes on the iPad though. This is covered in Chapter 6.

The App Store

The App Store is a goldmine for Apple and, according to some developers, it's a very profitable platform for app creators, too. This seems amazing sometimes, because a lot of content in the App Store is free.

There is a very important menu choice for users in the App Store when accessing the

Figure 2-7
The App Store inside of iTunes lists the top free apps.

site on a Mac or PC. It's the choice between iPhone and iPad. This option is positioned right in the middle of the screen at the top, and it switches between a list of apps developed for the iPhone and those designed for the iPad. Be sure that you click on iPad to see the apps developed for this device. There are new apps in the App Store every day.

The primary thing that separates apps from all the other media types is that apps contain content that gets updated. Developers add new features, fix problems and generally update their apps periodically for various reasons. At least the good app developers do. So

when an app is updated, you can download the new version in the iTunes Store, usually for free. Then, the next time you sync your iPad, the newer version of the app will overwrite the older version on your computer.

You can check for updates in iTunes anytime by visiting the App library and clicking Check for Updates, which is located on the bottom of the screen. This will automatically check for updates and open the App Store if it finds any newer versions of the apps you own. It's a good idea to keep your apps up to date, because many times the updates fix problems or add new features that you need.

Podcasts

Podcasts have grown in leaps and bounds since they were first offered on the iTunes Store back in 2005. Users can now search for and download podcasts on a huge variety of subjects—from tech news (some of my favorite subjects) to wine-making and automotive repair. The store looks just like the other iTunes stores with one key exception: All of the content is free.

Audiobooks

There are times when a good audiobook can make a long drive go by much faster … or at least seem that way. The iTunes Store offers a wide selection of audiobooks, ranging from political thrillers to autobiographies. The store is divided much like a regular bookstore—by fiction and non-fiction. But one really cool category is *Books Made Into Films*. I think this one is especially fun to browse. Check it out when you get a chance.

iTunes U

The iTunes U area of the iTunes Store was opened in 2007 and is a forum for educational materials. It allows educational institutions to distribute information through the iTunes

29

Store. The developer can limit access to its own institution or make it available to the general public. A ton of great free content is available in the iTunes U Store.

THE iTUNES APP

Buying content from Apple on the iPad is slightly more complicated than doing it on a computer ... or slightly simpler, depending on your point of view. Apple has split iTunes commerce into two different stores on the iPad: the iTunes Store and the App Store.

These stores mirror the content available on the iTunes Store that's accessible through iTunes on your computer. They might look slightly different and navigation is via finger instead of mouse, but the content available to you is the same ... with one extra. Apple offers an iBooks Store that's accessible only on the iPad (as well as the iPod Touch and iPhone). This store allows you to purchase iBooks right on the iPad.

On the iPad, the iTunes app is the place to buy and download music, movies, TV shows, podcasts, audiobooks and iTunes U content, while the App Store is dedicated to apps. Similarly, the iBooks Store is all about electronic books.

Let's start with the iTunes Store on the iPad. And before we go any further, please be clear that on the iPad, the app is just called *iTunes*.

iTunes

As stated above, the iTunes app is the place to search for and buy music, movies, TV shows, podcasts, audiobooks and iTunes U material on your iPad. All of this content is easy to find; the menu, organized by category, is laid out across the bottom of the screen. The different categories (or *stores*) look simi-

lar to the computer-based versions, but there are some small differences, and they can be really annoying. The stores that are available on the iPad's iTunes app include:

- **Music Store**
  You can search, purchase and download music right on the iPad. This works with both the Wi-Fi and 3G versions of the iPad. Find some music you want to buy by either searching for it using the search feature at the top of the screen or by navigating around as you would in the iTunes Store on the computer.

When you find music you like, you can download the album or individual tracks. Songs will be placed on the Downloads page. Remember, you get to enter your Apple ID and password before enjoying the sounds, so Apple can charge you for your purchases!

One thing to remember is that the screen on the iPad, especially when in landscape mode, doesn't show the full page of the store. So scroll down for more music choices.

The things that are different on the iPad version of the Music Store mainly consist of stuff that you *can't* do. The extra content and cool interface of the LP version of music files are not supported on the iPad, even if you buy the LP Album on your iPad. Also, when I click on the Complete My Album button at the bottom of the page, it never actually works. Instead, a dreaded *Cannot connect to iTunes Store* message pops up. But in perspective, these are slight inconveniences. The store works great most of the time.

- **Movie Store**

  This area of the iPad app allows you to purchase … or rent and download … movies to the iPad. One thing to keep in mind is that you need to be on a Wi-Fi network to do this, because the size of the movie files are far bigger than the allowable download size of the 3G.

  The Movie Store on your iPad looks just like the one on the computer, and it allows you to buy movies in both SD and HD. My suggestion here is that if you're planning to watch the movie on your iPad, stick with the lower-cost SD movies. If you're planning to enjoy the movie on a computer, the Apple TV or a HD television, then you might want to pay the extra coin for HD. I usually buy movies in SD, because I tend to watch them on smaller devices that don't benefit from the HD quality. Your call.

  But it's important to know that right now there are things you can't do with the movies you purchase or rent on the iPad. For one, you can't transfer movies that you rent on the iPad to a computer. If you rent it on the iPad, you have to watch it on the iPad. Another thing is that the iTunes Extras, which are available when you purchase some movies, do not work on the iPad … only on a computer … so just the movie content gets copied to the iPad. To watch the extra stuff, you need to be on the computer and watching the movie thorough iTunes.

- **TV Shows**

  The way things are progressing, all of my television viewing will soon be done on-demand and without advertisements. Through the iTunes TV Store, you can now buy individual shows and season passes in either HD or SD through the

iPad. But Apple still has a bit of work to do on the functionality of the TV content.

A glitch that exists right now has to do with season passes. Now I really, really want this to work, but it still doesn't. When you buy a season pass (on the iPad or on your computer) you can download the currently available episodes. But when subscribers get the e-mail about a new episode being available, clicking on the link in the e-mail (that's supposed to lead you blissfully to the new episode) opens iTunes on the iPad … only to reveal an error message that says the connection to the iTunes Store cannot be made and that no file is available for download. (Go ahead and throw your hat to the floor.) Right now, the only way to get your new episode is to download it to the computer and sync it to the iPad with the USB cable. (Groan.) Hopefully this will be fixed by Apple at some point … soon.

- **Podcasts**

  I have a favorite podcast or two. Actually, I have a whole collection of podcasts that I listen to when I have the time. I subscribe to the podcasts on the computer; but if there's something specific I'm looking for, I go searching through this Podcast Store.

  The only real downside here is that there's no way to subscribe to podcasts on the iPad. You can download single episodes, but you can't get the new ones automatically added to your library (as you can on the computer).

  Both audio and video podcasts are available, so the size of the downloads vary widely. A podcast's size will determine if it can be downloaded on 3G or if it can only be downloaded to your iPad when attached by Wi-Fi.

- **Audiobooks**

  I love a good audiobook, and having them available on the iPad just increases the value of the iPad in my eyes. The audiobook files in the iTunes Store are DRM-protected, so they can't just be copied and used anywhere. This means that the number of computers that can play an audiobook purchased from iTunes is limited to five; and all of them must be authorized under the same Apple ID. The good news is that your audiobooks can be played on as many iDevices as you want.

  When you find an audiobook you're interested in, play a preview of it. Many times, it really helps to have headphones or external speakers to get the best out of your audiobook, since the built-in speaker on the iPad 2 is better than the original iPad ... but is still not great.

- **iTunes U**

  Here is a great reason for students to have an iPad. You can access all of the iTunes U materials so easily! A really nice element of the iTunes U Store on the iPad is the set of three buttons in the middle that allow you to search by either:

  - Universities & Colleges

  - Beyond Campus

  - K-12

Tap on any of these three buttons and scroll through a list of school names and educational organizations. Tap on a school to see a listing of its content. What a great use of iTunes and a great use of the iPad!

App Store

I have no idea why Apple made the App Store a separate app on the iPad, but I like it. The

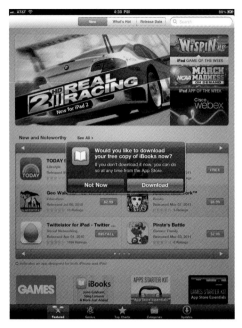

Figure 2-8

The App Store on the iPad makes it easy to find and purchase iPad apps.

setup makes it really easy to find and buy new apps. You can even check to see if the apps on your iPad are up-to-date and, if they aren't, the app will ask you to download the updates. Some updates will not be available unless you are on a Wi-Fi network (and not relying on 3G). This happens when an app is bigger than the 20MB per-app limit for 3G downloads.

Remember, if you've previously purchased an app on the computer or on your iPhone ... or other iPad ... using your Apple ID, then you can re-download it for free. Just go into the App Store and tap Buy. The iPad will act as if you are buying the app for the first time until it starts to download. Then it will tell you that you have bought the app before and ask if you want to download it again for free. This is really nice. It means that you can delete an app from your iPad; and, if you reconsider, you can just visit the App Store and get it again … for no additional cost.

iBooks Store

The iPad's iBooks Store is a rapidly growing electronic bookstore and the only place to buy books from Apple. I'm not sure that anything will ever replace the feeling I get when I wander through a bookstore, looking at new books for something to read. But the iBooks Store comes close.

This, however, is the most challenging of the stores to find, because it is not standard on the iPad. It is an extra app that has to be downloaded. Even then, it is still a semi-hidden part of the app. To gain access, tap the Store button in the library view of the iBooks app.

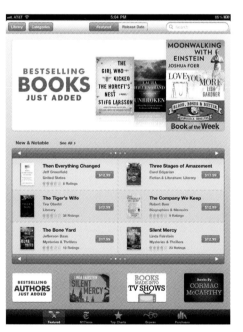

Figure 2-9
The iBooks Store is available inside the iBooks app.

This app gives users an opportunity to wander around a virtual bookstore and even download samples of books for free—just like flipping through a paper one. A really nice thing about the iBooks Store is that the book files are small, so they can be downloaded over 3G as well as Wi-Fi. This means you can grab a new book when you're just about anywhere.

Another very cool thing that is showing up in the iBooks Store is enhanced books, which include extra content like timelines, photographs and author Q&A for an extra fee.

DIFFERENT MEDIA, DIFFERENT TREATMENT

This is important: Apple treats your iTunes purchases differently, depending on what type of media it is. Here's what this means: Say you buy content in the form of music, movies or TV shows on the computer or your iPad … and they get deleted or lost … or you just decide to download the file a second time. When you go to download previously purchased media of these types, either on the computer or the iPad, you will get charged a second time.

I need to make this really clear, so here is a real world example. I went to the iTunes Store on the computer and bought the movie, "Hot Tub Time Machine" for $14.99. (I know, but I have a soft spot for anything with John Cusack in it.) Then, I decided to download the movie on my iPad, so I went to the iTunes Store on the iPad, brought up the same movie and tapped Buy Movie. I get a message saying that I've already purchased the movie and the question "Do you want to proceed with the purchase?" If I tap Buy, then I WILL PURCHASE THE MOVIE AGAIN. That is,

Figure 2-10
Since I had already bought these books under the same Apple ID, I was able to download them again for free.

iTunes will debit my credit card for another $14.99. This is true with music, TV shows and movies.

It's a different story when it comes to apps and iBooks. If you buy an app in the computer's version of the iTunes Store and then try to buy the app again on the iPad, Apple will allow you to download it the second time for free. For some reason, Apple has decided to keep track of your app purchases and allow you to re-download them at no additional charge ... as long as the device is logged in with the Apple ID that was used to purchase the app initially.

Now let's talk about iBooks for a minute. Apple has lumped them into the same category as apps. You can re-download any pre-

Figure 2-11
I had already bought *Faster;* but instead of getting the option to re-download the movie, I only get an option to buy it again.

viously purchased book on the iPad as long as you are signed in with the Apple ID that was used to first purchase the book. This makes it really easy to have the same book on multiple devices ... if they all have the same Apple ID associated with them. For example, I have an iPad and my wife has an iPad, and both are tied to the same Apple ID. This means she can download to her iPad any iBook I buy on my iPad ... for free. The same goes for apps—but not music, movies or TV shows.

To recap, iBooks and apps can be re-downloaded at any time for free, but music, TV shows and movies cannot. If you re-download content that's not an iBook or app, then you will get charged a second time.

TRANSFER CONTENT

As we've seen, it's easy to buy content for the iPad *on* the iPad. And it's also easy to take that content off the iPad and put it into your iTunes account. Especially because some content (like iBooks) can only be purchased on the iPad, this is important.

With the iPad connected and iTunes running, you can transfer files to your computer by clicking on File > Transfer Purchase from iPad. Or, you can right click (or, for a Mac, control click) on iPad in the Device list and then click on Transfer Purchases.

After you've purchased and transferred content to the computer from your iPad, notice a new list in the Store section of menu bar; it's called Purchased on iPad. This list shows all the content (other than apps) that you've purchased on your iPad. The content that you buy on the iPad is also transferred to the computer when you sync the device.

BACK IT UP

Apple might not consider your iPad a personal computer, but in some ways it's mighty close to one. For example, you can lose the information that's stored on your iPad (just like you can lose the files and data that are on your computer). So, you need to back up your iPad once in awhile.

Apple makes it very easy to back up your iPad content. In fact, your computer backs it up automatically when the device syncs with iTunes. You can also back up anytime by right clicking (PC) or control clicking (Mac) on iPad in the Device list and choosing Back Up. The backup includes your settings and some data in the iPad, but it doesn't actually make new copies of the media you have there. Rather, the media (e.g., music, movies,

Figure 2-12
Access the backup option by right clicking (PC) or control clicking (Mac) on the iPad in the Device list inside iTunes on your computer.

apps and photo content) are already on the computer and will be reloaded when the iPad is restored.

In case you want to know where iTunes stashes your backups, find them here:

- **On a Mac:** ~/Library/Application Support/MobileSync/Backup/
- **On Windows XP:** \Documents and Settings\(username)\Application Data\ Apple Computer\MobileSync\Backup\
- **On Windows Vista and Windows 7:** \Users\(username)\AppData\Roaming\ Apple Computer\MobileSync\Backup\

RESTORE

Sometimes things go wrong. It happens. And when it does, the best course of action is to restore your iPad, so that it goes back to the factory settings and then restores from a backup. You can also restore from a backup by right clicking on the iPad in the Device menu and choosing Restore from Backup (PC).

When you use the Restore function for your iPad, be aware that all the data is deleted from the device. This includes the music, movies, contacts, photos and calendars. All the settings are then set to the factory defaults. From there, you can reload your data from a backup. Restoring your iPad can take awhile, so be patient.

To restore your iPad:

1. Open iTunes and plug in the iPad.

2. Select the iPad from the Device list.

3. Select the Summary tab and click on the Restore button.

From here, you will be prompted to back up your settings before restoring the device to the factory defaults. Whether or not you take the advice and back up depends on how recently you backed up your content and settings—and how valuable you think your content is.

WARNING

If you sync your iPad to another computer, all your preexisting media will be removed from the device.

The prompt to restore the iPad will be: "Are you sure you want to restore the iPad to its factory settings? All of your media and other data will be erased." I know, it sounds ominous; but if you need to do it and have a backup, then go for it.

Once the restore process is complete, you'll be asked if you want to use the backup to reload your info onto the iPad. Go ahead and use the backups. Or, if you want a clean slate, just say no.

There you have it, a backup and restore for the iPad. My advice is to make sure the iPad is backed up every so often, because it can be a real pain to get everything back exactly the way you want it if you do have a crash.

NO MULTIPLE iTUNES ACCOUNTS

I have a bit of bad news. But if you know Apple, then it shouldn't come as a surprise: The iPad cannot access multiple iTunes accounts. This device is not designed to be shared. Once it is tied to an account, it can't sync to another. Knowing that some people want to use the iPad as a laptop replacement, I think it's important to know about the single-account limitation.

Real life scenario: I have an iTunes account. It's the account I use to buy movies, rent TV shows, buy music, buy apps and gather iBooks. It's the same account that's tied to my computer. I sync my iPad to the same computer, so all the movies and media that I purchase from Apple is available on the iPad … and my computer.

The problem starts if I want to share the iPad with someone who has a different iTunes account. Once the iPad becomes synced to another account, none of my media is accessible.

Another problem related to the single-account issue happens if you have two people trying to share the device. This is especially thorny if both users have separate MobileMe (.me) accounts from Apple. The MobileMe service controls a user's e-mail, calendar, web bookmarks and notes. And because the iPad can deal with only one account at a time, you have to decide whose information will be on the iPad. Of course, you can always get a second iPad to ensure both .me accounts are on an iPad. And that just might be Apple's master plan! Eureka!

MOBILEME

MobileMe is a cloud-based Apple service that not only provides an e-mail account but also helps keep a user's information synced among the computer, MobileMe website, iPad and iPhone—automatically. So if your read your e-mail on the iPad, it automatically updates the e-mail account on your computer and iPad. If you add a contact on the iPad, the same info will be instantly available on your computer and iPhone. You get the idea.

I've been using and paying $99 a year for MobileMe service since it was called .Mac in 2002, and I'm really happy with the service. The name was changed in 2008 to MobileMe, and all the .Mac accounts were automatically transferred to .Me accounts. As I sit here and write this in Spring 2011, it's no longer possible to purchase MobileMe, which is fueling rumors that Apple will soon unveil a free version of the MobileMe service. Stay tuned ...

Photography

The Skim

I am a photographer. I spend most of my time shooting pictures, writing about photography and teaching other people how to take better pictures. So when the original iPad was released, I was excited by the buzz in the photography community about what this device could do to change the way we display our images, especially portfolios. The iPad does not disappoint.

With very little work, anyone can have a professional-looking portfolio in minutes. So while there are times when a printed portfolio may be better than a digital one, the ability to display your images on the iPad is fantastic. We'll cover the details in this chapter.

But it doesn't stop there, of course. Along with the image-display features of the iPad are many choices for editing images on the device, including an app from the biggest name in photo editing: Adobe.

And now, with the release of the iPad 2—which has two built-in cameras—Apple has definitely upped the ante. Not only can you view and edit your images on the new iPad; you can also shoot them. If you have the original iPad, you can view and edit images; but I'm sorry, there is no way to take photos with the original version of this device.

RESOLUTION

I know you want to get right to the details of taking, editing and managing photos. But before we can get into all that, we need to cover some technical details about the resolution of the iPad's screen and its two cameras. This will help you use the iPad's photography capabilities appropriately and efficiently.

iPad Screen

The original iPad and the iPad 2 have the same screen with the same resolution. It's a 9.7-inch diagonal LED-backlit glossy screen with a resolution of 1024x768 pixels at 132 pixels per inch (ppi). These numbers are important, especially when it comes to tweaking your images to look their best on the iPad, so we'll cover this in detail a little later in the chapter.

I know many photographers (and others) were hoping that Apple would upgrade the iPad screen with the release of iPad 2—maybe even use the same type of super-high resolution screen that was introduced with the iPhone 4—but this didn't happen. And I don't have a single problem with this, because I think the screen on my iPad is fantastic as-is for viewing images.

iPad Cameras

Let's look at the resolution for the iPad cameras. That's right; there are two cameras on the iPad 2.

- The first is located on the front of the device. The front-facing camera takes photos that are 640x480 at 72 ppi. This is a lower resolution than the other camera.

- The second camera is on the back. The rear-facing camera takes photos that are 960x720 at 72 ppi. This is still a lower resolution than the camera on the iPhone 4.

This means that photos taken with the iPad have a lower resolution than the iPad screen, so when viewed on the device at full screen, they will never look great. Some people are very unhappy with this; but I'm not bothered, because I just don't see the iPad as a still-image capture device. The built-in cameras are really better used for the video applications.

That said, Apple could have at least made the camera equal to the iPhone 4, which has a resolution of 2492x1936 at 72 ppi—much higher than the iPad 2. Oh well.

TAKE PHOTOS

The easiest way to get images onto the iPad 2 is to take them with the built-in cameras. As explained above, this is not going to give you the best quality images, but it is really easy.

1. Turn on the iPad 2.

2. Tap the Camera app.

3. There's a button on the top right of the screen that switches between the front and rear cameras. Tap the button to select the camera you want to use.

4. If you have one of the Apple Smart Covers on your iPad 2, it will interfere with the visibility of the rear camera. So you have to remove this cover in order to use the rear camer you want to use.

5. Tap on the screen to pick the focus point. This also helps to get the best exposure. When using the rear-facing camera, a scrubby slider will appear to allow you to zoom the camera. But don't do it! The quality of this zoom will deteriorate your image very quickly into the unusable range.

Figure 3-1

This is the view when using the built-in camera. Notice the button that allows you to switch between the front and rear cameras. Also note the big shutter release button on the bottom.

6. Across the bottom of the display are three buttons:

- Press the middle button to take a photo.
- On the left is the thumbnail of the last photo you took. Tapping it opens the Camera Roll of the iPad's Photo app, which is covered a bit later.
- On the right is where you switch between stills and video.

SCREEN CAPTURES

Want to share something on your iPad screen with someone else? You can do this by taking a screen capture of your iPad screen. It's really useful; at least it is for me, as most of the images in the book were created using this feature.

To take a screen capture, just press the Home button and the Power button on your iPad at the same time. The screen will flash white, the iPad will make a camera shutter click sound, and you're done. Now just go back to what you were doing.

The screen capture will be available in the Camera Roll of the Photos app. Select it to e-mail it through the Mail program.

ADD EFFECTS WITH PHOTO BOOTH

The Photo Booth app (only available on the iPad 2) adds effects to images that are taken with the iPad 2 cameras. When you open the app, it uses the front-facing camera to show off the various effects in a three-by-three grid.

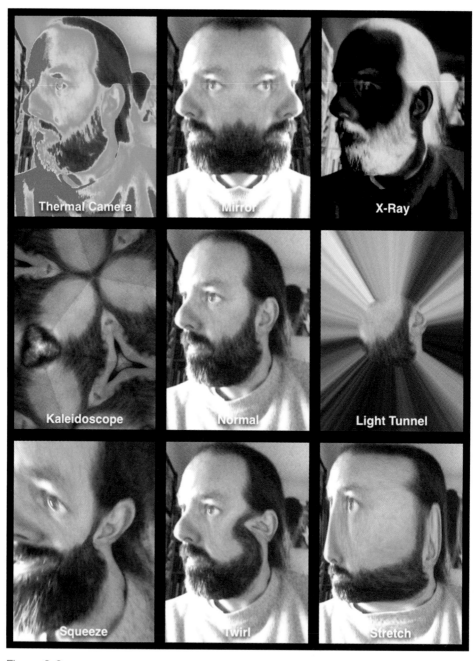

Figure 3-2
The Photo Booth effects (L to R, top to bottom): Thermal, Mirror, X-Ray, Kaleido-scope, Normal, Light Tunnel, Squeeze, Twirl and Stretch

Once you pick an effect, the screen changes to a full-screen preview and gives you the option to switch to the rear camera. The button used to actually take a photo is on the bottom of the screen in the middle. You can go back to the Effects page with a tap on the thumbnail (bottom left).

All in all, while this app is free and could be fun for a while, it seems a little dated.

THE PHOTOS APP

The Photos app is the built-in app for dealing with images and videos on your iPad. All the images you shoot with the iPad 2 cameras or transfer to your iPad are located in this app. The thing is that this app just shows you the images; it doesn't handle any editing. And you can't move any of the photos around on the iPad or iPad 2. The Photos app is a clean and simple program that shows off your images very well. You don't *have* to use any other portfolio apps to display your photos, but I cover that a little later anyway.

The Photos app is divided into six sections … if you happen to use all the features of iPhoto '11 and have a camera attached through the Camera Connection Kit. If you use a different photo program or are on a PC (which doesn't have iPhoto), then some of these sections will not appear.

Each of the sections lets you look at your photos in a slightly different way. When you first tap on the Photos app, it will open in the Albums view … if there are albums present. If not, it opens in the Photos view.

Here's an overview of the six sections.

- The **Photos** view shows all your photos that are on the iPad in a thumbnail view. If the photos were not sorted into albums before you loaded them on to the iPad, then this is the only view you get.

Figure 3-3
The Photos app offers up to six sections.

- The **Albums** view shows all the albums on your iPad. If you have used the Camera Connection Kit, there will be an additional two albums that the iPad created automatically. Those are the Last Import album and the All Imported album. These two albums contain images that have been imported into the iPad using the Camera Connection Kit. Another album created by the iPad 2 is called Camera Roll. It contains images saved to the iPad from the built-in cameras as well as any screen captures and images saved from websites. On the original iPad, this folder is called Saved Photos.

- The **Events** section is for iPhoto users only. In recent versions of iPhoto, you have the option to sort your photos by events. This is very much like an automatic album creator; and if you sync an event to the iPad, then it will show up here.

- **Faces** in iPhoto 09 has a very interesting face-recognition feature. You can tag people in your images and the program will try to find other photos you may have in your collection that show the same face. If you use the Faces feature in iPhoto 09, then it will show up here ... as long as there is at least one image that has a face tagged in it.

- The **Places** section might be one of the coolest interfaces available for looking through your images. If you geo-tag your images—either by using a camera that is GPS-enabled (including the iPhone and iPad 2) or by using the Map tool in iPhoto '11—then when you load your images onto the iPad, you can search for them by using Places. The Places view shows, on a map, where your images were taken. Each location is marked with a red pushpin. Tap on a pushpin to see the photos from that location.

- The **Camera** section is visible when you connect a camera to the iPad with the optional Camera Connection Kit (described later in this chapter). This allows you to select the images on your camera for import onto the iPad or to be deleted.

Viewing Photos

The real fun with the Photos app is in viewing the individual photos. No matter which view you use to access the photos you want to show, just tap on the thumbnail to open the image. With the image open, you have the following tools:

- **Filmstrip:** When you first tap on an image to open it, you will see a filmstrip view across the bottom of the screen and some menu options on the top. These will fade from sight after a few seconds but are eas-

Figure 3-4
The iPad Photos app is showing a single image.

ily brought back up by single tapping on the screen. You can now use your finger to scroll through the images and release on the one you want to pick that image and display it in full screen view.

- **Scroll through Images:** With an image file open, slide your finger from right to left to go to the next photo or from left to right to go to the previous photo. Just keep in mind that when you are at the first image, you can't swipe left to right and when at the last image you can't swipe right to left. Well, I guess you can, but it won't reveal a new image.

- **Slideshow:** One of the menu choices is to run the images as a slideshow. More on this feature later in this chapter.

- **AirPlay.** You can send image(s) to an Apple TV and show them on a big screen. This is a great way to show off your work, and you can control the image on the screen with the iPad.

- **Double Tap:** Double tap on an image to fill the screen with that image. Note though: If you are holding the iPad in landscape mode and looking at a photo taken in portrait orientation, there will be black bars on either side of the photo. Double tap the screen to make those bars disappear and zoom the image to fill the screen, but this does not change the proportions of the image. The problem with this is that you are now missing the top and bottom of the image. You can use a finger to move the image around, but you won't be able to see all of it at the same time. Double tap the screen again, and the view will return to a size that fits inside the screen.

- **Zoom In:** To zoom in on a photograph, put two fingers on the screen … close to each other. Move your fingers apart at the same time. This enlarges the image to reveal more detail.

- **Zoom Out:** To zoom out on a photo and see the whole image at the same time, place two fingers on the screen far apart and pinch them together. If you zoom out further than the photo boundaries, it will release the image and go back to the thumbnail view.

Moving Photos

When a photo is open in the Photos app, on the top right of the screen is an Export button. It looks like a box with an arrow coming out of it. When you tap this, choices appear for how you can move the currently visible image. These options include:

Figure 3-5
The Export menu in the Photos app offers many ways to share your image.

- **E-mail Photo:** Tap this to copy the image into an e-mail message. Done. Really nice and simple. More on e-mailing photos a little later.

- **Send to MobileMe:** This publishes the image to your MobileMe account and adds it to a gallery. If no other images are there, MobileMe will ask you to create a gallery and name it.

- **Assign to Contact:** This allows you to use the current photo as the image for any of the contacts in your Address Book.

- **Use as Wallpaper:** Change the wallpaper background of the iPad's Home screen or the lock screen (or both) by tapping on the Wallpaper button.

- **Print:** If you have an AirPrint-enabled printer, you can send the image directly to it and print a copy.

- **Copy Photo:** This allows you to copy the photo into the iPad's memory to be pasted later.

Figure 3-6
Once you select five images, you no longer have the ability to add more to an e-mail; the button becomes grayed out.

Managing Multiple Images

There are times when you'll want to select multiple images ... maybe to e-mail them out together or to delete them. Apple has you covered here, but the controls are a little difficult to find.

In the thumbnail view of your images, tap the icon on the top right of the screen. (It's the little box with an arrow coming out of it.) This brings up the Select Photos screen, which looks just like a regular thumbnail screen except for the words *Select Photos* across the top. Tapping on a thumbnail selects it. Each selected image will have a blue and white check mark in the bottom right corner. Tap the image a second time to de-select it.

When you've selected at least one image, the E-mail and Copy menu choices are suddenly active. So you can now e-mail or copy the images that have been selected. There is a catch though: If you select more than five images, the e-mail option disappears. You can only e-mail up to five images at a time.

If you want to delete photos from your iPad, you can ... except for those that were synced directly from iTunes. The only way to delete or remove those photos is to uncheck them in iTunes. If you do this, the next time your iPad is synced, they'll be removed.

To delete images that you've imported into the iPad using e-mail, the Camera Connection Kit or the Photo Transfer app:

1. Open the Photos app on your iPad.

2. Tap on Albums on the menu across the top of the screen. (If Albums is not present, then you have no saved images on your iPad that can be deleted.)

3. Tap on the Camera Roll album ... or the Last Import album or the All Imported album. (These are the only albums from which you can delete photos on the iPad.)

4. Tap on the file icon at the top right of the screen to access the Select Photos screen.

5. Select the images you want to delete.

6. Tap on the red Delete button. A second button will appear to ask if you really want to delete the selected photos.

7. Tap on this button to delete the images, or tap the Cancel button on the top right to stop the deletion process.

Be careful. When the images are deleted, they are gone. There is no Undo.

When you're browsing through images in the Camera Roll, the Last Import and All Imported albums, you can delete any single photo you see by tapping on the Delete icon at the top right. It looks like a little trashcan. Tapping it brings up a Delete Photo button. Tap this to delete the image, or tap anywhere else on the screen to cancel.

App Limitations

There is no way to create albums on the iPad and no way to move images from one album to another. This means that if you import images to a certain album, they are stuck there. So, if you have an album of concert images on your iPad and you want to show someone only the images of the guitar player, you need to create another album in iPhoto on your Mac and then sync the images over to your iPad in a new album using the USB cable. What a pain! Fortunately, there are portfolio apps to remedy this, and these are covered a little later in this chapter.

IMAGE EDITING APPS

Taking, storing and seeing your images on the iPad is one thing; editing them is another. Here, we'll explore two image-editing apps that are free. That's right, free ... as in *gratis*—no money needed.

Adobe Photoshop Express

When it comes to editing images on the computer, Photoshop is the leader of the pack. And while it would be impossible to run the full version of Photoshop on the iPad, Adobe has an editing program for the iPad that allows you to do basic edits like crop, straighten, rotate, flip and adjust exposure. You can also change the colors, turn an image black and white, and add a variety of filters and borders.

The Photoshop Express app allows you to edit your images very quickly and easily. Here's how to get started:

1. Open the Photoshop Express app.

2. A Select Photo button appears in the middle of the screen.

3. Tap Select a Photo to bring up a list of albums that are saved on your iPad.

> **TIP**
>
> The Adobe Camera Pack adds noise reduction, which will help the quality of the iPhone/ iPad images. And it offers camera functionality, including a self timer ... that does not work with the iPad camera yet. According to Adobe, we can expect that functionality to be available with the next major upgrade.

4. Navigate to the image you want to edit, and tap on it.

5. Notice the four icons across the bottom left of the screen. They control your editing:

   - The **Crop** menu allows you to Crop, Straighten, Rotate and Flip.

   - The **Exposure** menu is where you adjust Exposure, Saturation, Tint, Black & White effects, and Contrast.

   - The **Effects 1** menu offers effects such as Sketch, Soft Focus and Sharpen as well as Reduce Noise (if you purchase the Adobe Camera Pack).

   - The **Effects/Border** menu offers seven preset Effects and eight different Borders.

6. Add whatever effects you like and, here is the fun part, just slide you finger up and down or left and right to increase or decrease the effect on the image you've selected.

7. When you're done, you can either tap Save or Cancel. Or, you can upload the image directly to Photoshop.com or to Facebook, if you have live accounts.

8. If you click the Share button on the top left of the screen, the Upload page will open with the Adobe, Photoshop and Facebook icons on the bottom of the screen.
   - Tap the Adobe icon to select the destination for the image on the Photoshop Express website. You can enter a caption for your image, if you want.
   - Tap on the Facebook icon to open a menu that allows you to log into your Facebook account. You'll then need to allow Photoshop Express to post to your Wall by tapping the Allow button. Then, add a caption and tap Upload.

This app works well and does a good job with basic editing and enhancement of image.

PhotoPad by ZAGG

I really like this app and I love the price. C'mon, who doesn't love free? PhotoPad by ZAGG allows you to do basic editing functions, including image rotation, image resizing, drawing/ sketching, paint bucket, color selection, color swap, cropping, threshold levels and posterizing. You can also adjust the color, contrast, tint, chromaticity, saturation and red eye.

This app is free, because ZAGG sells a product called ZAGGskin and you can buy device skins through the app. There is a button on the top of the screen called Create ZAGGskin, which allows you to pick a device and create a skin for it. This includes products like the Apple iPhone and the iPad.

This app is simple and powerful, which makes it great for editing your images on the iPad.

Figure 3-7
The tools in the PhotoPad app are easy to find. Just tap the tools menu and scroll with your finger.

To edit images on the iPad:

1. Open the PhotoPad app.

2. Tap on Images to load an image from your iPad albums.

3. Tap on Tools and begin editing.

4. When you're done editing, tap on either the green check sign on the top right (to apply the changes) or on the red x on the top left (to cancel them).

5. Once the image is adjusted to your liking, tap the Save button. This will save the image as a copy in the iPad's Camera Roll.

This app even allows you to e-mail your edited image out of the app by tapping on the Email button at the bottom of the tools list. This opens a page that allows you to add photos to an e-mail—without leaving the app!

PRO APPLICATION INTEGRATION

Most pro and serious amateur photographers do most of their photo editing on computers—not directly on the iPad. If you are in these categories, then you too were probably very excited about what the iPad could offer for image management and sharing. At the same time, you were also probably quite disappointed at the lack of options available for display, organization and editing photos in the Photos app.

In the end, the critical thing is to get your photos sized correctly for use on the iPad. It doesn't matter if you're using the Photos app or one of the portfolio apps; it's important to make sure that you are working in the right resolution. We covered resolution briefly at the beginning of the chapter.

The program I use for 99% of my image sorting and editing is called Adobe Photoshop Lightroom. It was created for professional photographers and serious amateurs. Lightroom is a very powerful workflow program that can help photographers tag, sort and edit images.

When it comes to creating images to be shown on the iPad with Adobe Lightroom, you can create an export preset so that the images will be sized properly every time. Since we know the size and resolution of the iPad screen, we can create images to perfectly suit it.

Actually, there are two different presets we can create for images on the iPad. One preset could export the biggest possible photo files that the iPad can deal with. This allows you (and other viewers) to zoom in and see details in the images. The second preset could create files that fit the iPad exactly … without tak-

Figure 3-8
Here is the Lightroom export panel with the longest edge set to 2304 and the quality set to JPG.

TIP

Since the iPad 2 has built-in cameras, it will only be a matter of time until the camera apps that are available for the iPhone will become available on the iPad. Shouldn't be too long …

ing a ton of space on the device. When using Lightroom, you can create presets so you don't have to go through all the same little steps to format an image over and over again.

The key setting is the Image Sizing menu, which is in the Export menu.

To format an image for the iPad screen, set the Long Edge to 2304 pixels. This will

Figure 3-9

When you get an e-mail with a photo attached to it, just press and hold your finger on the photo to open the Save Image/ Copy menu.

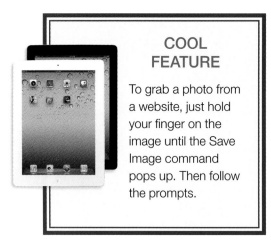

COOL FEATURE

To grab a photo from a website, just hold your finger on the image until the Save Image command pops up. Then follow the prompts.

automatically keep the aspect ratio of your images correct while keeping the size as big as possible. If you want to make the images just big enough for the iPad screen, then the Long Edge needs to be set at 1024. This works for both landscape and portrait images.

For both presets, set the resolution to 132 ppi (the same resolution as the screen) and the file type to JPG at a quality of 80 or higher … with a Color Space of sRGB. I also like to set Sharpness for *screen* and Amount as *standard*. That's it.

Your images that are now exported from Lightroom can be transferred to the iPad as the correct size.

E-MAIL PHOTOS

Who hasn't e-mailed a photo at some point? Even my parents, who use the computer on occasion—to e-mail, browse the Internet and write a letter or two—know how to attach a photo to an e-mail and send it. And they even know how to save those incoming photos into iPhoto. What I'm saying is, it's really easy to use e-mail to get photos on and off your iPad.

When you receive an e-mail with a photo that you want to transfer to your iPad, just press and hold your finger on the image until the Save Image/ Copy menu to pop up. Tap Save Image to copy the photo to the Camera Roll in the Photos app.

At times, you might receive an e-mail with multiple images; don't worry. Apple understands this happens. If there are multiple images attached to a message, press and hold your finger on one of the images. You'll get a pop-up dialogue box that asks if you want to save them all. Find more on iPad e-mail features in Chapter 8.

TRANSFER PHOTOS WITH iTUNES

If you want to move a group of images from your computer onto the iPad or iPad 2, the best way is through iTunes. This works especially well if you keep your images sorted on your computer using a program like iPhoto, Aperture (Mac) or Adobe Photoshop Elements (PC or Mac). It also works well if you keep your images in a specific folder on your computer.

To transfer images from your computer to your iPad using iTunes:

1. Connect the iPad to the computer with the USB cable.

2. Open iTunes on your computer.

3. Select the iPad from the Device list.

4. Click on the Photos tab.

5. Click Sync Photos From checkbox.

6. In the drop-down menu, select the source for your images. This is where you have specific options, depending what software you use to organize your photos. You can also select the folder you use to store your images if you don't use any of the supported software.

   • **iPhoto:** You can select All photos, albums, events and faces … but I don't recommend it, especially if you have a lot of images. This will fill the space on your iPad in a snap. Instead, choose to select albums, events and faces and to automatically include events, using a drop-down list of choices. If you pick this option, you can go through your collection and choose certain albums or events, so you transfer only the images you really want on your iPad.

Figure 3-10
A menu in iTunes shows where you can pick images in iPhoto to be synced to the iPad.

   • **Aperture:** You can select All photos, projects and albums or, as above, choose to transfer only selected photos, projects and albums. Once again, I recommend picking selected images in order to retain some control over the amount of space you use on your iPad for this type of content.

   • **Photoshop Elements:** Again, you get to choose between a full transfer of all photos and albums or selected albums only. At the risk of being repetitive, if you choose All photos and albums, it can fill up your iPad very quickly; so I advise against this option unless you have very few image files on your computer.

7. Click Sync. Or, if this is the first time you are syncing photos, click Apply.

iTunes will now optimize your selected images for display on the iPad. This means that larger images will be compressed in order to make the best use of the limited space available on your iPad. This doesn't actually change the images on your computer; it just adjusts the file versions that are going onto your iPad.

TIP

You can only sync photos to your iPad from one computer. If you attach your iPad to another computer and sync photos from it, the photos that are currently on the iPad will be erased and the new library's selections will be transferred. No other apps, music, media or content will be affected unless you also choose to sync those areas from the new machine as well.

Figure 3-11
When a camera is plugged in, the iPad opens the Photos app. Notice the Camera tab at the top.

CAMERA CONNECTION KIT

Apple has a Camera Connection Kit available for $29 for the iPad and iPad 2, and this is the best way to move images from your camera to your iPad without having to use a computer.

This kit contains two separate pieces: one is for importing images to the iPad from an SD (Secure Digital) card, and the other allows you to use your camera's USB cable to import photos. The kit plugs directly into the iPad connector and, when images are present, you can save them directly to the iPad. It is very simple to use this accessory and it works great.

When you plug the Camera Connection Kit into the iPad or iPad 2 and attach either a camera with a USB cord or insert an SD memory card, the Photos app on your iPad or iPad 2 will launch automatically. The iPad supports most standard photo formats, including JPEG, TIFF and certain RAW file types. Find

more on the file formats supported by the iPad in Chapter 1.

You can now either import all the images or select specific files to import. The iPad will ask if you want to keep or delete the photos on the memory card or the camera when the images have been downloaded. This is your choice. I usually like to keep them on the memory card until all the photos are backed up onto my main computer.

I use 16GB CompactFlash memory cards in my camera, and there is no way to load a full 16GB card onto the iPad unless you have a 32GB or 64GB model that's empty. And if I happen to fill two or three cards, which is easily done on vacation or a professional shoot, then the iPad is definitely not able to store them all. So while it is possible to load images from the camera to the iPad, I seldom add more than a handful at a time due to the space limitations. Instead, I load my images onto my computer at home. I sort and resize the images and load just the keepers onto the iPad.

So why bother using the Camera Connection Kit at all? Well, it can be a great way to show off images you've just taken.

Here's a practical example for this: Say you're a wedding photographer. After the ceremony, you could load a selection of the images directly from the camera to the iPad and allow the bride and groom (and other guests, who are all prospective clients, by the way) to look through the ceremony images during the reception. What a great use for the iPad!

WIRELESS TRANSFER SOLUTIONS

There are a few ways to get images from a computer (or other device) to your iPad without having to plug your iPad into your computer or sync it through iTunes.

Photo Transfer App

The best solution I have found for wireless iPad transfers is a cool little app called Photo Transfer. It moves photos and videos to and from the iPad using a Wi-Fi network. The app isn't free, but I've found that for $2.99, it works really well doing its thing.

Remember earlier when I said that the iTunes sync function allows you to use only one computer's photos? Well, this program allows you to add photos from *any* computer … as long as it's on the same Wi-Fi network as your iPad. Just follow these simple steps.

1. Turn on the iPad.

2. Start the Photo Transfer app.

3. Tap PC on the bottom of the iPad screen.

4. Two URL addresses will appear in the middle of the screen: one is for Apple computers and the other is for Windows-based computers.

5. Type the appropriate address into the browser on your computer.

6. Click on Transfer Photos (or videos) in the browser window that opens.

> **TIP**
>
> Photo files require a lot of space, so you can fill the iPad quickly with them. This is especially true if you use the RAW file type.

> **TIP**
>
>
>
> You can use the iPad's Camera Connection Kit to download photos from your iPhone to the iPad. Just attach the iPhone to the USB cord and then plug the USB cord into the Camera Connection Kit. Attach the Camera Connection Kit to the iPad. The Photos app will launch, because it sees your iPhone as a camera, and it will transfer your images.

7. Select the images (or Transfer Videos) you want to transfer.

8. Click Open.

9. The images and/ or videos will then transfer to the iPad's Photos app.

The cool thing is that you can use this app to transfer images from one iDevice to another. You just need to have the Photo Transfer app

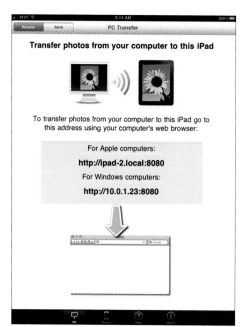

Figure 3-12

This Photo Transfer app screen shows the address of the iPad.

running on both devices, and they need to be on the same Wi-Fi network. But think how cool it is to transfer photos from one iPad to another or from an iPhone to an iPad ... or from an iPad to the iPhone, etc.

To receive files from another device:

1. Turn on both devices.

2. Start the Photo Transfer app on both devices.

3. On the device receiving the images, tap Device at the bottom of the screen, and then tap Receive (located at the top left).

4. A list of devices that the Photo Transfer app can see will appear in the middle of the screen.

5. Select the device that is providing the images, and tap Get Photos or Get Videos. The images or video files will transfer.

To send images from your iPad to another device:

1. Open the Photos app.

2. Tap on the file icon in the top right corner.

3. Select the images to send.

4. Select the photos you want to transfer by tapping on them. A white checkmark will appear in the lower right corner of each selected thumbnail.

5. Tap the Copy button. Depending on the size of the images, this could take a minute.

6. Close the Photos app and open the Photo Transfer app.

7. Tap on Device at the bottom of the screen.

8. Tap Send.

9. The middle of the screen will show the number of images to be transferred and the name of your iPad, which is the device that is sending the images.

10. On the device that is going to receive the images, open the Transfer Photos app and tap on Device. Then, tap Receive and tap on the device name.

11. The images will be transferred.

You can also use this app to transfer photos off the iPad to a computer without having to use a USB cable.

To send images from your iPad to the computer:

1. Open the Photo Transfer app.

2. Tap the Send button on the top left.

3. Tap the PC button on the bottom left.

4. Tap Select Photos and Videos in the middle of the screen.

5. Open the web browser on the computer to which you want to transfer the images.

6. Go to the address shown in the middle of the iPad screen.

7. The images that you selected for transfer will appear as thumbnails and you'll be able to download them to your computer.

Note: The computer and the iPad need to be on the same Wi-Fi network for this process to work.

This app makes it so easy to transfer photos that I now use it all the time to get photos off my computers and onto the iPad. It also makes it easy to transfer photos from my iPad to my wife's iPad.

SLIDESHOW

The iPad has a built-in slideshow feature. Yup, built right in … no app to buy. Granted, it's a very simple slideshow, but it does a great job for the price. I did mention that it is free, right?

While there are a few settings that you can access when running the slideshow, the main menu to set up the slideshow is in the Settings app of the iPad. You'll see that there are only three options. You can:

• Control the length of time that each slide is visible (2 seconds, 3 seconds, 5 seconds, 10 seconds or 20 seconds)

• Turn Repeat on or off

• Turn Shuffle on or off

That's really about it. To play your slideshow, just select an album or group of photos using one of the five selection options: Photos, Albums, Events, Faces or Places. Then tap on the Slideshow button, which is located at the top right of the screen.

This opens a set of slideshow controls that includes an option to play music with your

Figure 3-13
The slideshow options appear when you tap the Slideshow button at the top of the screen.

slideshow and even pick the music to use. This is also where you can pick the style of transition between slides. There are five choices: Cube, Dissolve, Ripple, Wipe and Origami.

Tap the Start Slideshow button to play the images. It doesn't matter if the iPad is in portrait or landscape orientation; the slideshow works in either. And if you change orientation in the middle of the slideshow, the image display will adjust automatically.

If you have an Apple TV on the same network, you can turn on AirPlay to show your slideshow on the connected television.

PORTFOLIO APPS

As I mentioned at the beginning of this chapter, I'm a photographer. And I was really looking forward to using the iPad to show off my work. But after using the Photos app for awhile, I felt that it just wasn't professional enough for what I wanted.

When I went in search of a portfolio app, I was relieved to find that there are quite a few to choose from. They range in price quite a

TIP

In the Portfolio app, you can lock the portfolio. This is help-ful in cases when you might hand over your iPad to someone to view. If locked, (s)he can't change any of the images or settings.

Figure 3-14
This screen shows the main images and their dimensions. And with the lat-est version of this app, you can also change the colors of the background, thumbnail strip, slideshow background and gallery list background.

bit, but none are really cheap. And in this case, you really do get what you pay for.

The portfolio apps listed below are all great. Each has a good interface and better layout options that the Photos app:

- Portfolio for iPad ($14.99)
- FolioBook (7.99)
- Padport ($9.99)
- Mediapad Pro ($14.99)
- PadFolios ($9.99)

Portfolio for iPad ($14.99)

The app that I use most of the time is Portfo-lio for iPad. The ease of use and customizable options make it perfect for me. I realize that it is also the most expensive app listed, but I've been able to easily create a portfolio that I'm proud to share.

I think it's important to grab viewers' atten-tion the minute they look at your portfolio, so I really like the way Portfolio for iPad deals with the main image. Instead of just trying to use a regular image, the app allows you to set a specific image for the main page. Moreover, it gives you the exact dimensions to help you create an image that fits—whether it's in

portrait or landscape orientation … or attached to external monitor.

After you open the Portfolio app, tap on Configure to manage the galleries, change the front image or read the Help file. You can also lock the Configure menu here by entering a four-digit passcode. Don't forget the code, because there is no way to get it back. If you lose the code, you'll have to delete the app and start over.

When you tap Manage Galleries, you can add galleries and add photos to each gallery. The really nice part of gallery creation here is that you can choose images for the gallery

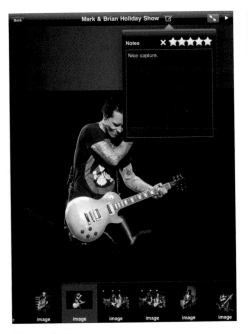

Figure 3-15
Rating and commenting on a photo in the Portfolio for iPad app is as easy as tapping on the Comment button and typing a message.

TIP

The Portfolio app allows you to export your portfolio so it can be imported onto another iPad. This allows you to create a portfolio once and install it on multiple iPads. Just tap on the Import/ Export library button in the Configure menu and follow the directions.

from the images on your iPad in the Photos app. You can also use Dropbox to get the images in your portfolio. You can even load images using a URL if the image resides on the Internet.

To use a URL, grab an image from the Internet and put it in the portfolio. Tap on any photo in this portfolio app to set that image as the gallery cover, edit the keywords associated with it, or rename the photo.

For those who get to see your portfolio, this app offers some nice touches. The one that really stands out to me is the ability for viewers to leave notes and ratings on any image.

To leave a note on a photo you're viewing, tap on the screen and then tap the file icon

at the top of the screen (next to the portfolio name). This opens a Notes window that allows you to leave a message and rate the image. This is an especially useful feature if the person viewing the portfolio is not with you. When you get the iPad back from the person viewing your images, go back into the Manage Galleries section, click on a gallery, and either:

• Clear Ratings and Notes

• E-mail Ratings and Notes

When you e-mail the Ratings and Notes, the iPad creates an e-mail message that you can send to anyone. The message will contain the name of the image(s), a thumbnail, its ratings and any notes that viewers left—in either a PDF or a HTML5 file. You can't edit the information, but getting feedback … even if it's something you don't love … is good, right?

Video

The Skim

When the iPad 2 was released, one of the biggest changes from the original iPad was the inclusion of two video cameras: one on the back of the device and another on the front. Both can be used for still photography, but these two cameras are not equal.

The front-facing camera only shoots VGA-quality video and is designed to be used mainly for video teleconferencing—called FaceTime on the iPad 2. The rear-facing camera can shoot 720p HD video at 30 frames a second. (Information on using these cameras for still photography is provided in Chapter 3.)

And there's more. Along with the new video camera capability, Apple created a mobile app version of its iMovie video-editing application and added a FaceTime app, which allows for easy video communication among Apple products.

VIDEO CAMERA

The iPad 2 uses the same Camera app to take stills and video. This allows you to change between the two easily. For those who use the Apple iPhone, this will look very familiar.

Figure 4-1
Here is the full-screen view of the camera/ video app. Notice the Record button, located bottom center, and the switch that allows you to change the camera from still to video (bottom right). Switch between the two cameras with the button on the top right.

To use the iPad's cameras to shoot video:

1. Turn on the iPad.
2. Tap on the Camera button.
3. To switch between still camera and video camera, use the slide button on the bottom right.
4. Slide the switch to the right to use the camera for shooting video.
5. Switch between the front- and rear-facing cameras by tapping the Switch Camera button on the top right of the screen. Once you start to film, you can't switch cameras.
6. Tap once on the Record button, which is located at the bottom center, to start recording. Tap it again to stop recording. There is no zoom function when using the video camera.

Your video footage is automatically saved in the Photo app's Camera Roll. It will stand apart from still images by a small video camera icon and time stamp at the bottom of the thumbnail. Tap the file to open it, and tap the Play button (in the middle of the screen) to watch it.

Once a video clip is in the iPad, you can edit it using the iMovie app.

iMOVIE APP ($4.99)

Apple iMovie has been a staple on Macintosh computers for years, and it's now on the iPad 2. Officially, the iMovie app is only supported on the iPhone 4, the iPad 2 and the iPod Touch 4th generation or later, which means that the iMovie app will not load onto the original iPad through the App Store or iTunes. See sidebar on the next page for the workaround.

NOTE: *All directions for iMovie assume that the iPad 2 is in horizontal position.*

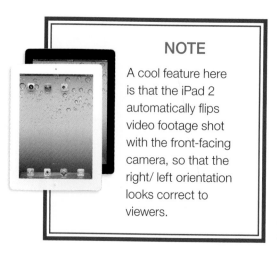

NOTE

A cool feature here is that the iPad 2 automatically flips video footage shot with the front-facing camera, so that the right/ left orientation looks correct to viewers.

INSTALL iMOVIE ON THE ORIGINAL iPAD

The original iPad can run iMovie, but it will operate a little slower there than on the newer, faster iPad 2. But that's no reason to not have it on your iPad if you want to use it. Of course, there may come a time when the original iPad will not be able to run iMovie, but for now, go ahead and enjoy it.

You can load it legally without having to jailbreak or alter your iPad in any way; you just have to use a different tool—not the App Store or iTunes—to do it. This tool is the newest version of the iPhone Configuration Utility software. It runs on your computer and will allow you to load applications onto your iPad without using iTunes. Find it for Mac at http://support.apple.com/kb/dl851 and for Windows at http://support.apple.com/kb/DL926. You'll also need to buy the iMovie app in iTunes on the same computer that you use to download the iPhone Configuration Utility Software.

Once you've installed the iPhone Configuration Utility Software, and the iMovie app is in iTunes, just follow these instructions to get the iMovie app onto your first generation iPad.

1. Plug your iPad into the computer with the USB cord.

2. Run the iPhone Configuration Utility Software. (On a Macintosh, it will be in Applications > Utilities. On a PC, it will be wherever you decided to save it.)

3. Click on the Applications button on the left.

4. Click the Add button on the top left.

5. Navigate to the app's location on your computer. Usually, you can find this by going to Music > iTunes> Mobile Applications.

6. Click on iMovie from the list on the right.

7. Click on iPad from the Device list on the left.

8. Click on Applications from the tabs across the top and scroll until you see iMovie.

9. Click the Install button.

iMovie is now on your original iPad. Of course, you can't use the original iPad to shoot any video; so to edit clips, you'll need to use a different video camera and load those clips onto your device … either through iTunes or through the Camera Connection Kit.

Create Video

There are two ways to get video into the iMovie app. The first and easiest way is to shoot the footage with the built-in camera. You can also transfer videos using iTunes on your computer. We'll cover that in the next section.

Before you can import any video, you need to open a project. So when the iMovie app starts, tap the (+) sign at the bottom of the screen. This will open the main work screen. Tap on the Video Camera icon to open the built-in video camera.

Start filming by pressing the red button on the bottom of the screen. This starts the

video capture. When you've filmed all the footage you want, tap the button a second time to stop. You can now retake the clip, play or use it. If you tap Use, the video clip will automatically be imported into your iMovie app.

Import Video

The iMovie app can use video clips that you have on your computer. The key is to put those movie clips into iTunes and then sync them to your iPad with the Photos setting. Doing that makes the video clips accessible in the iMovie app.

EDIT VIDEO CLIPS IN iMOVIE

To access video clips that are in your photo library to edit them, open the iMovie app and tap the (+) symbol to open the main editing screen. Then tap on the icon that looks like a small frame (located on the left side of the screen in the middle). This brings up the video clips on your iPad that can be used

TIP

When shooting and editing video, I like to use the iPad in the horizontal orientation, because that matches the dimensions of a TV.

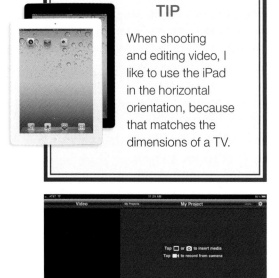

Figure 4-2
The blank workspace is just waiting for you to start your movie project.

Figure 4-3
The Photos tab in iTunes is where photos are transferred. Be sure that the Include Videos checkbox is marked when you sync.

with the iMovie app. This will include videos taken with the built-in camera as well as clips that have been imported.

Trim Clips

When you tap on a clip, it will be outlined in orange. Also, little orange dots will appear on the top left and bottom right, and a blue arrow will extend through the middle. The orange dots allow you to trim the clip before entering it into the editing pipeline.

Put your finger on one of the orange dots, and the preview window will show the selected clip. Now just slide the dot to the left or right to trim the clip. The video in the preview window will show you exactly where you are in the clip, so that you can make the edits exact. Once the video's start and stop points are set, tap on the blue arrow to insert the video clip into the editing timeline.

Tweak It

Before adding another clip, let's look at what we can do in the main editing widow to the imported clip.

- Tap on the clip once. The two orange dots will appear again, allowing you to fine-tune the clip. Slide the orange dots to edit the start and end point of the clip. Keep in mind, for good transitions, you'll want to leave a little space at the start and end of each clip.

- Double tap on the clip to access the Clip Settings menu. This is where you can add a Title Style, add a location and adjust the volume. You can also delete the clip if you want. This won't delete it from the iPad ... just from the timeline.

Add a Second Clip

To add a second clip to your movie, you first have to decide if it goes in front of or behind the current clip. All you do is slide the current clip either left or right until the red line (which represents the play head) is at the beginning of the current clip or the end. Then tap on the clip you want to add to your movie, and adjust the start and end points as you did with the previous clip; then tap on the arrow, and the clip will become part of the movie with a transition already applied.

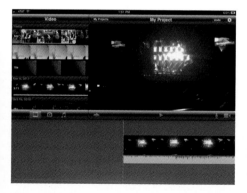

Figure 4-4
The selected video on the top left of the screen shows orange circles. These allow you to trim the clip before importing.

Figure 4-5
Tap on the selected clip once to bring up the trim controls. Tap twice to reveal the Clip Settings.

Transitions

Good transitions make a home movie look polished and professional, and they're automatically applied when you add a second (or third or fourth, etc.) clip to the movie timeline. It's easy to edit the transition:

- Single tap on the transition (it looks like two arrows pointing at each other between your clips) to bring up the transition editor, which allows you to change where the transition starts and ends. This icon appears as two orange arrows that appear below the transition icon. (These arrows face down and up instead of right and left.) Tap on these to open the editor. You can now use those orange dots to adjust the transition. Zoom in to make it easier to make good edits.

- Double tap the transition to access the Transition Setting menu. This is where you can control the length of the transition and the style. The default is Cross Dissolve, but you can also choose None or a Theme transition. You can set the length of transition from 0.5 sec to 2.0 sec.

Add Still Photos to a Movie

If you want to add still images to your movie, then Apple has you covered. You can easily add any still photo that's on your iPad to your movie. Right next to the Video button is a Still Photo button. (It looks like a camera.) Tap on it and the video files on the top left will be replaced with the photos stored on your iPad 2 ... sorted by folders. Tap on a folder and the images from that folder will appear. Hold your finger on an image to preview it. Tap on an image to insert it into the timeline.

When you add a still image to the timeline, the default setting is for the image to stay visible for three to five seconds, depending on your transitions setting. You can adjust the length of time that the photo is visible in your movie by using the orange dots to trim or expand the frame. The photos all have the Ken Burns effect (Apple's term for *panning*) applied automatically.

To edit the clip:

1. In the timeline, tap the photo you want to adjust.

Figure 4-6
The Transition Settings menu allows you adjust the transition between clips.

Figure 4-7
The image was inserted between the clips. Double clicking on it opens the Photo Settings clip.

2. In the Preview window are Start and End buttons that can be used to set where the image movement begins and ends.

3. To set the start of the Ken Burns effect, tap the Start button. It will dim.

4. Drag the image around the viewer and use your fingers to zoom in. This will be the start point of the effect.

5. Set the End button to show how the Ken Burns effect will end up. Tap the End button to select it and then drag the image around the viewer and pinch to zoom in or out on a specific portion of it. This will set the endpoint of the effect.

6. Tap Done.

If you set the start and end to look the same, there will be no effect on the image.

Add Sound

What's a movie without sound? A boring one, that's what! Fortunately, iMovie allows you to add background music, sound effects and voiceovers to your movie. Here's how:

- **Background music:** There are two types of background music. The first is theme music, which changes depending on what theme you use. The other is music taken from your iPad 2 iTunes library. To add background music:

  1. In iMovie with a project open, tap the Audio button.

  2. Tap Theme Music to choose any of the built-in theme music, or tap any one of the other categories to find music that you've loaded onto your iPad 2.

  3. Tap on the song/ music you want to play in the background of your video. It will show up as a green bar behind the video clips.

TIP

You can have only one music track in your project with background music looping turned on. If you want more than one background music track, then looping must be turned off.

4. Adjust the volume of the music by double-tapping the green bar to open the Audio Clip Settings window. Use the volume slider to find a volume that's appropriate for your video.

5. Turn music looping on or off by tapping the Project Settings button (it's the little gear on the top right) and selecting on or off for Loop Background Music.

- **Sound Effects:** iMovie comes loaded with some special audio effects. Add them to the movie using the same process that's described above for adding background music. But instead of a track that runs behind the clip, you'll see a small audio clip on your timeline. Tap it once to adjust the length of the effect; tap it twice to adjust its volume. Or, if it doesn't work out as you'd hoped, you can delete it.

- **Voiceover.** The iPad 2 has a Microphone button that, when tapped, allows you to record any sound through the built-in microphone (or through one of the headphones with the built-in microphone plugged into the headphone jack). The

Figure 4-8
The background music is green, while the inserted sound effect is blue.

Figure 4-9
Here is a look at the Themes menu in iMovie.

recorder comes up with a volume display, showing you are ready to record. Tap the Record button. You'll get a three-second countdown to begin recording. Once it's done, you can discard, retake, review or accept the recording. If the recording is accepted, it enters the timeline.

To move the audio clips around the timeline, press and hold your finger on the audio clip until it pops off the background. Move the clip with your finger to a new spot, and then drop it.

Themes

iMovie comes with eight built-in themes to help you create good-looking movies. Each theme is a set of coordinated transitions, music and titles. The Modern Theme is the default. When you change the theme, any previous theme elements in your project will be changed to the new theme, including any music if the theme music is turned on.

To access the theme settings, open the Project Settings menu. This is located on the top right and looks like a little gear. There are five options here:

- Choose a Theme
- Activate Theme Music (or turn it off)
- Loop Background Music (or turn it off)
- Set to Fade In from Black (or turn it off)
- Set to Fade Out to Black (or turn it off)

Titles

You can add a title to any video clip or photo in the iMovie timeline. And your text will be on the whole clip or photo. There is no way to adjust the period of time that the text is visible. It's either on the whole clip or none.

To add a title:

1. Open iMovie.

2. Double tap the clip or photo to open the Clip Settings menu.

3. Tap on Title Style to access options for font treatments.

4. Pick a style. A preview of the selection will appear in the preview window.

5. Tap on Title Text Here in the preview window.

Figure 4-10
The Title view shows where text
is edited.

Figure 4-11
You can share your movie in a variety of
ways with the tap of a finger.

6. Type in the title.

7. Tap Done on the keyboard to return to
general editing.

8. Each clip can have only one title.

SAVE AND TRANSFER iMOVIE FILES

Video files in iMovie are saved automatically
... as you create them. So when you're done
creating and editing a movie on your iPad 2,
tap on the My Projects button. This takes you
back to the My Projects screen, where you
can scroll sideways through your saved movies by swiping your finger left or right.

The first thing I like to do is change the name
of a new iMovie project to something more
descriptive than *My Project*. It's easy to do;
just tap on the title on the movie marquee.
You can't change the date or time that's under
the name, but that's okay. It's the date of the
last edit and the running time of the movie,
which are helpful bits of information.

There are six buttons across the bottom of
the screen. Here's what they do:

- **iMovie Help** is the user manual for
iMovie. It will walk you through everything—from the navigation gestures to
audio adjustments.

- **New Project** is the (+) sign that starts
a new project. Tap it to open a new
project window.

- Tap **Play** to show the selected movie.

- **Export/ Share** opens the Share Movie To
menu. Here, you can export your movie
to the iPad 2 Camera Roll or to YouTube,
Facebook, vimeo and/ or CNN iReport.
You can also send the project to iTunes for
editing on the computer.

- **Import Menu** allows you to import video
files to your iPad. (Steps for importing
are provided below.) So if there are any
iMovie projects in iTunes that you want
to edit on the iPad 2, use this button to
move them.

To move iMovie projects from iTunes on your
computer to your iPad 2, attach the iPad to
your computer, open iTunes and then:

1. Click on the iPad in the Device list.

2. Click on the Apps tab at the top of the screen.

3. Scroll down the page until the File Sharing window appears.

4. Click on iMovie in the apps list.

5. Click Add (at the bottom of the window) and navigate to the project you want to transfer.

6. On the iPad, open iMovie and tap the Import button.

7. A list of compatible iMovie projects will be there. Just tap on the one you want to import.

FACETIME

FaceTime is the video-conferencing technology that Apple introduced in the iPhone 4. Alas, it made its way into the iPad 2. So with a simple tap, you can use the iPad 2 to call any of the FaceTime-enabled devices, including the iPhone 4, another iPad 2, iPod Touch or Mac computer, over Wi-Fi.

When I was a kid, I read a lot of science fiction. Actually, I still do. And this technology is what I always envisioned when thinking about phone calls in the future. It's great. But of course, there are drawbacks to FaceTime.

NOTE

FaceTime is not available on the original iPad. There's no video camera.

The most notable is that it only works over Wi-Fi. But the fact that you can have a video conference using your iPad 2, iPhone 4, iPod Touch or Mac computer is just amazing.

Set Up FaceTime
Setting up FaceTime is not difficult. All you need is an Apple ID and an e-mail address.

The first time you run FaceTime on the iPad 2, it will ask you to sign in with your Apple ID … or to create a new account. After you sign in, you'll need to pick an e-mail address to use for FaceTime calls. This address doesn't have to be the same address you use for the Apple ID.

Now, this is important, if you have multiple devices that all have FaceTime capability—

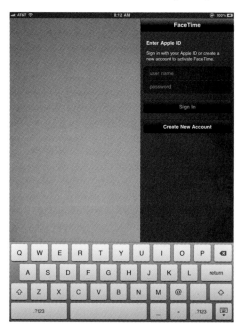

Figure 4-12
The FaceTime sign up screen requires you to enter your Apple ID and password once. From there, the iPad 2 will remember it.

and you want them all to ring when called—then use the same e-mail address for all of them. If you have multiple devices but want them all to be considered separate, then use different e-mails.

Here's an example. I have a MacBook Pro that has FaceTime. And I have an iPhone 4 with FaceTime installed. If someone wants to call me on the iPhone 4, then they call using the iPhone's telephone number. If they want to call me on the computer, then they use my main e-mail address.

When I set up my iPad 2, I wanted it to have a different identity, so that people could call it separately from the computer. So my iPad 2 uses a different e-mail address ... even though it uses the same Apple ID as the computer. This means that the computer can call the iPad 2, and the iPad 2 can call the computer—again, because they use different e-mail addresses for calls.

But there is a trick involved with getting an iPad 2 to FaceTime with a computer when both are using the same Apple ID. You have to change the Caller ID in the Settings app. Here's how:

1. Turn on the iPad 2.

2. Tap Settings.

3. Tap on FaceTime from the list on the left.

   • You can turn FaceTime on or off here. Turn it off if you don't want to be disturbed.

   • See the Account e-mail that is your Apple ID.

   • Notice the e-mail that you entered as the address to use for calling the device.

   • Find the button that allows you to add another e-mail.

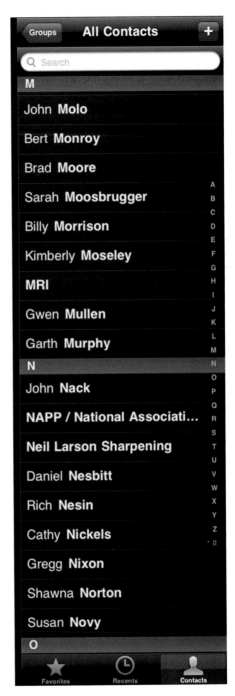

Figure 4-13
This is a list of contacts on an iPad 2.

- If there is more than one e-mail address entered here, there will also be a Caller ID field. This needs to be set to the e-mail address you want to be used for calling your iPad 2.

4. Tap on the caller ID field to pick (from the e-mails listed) the one to use as a unique identifier for the device.

Make a Call

Once you have FaceTime set up, use your contact list to call someone. Making a call with FaceTime is very easy; Apple has kept the processes simple. All you do is start the FaceTime app and click on one of your contacts. The video camera will turn on automatically; there are no settings to adjust.

The person being called will hear a ringing sound. FaceTime will ring even if it isn't currently running on the recipient's machine. A message on their screen will ask if they want to accept or decline the FaceTime call. That's it. The recipient just needs to tap the Accept or Decline button on the bottom of the screen.

When using FaceTime, it's possible to switch between the front-facing camera and the rear-facing camera … just by tapping the Change

NOTE

Currently, FaceTime does not work with other video services like AIM or iChat.

Camera button. This capability allows you to go from a face-to-face conversation to showing the person you're talking to what's going on around you with the tap of a button. So, for example, I could be having a face-to-face conversation on my iPad and decide to show the person I'm talking to something that's going on. I don't have to turn the device around and try to aim a camera blindly. Instead, I can just tap the switch that changes to the other camera.

When you're on a FaceTime call, the FaceTime interface uses the whole iPad 2 screen.

Add a Contact

When you start the FaceTime app, you'll see a list of contacts on the right side. Or, you'll see a list of favorites or the most recent calls (if you select those views, as described below). Add a contact by tapping the (+) sign on the top right when you're in the contacts view. Any contact you enter here will appear in your address book on the iPad 2, and all the contacts from the address book on the iPad 2 will be shown here.

At the bottom of your contact list, there are two other options. You can view a list of recent calls and a list of Favorites. The Recents list can show all the calls made and received on your device, or it can limit the list to just the missed calls. Tap the Clear button on the top right to erase all the listings in the Recents screen.

To mark a contact as a favorite:

1. Open FaceTime.

2. Tap on Contacts on the bottom right.

3. Tap on the contact you want to mark as a favorite.

4. On the bottom of the contacts information are two buttons: Share Contact and Add to favorites. Tap Add to Favorites.

5. A pop-up menu will appear that asks which of the contact's phone numbers or e-mails you want to add.

6. Tap on the contact info you want added as a favorite.

To remove a favorite:

1. Open FaceTime.

2. Tap on favorites on the bottom left.

3. Tap the Edit button on the top left of the Favorites list.

4. A white (–) sign will appear next to each entry. Tap on the sign next to the entry you want to remove from Favorites.

5. Tap Done when you're finished editing.

The video quality of FaceTime is pretty good; but like all live video over the Internet, the quality is dependent on the connection speed. The better the connection and the higher the speed, the better the quality of the video.

As Apple releases new products, expect to see FaceTime integrated into all the iDevices … along with improvements to the camera and software. The MacBook Pro laptops that were released in early 2011 come equipped with 720p video calls.

PART 2

Entertainment Content

eBooks

The Skim

iBooks • Kindle • nook • Stanza • Bookmarks
Sharing eBooks • Self-Publishing

I have been using the iPad as an electronic book reader since the day it came out. And I absolutely love it. Yet the iPad 2, almost unbelievably, makes reading even more comfortable. The lighter, thinner device is so much easier to hold!

The volume of selections at the iBook Store on the iPad is larger now, too. And, of course, Apple would like it if you purchased all your electronic books through its store. But admittedly, this outlet doesn't have nearly the same number of titles as the Amazon Kindle store. It is growing though. In fact, bestselling titles from publisher Random House started to appear in the iBooks Store recently.

There's been a lot of discussion about the different book-reading apps available for the iPad, especially since Apple rejected the Sony reader app and is now enforcing its terms of service for other publishers. In a nutshell, Apple's terms might force the Kindle and nook apps off the iPad, which would be a great loss.

But Apple is used to getting its way when it comes to what content is available on its devices. And in the past, a lack of competition made Apple king of the hill. For example, when the iTunes Store first started selling music, there was no other company doing it. But with digital books, both the Kindle from Amazon.com and the nook from Barnes & Noble have been around longer than the iPad. And these products are

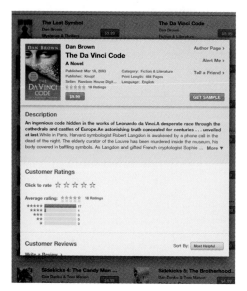

Figure 5-1
The best seller *Da Vinci Code* is now available in the iBooks Store due to the Random House deal.

actually better for consumers than the iPad in terms of functioning as an eBook reader.

In early 2011, Apple began tightening its policies related to eBook apps on the iPad. The company rejected the Sony reader app because it only allows customers to purchase content in a web browser; it doesn't allow for in-app content purchases. Now, while this doesn't seem like a big deal, it violates the Apple developer guidelines by cutting Apple out of the profits.

According to Apple's guidelines, any purchases that can be made outside of the app must also be available inside the app … at the same or a cheaper price. Moreover, the content purchase is subject to a 30/70 revenue split with Apple.

The problem is that when a user wants to purchase an eBook through the Kindle or

nook app, both programs open a web-browser window. If Apple holds true to the new stricter interpretations of its developer guidelines, then the Kindle app and the nook app are likely to disappear from the iPad. Therefore, I recommend that you download the apps from these companies as soon as possible!

iBOOKS

The iBooks app is an electronic book reader and bookstore all in one, but you won't find this app on your iPad when you take it out of the box. You have to install the iBooks app just like any other app—either through the iTunes Store on your computer or the App Store on your iPad. But the good news is that it's free.

Install iBooks

There are a few different ways to get iBooks onto your iPad. You can get it while on your iPad or via your computer.

- **On the iPad**

  Tap the App Store icon. An offer to download a free copy of iBooks should appear. Tap Download to get the iBooks app. If you don't get the invitation, just click in the search bar on the top right of the screen and enter *iBooks*, and then tap Search. The iBooks app from Apple will be the first choice. Tap on the FREE button to begin downloading the app.

- **From iTunes on the Computer**

  Start iTunes and click iTunes Store on the left side of the window. Click on the App Store tab at the top of the window and search for iBooks. Once you've downloaded the iBooks app, just sync the iPad to install the app.

With the iBooks app on the iPad, you can start enjoying your iPad as an electronic book reader.

Use iBooks

To see how iBooks works, I recommend downloading a free iBook. Just follow the steps below to get a free version of *Winnie-the-Pooh*:

1. Tap on iBooks.
2. Tap Store.
3. Tap on the Top Charts button on the bottom of the screen.
4. The top free book is *Winnie-the-Pooh*— at least it is as I'm writing this. Tap on Download.
5. You will have to enter your iTunes password but you won't get charged.
6. You now have a free iBook to read.

Just tap the cover to open your book. When an iBook is opened, the screen will show a menu bar across the top and a slider along the bottom with the page count. Both of these tools will fade from view after a few minutes, but you can easily bring them back by tapping on the top of the page.

The controls at the top of the page make the iBook reading experience really enjoyable.

- Tap the **Library** button to get back to your library of books.
- Tap **Table of Contents/ Bookmark** to bring up a menu that allows you to choose between the Table of Contents (which includes links to the start of each chapter) or to a list of bookmarks that you've set in the current book.
- **Buy** is only visible when you're reading a sample chapter. This button allows you to immediately buy the book you're sampling … with a simple tap.
- Tap **Brightness** to change the strength of light for the page in your eBook, which

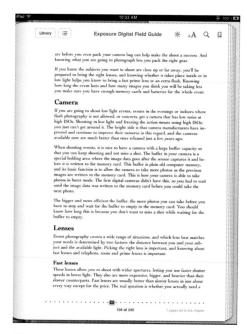

Figure 5-2

This is a page of a book as shown in the iBooks app. Notice the menus across the top and the controls across the bottom.

is really useful when reading in low light, when the device doesn't need to be very bright. Note that the brightness level you choose here affects only the material in your iBooks app and not the whole device. There is a different brightness setting in the system menu that affects the rest of the whole iPad.

- The **Type Size, Font and Page Color** settings adjust the size of the text, the font used for displaying text, and the color of the paper (white or sepia).
- Tap **Search** to look for specific terms in the eBook.
- The **Set a Bookmark** button looks like an old-fashioned page marker. And it

CONNECT

You need to be connected to the Internet in order to access the iBooks Store. This means that you need to be on a Wi-Fi network or have the iPad 3G model as well as an active account and cell signal.

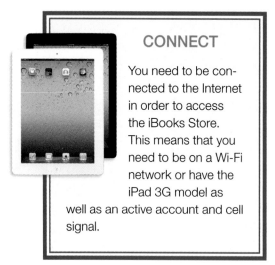

Figure 5-3
The iBooks Store looks a lot like the iTunes Store, making it familiar to anyone who has purchased music or movies on a computer.

functions as one, too. Just tap it. There are other ways to set bookmarks, and we'll explore those processes a little later, but this is a good option.

- **Bottom Slider:** The small brown slider on the bottom of the page is a quick and easy way to flip through a book until you get to a specific page. Hold your finger on the little box and move it left or right to page quickly. Notice the page count on the bottom. Chapters and page numbers are visible right above the little brown box.

To turn a page in iBooks, swipe your finger across the page in the direction you want the page to turn. You can also turn a page by tapping on the edge of the page you want to flip. One little thing to keep in mind is that if you tend to swipe across the bottom part of the screen to turn a page, there's a chance you'll inadvertently activate the slider there … and find that you've jumped back or forward by whole sections instead of a single page. I know it seems like it wouldn't happen. In fact, that's what I thought until I did it by mistake. Twice.

iBOOKS STORE

There is only one iBooks Store and it's part of the iBooks app. There is no place to buy iBooks on your computer or through the iTunes Store. To access the iBooks Store, tap on the Store button that's located on the top left of the screen in the iBooks library view.

If you've used the App Store or the iTunes Store, then the iBooks Store will look very familiar. You won't see any video or music offerings; instead, you'll find a growing selection of electronic books.

The menu across the top of the screen offers a range of helpful options:

- Tap the **Library** button to return to your collection of books and PDFs on the iPad.

- **Categories** allows you to jump directly to a specific type of book (e.g., Classics, Nonfiction, etc). Picking a classification here will change the information presented in the main part of the window.
- **Featured/ Release Date** enables you to display content by items that Apple wants to feature or by the most current release date.
- **Search** allows you to explore the whole iBooks Store by author, subject or anything else you can think of to distinguish your selections. Apple will try to help by automatically filling in the rest of the search string as you type.

The middle section of the screen features a display of eBooks that are available for purchase. One odd thing about the navigation here is that swiping your finger across the page doesn't work. You need to use the little arrow icons to browse the pages of eBook listings.

The menu across the bottom of the screen includes the following options:

- **Featured** is the main display in the iBooks Store. This gives you the latest and greatest offerings in the store.
- Tap **NY Times** to see the *New York Times* Best Seller lists. This iBooks list gets updated once a week, when the publication updates its list.
- **Top Charts** show you the paid and free books that are popular and selling well in the iBooks Store.
- Tap **Browse** to access a search feature that allows you to scroll through the Top Authors in the paid and free books as well as the different categories. This is very much like browsing the shelves of your local bookstore.
- **Purchases** shows which books you've already purchased and allows you to re-download them if you want.

Figure 5-4
The book information page gives you the option to buy the book (by pressing on the price) or getting a free sample (by selecting Get Sample).

Once you've found a book that looks interesting, just click on the book's icon to bring up more info about it. You can go ahead and buy the book by tapping on its price, which turns into a Buy Now button. If you tap Buy Now, you'll be asked to enter your iTunes account name and password, so Apple can charge you.

Or, get a sample chapter before buying by tapping Get Sample. I like to get a sample before I buy an eBook ... to make sure it is what I want. I really love the try-it-before-you-buy-it concept, and iBooks has done it right. If you click on Get Sample, the bookstore will automatically launch your library with the requested book on the shelf (marked as a sample).

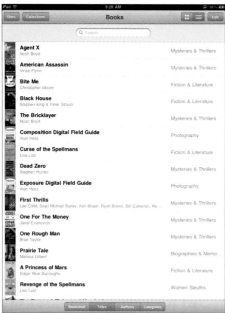

Figure 5-5

The two views of the iBooks Library screen show the same library. I prefer the book-cover view, but it's nice to have options.

That's how easy it is! And, even better, you can download as many samples as you want. Apple's savvy like that. The company understands that you are much more likely to buy a book after you read a chapter or two.

iBOOKS LIBRARY

The iBooks library has some neat features. For starters, it has two different views. For those who like the visual of a book case with covers facing out, that's the default look (shelf view). And for those who prefer a list, that view is also available (list view). Select your preference by choosing a button on the top right side of the library view.

Arrangements

When using the library list view, you can decide how to sort your books on your bookshelf. Arrange by title, author or category. Find these sorting options on the bottom of the screen when the library is in list view.

There is a way to sort your books when in the shelf view, too, and it's pretty cool. Just hold your finger on the book you want to move and wait for it to get bigger. Then, drag it around the bookshelf and drop it where you want it. It's like sorting books on a real bookshelf, which is really useful when you have a lot of books and want to keep them in a specific order that's not available in the list view menu.

Collection Management

Notice the Edit button on the top row. Tap this to delete a book from your iPad. The nice part about this is that if you buy a book and delete it, you can re-download it later at no additional cost. This is a massive departure from the usual Apple policy that makes you responsible for keeping the media content you buy.

Figure 5-6
Switch collections with a tap of
your finger.

The other button on the top of the screen is
the Collections button. Tapping this allows
you to sort your books into different collections. If you have PDFs loaded into your
iBooks app, then this is where you find them.
I've created a few collections. The first is
called "Dresden," and it's where I keep all my
Dresden File books by Jim Butcher. The second is a Stephen King collection that holds
the few Stephen King books I have on my
iPad.

So how do you get books into the different
collections? That's simple; you have to use
the Edit button.

1. Tap the Edit button on the top right of the
   screen.

2. Tap on the eBooks you want to move into
   a collection.

3. The selected books will look grey with a
   white checkmark in a blue circle in the
   bottom right corner.

4. Now, tap on the Move button that's
   located on the top left of the screen. But
   be careful not to tap on the Delete button,
   which is right next to it.

5. A list of collections will open, and this
   allows you to create a new collection.

6. Tap on the collection to which you want to
   move the eBook.

7. Enjoy watching the cool animation as the
   book flies from the old collection to the
   new one.

An iBook can only be in one collection at
a time.

eBOOK READER APP OPTIONS

The iPad allows you to read eBooks through
the iBooks app on your iPad as well as those
purchased on other electronic book readers, specifically the Amazon Kindle and the
Barnes & Noble nook. This is because there
are Kindle and nook apps for the iPad.

Amazon Kindle App

The most popular electronic book reader on
the market is the Kindle from Amazon. While
the iPad is making inroads into the eBook
market, it has a long way to go to catch up
to the Kindle. And part of the challenge for
Apple is that the Kindle Graphite with Wi-Fi
is $139—not $499. But of course the Kindle
is just an eBook reader and can't do all the
other stuff that the iPad can do.

The Kindle app for the iPad allows you to read
your Kindle books on the iPad. You can also
buy Kindle books, browse the Kindle bookstore
and add any of your previously purchased
Kindle books to your iPad through this app.

Figure 5-7
The Kindle app shows the books
that have been purchased and those
that are just samples.

Figure 5-8
The Kindle bookstore has a huge variety
of content, all available for immediate
download.

TIP

You don't need to
actually own a Kindle
to run the iPad Kindle
app. The Kindle app
effectively turns your
iPad into a Kindle,
allowing you all
the benefits of this
device, including an ability to
shop the Amazon Kindle store.

One main difference between the iBooks app
and the Kindle app is that the Kindle app
launches the Kindle website, which is a subset
of the regular Amazon.com website. When
you find a book through the Kindle app, you
buy it from the website and it automatically
loads into your Kindle app. As mentioned
earlier in this chapter, the Kindle app's lack of
in-app purchase options might mean that it'll
disappear from the iPad.

As with the iBook Store, when you find a
Kindle book you want to buy, you can either
purchase it or download a sample. Then you
have the option to go back to the bookstore
or return to the iPad Kindle app. The whole
process is really very easy.

Keep in mind that the Kindle app will not allow you to get new books or connect to the store unless you are connected to the Internet, either through Wi-Fi or 3G.

nook App

The Barnes & Noble eBook reader is called the nook, and it too has an app for the iPad. The nook app allows you to shop in the Barnes & Noble online store, download sample chapters, sync books over multiple devices and, of course, read your electronic books on your iPad. Two different versions of the nook are available, and both are significantly less expensive than the iPad:

- Color version runs about $249.
- Black and white version costs $149.

Before you can use the nook app, you'll need to either sign in with an existing account, or tap to set up a new account. Once you are signed in, the nook will walk you through a series of screens that show how the app works. If it doesn't, or you want to see the instructions again, just tap on the Welcome to eBooks button.

Tap the first button, Shop, to visit the Barnes & Noble Online nook Store. This is very much like the Amazon online store; it allows you to search for and buy eBooks. All you need is a credit card. And once you purchase a book, there are links on the page that allow you to download the book into iTunes or start reading it immediately on the iPad in the nook app.

Now, since we are doing everything through the iPad here, click on that link. The nook app will open, and the newly purchased book will start to download to your iPad. Because the nook app sends users to a web browser for purchasing eBooks (like the Kindle app), there is a chance that Apple will pull the plug

Figure 5-9

Buying a Kindle eBook is really easy. And you can go straight from the store back to your iPad.

Figure 5-10
The nook app shows the Store button as well as purchases, samples and the Welcome to eBooks button. After a book has been purchased, you can see the links to download the book.

Figure 5-11
The nook online store is really well-designed. I found it easier to use this store than the Kindle store. The cool part is that you can download samples, so you can try before you buy.

on the nook app … unless it starts to offer in-app purchases as well.

The nook app will not allow you to get new books or connect to the store unless you are connected to the Internet, either through Wi-Fi or through 3G.

Stanza App

Another option for reading electronic books on your iPad is the Stanza app. This is less well-known than the Kindle app or the nook app, but it's a really nice eBook reader. The Stanza app has the ability to access a range of different bookstores, including a wide selection of free books. This is by far the easiest way to access a huge volume of free electronic

book content right on the iPad.

Open the Stanza app, and click on the Get Books button at the bottom of the screen. Then tap on the Catalog button on the top of the screen to see the four bookstores:

- BooksOnBoard eBook Shop
- O'Reilly Ebooks
- All Romance eBooks
- SmashWords

There is also a much more comprehensive free eBook list with providers such as:

- Project Gutenberg
- Random House Free Library
- Sheet Music from Mutopia

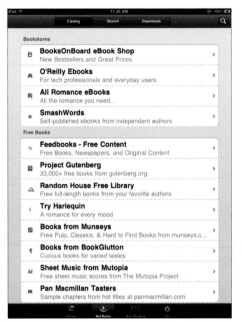

Figure 5-12

Here is the list of eBook sources inside the Stanza app. Just tap on a store to browse their collections.

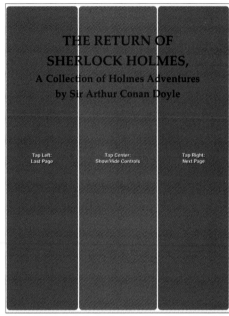

Figure 5-13

The Stanza app controls are shown when you first open an eBook.

Once you've found a book or two that you want to read, the Stanza app allows you to download them directly into your iPad. I love a good mystery, and there are none better than good old Sherlock Holmes. Within a few minutes of looking through the Stanza collections, I found *The Return of Sherlock Holmes*. Following the instructions for that store, I was able to download the eBook right into Stanza and begin reading.

After you install the Stanza app, you can transfer eBooks from your computer to the iPad and from the iPad to the computer. Because you can transfer files in and out of the Stanza app, you can actually get free books in the Stanza app and transfer them to your computer and back into iTunes, and then load them into the iBooks reader.

TIP

Each of the bookstores in the Stanza catalogue is independent and may have a different method for you to purchase content.

You don't have to do this, but you can. Here's how:

1. Download the Stanza app onto your iPad.

2. Open the Stanza app and tap the Get Books button at the bottom of the screen.

3. Download the books you want to read.

4. When you're back at your computer, plug in the iPad and launch iTunes.

5. In iTunes, click on File > Transfer Purchases from the iPad.

6. Select iPad in the Device list on the left side of the screen.

7. Click on the Apps tab in iTunes.

8. Scroll to the bottom of the page to find the File Sharing section.

9. Click on the Stanza app on the left side under File Sharing, and you'll see all the books you've downloaded to your iPad using Stanza.

10. Select the books you want to transfer and click the Save To button.

11. Select a spot that you'll be able to find later. I use a folder called *Stanza Books*.

12. Once the files have been saved, click on File > Add to Library … and navigate to the saved books.

13. Now click on the Books tab to see the books you bought on Stanza. Make sure they are selected and sync the iPad.

14. The books you got with Stanza are now in your iBooks library and can be read like any other book in your iBooks app on the iPad.

An additional note about Stanza: Not only can Stanza read ePub-formatted books, like those in the iBooks Store; it can also read PDF files, HTML documents and even Comic Book Reader (.cbr)-formatted books and documents!

BOOKMARKS

Bookmarks are important; they allow you to pick up right where you left off … when you get back to your paper book or eBook.

But eBooks are different from paper books because they can be in two places at the same time, and this makes electronic bookmarks even more helpful.

For example, I can have the same eBook loaded on my iPad and iPhone 4 as long as both devices use the same Apple ID. This is perfect for me, especially when I photograph a concert (which I do often). At times this job entails sitting around with nothing to do while the band sets up. So I use my iPhone to read a chapter or two of whatever eBook I'm into at the time. And the cool part of this technology is that the next time I open that book … even if it's on my iPad or other device (again, that uses the same iTunes account) … the eBook will open to the spot I left off.

The first time you run the iBooks app, you'll be asked if you want to Sync Bookmarks. This allows you to keep the same Bookmarks and Notes on multiple devices … as long as they all have the same iTunes account. Just tap "Sync" or "Don't Sync." You can turn this on or off at any time using the following steps:

1. Turn on your iPad.

2. Tap on Settings.

3. Select iBooks from the apps list on the left.

4. Turn on (or off) Sync Bookmarks.

While we're covering iBooks settings, note that this is also the place to activate or de-activate other functions, like:

- **Collections Syncing:** This syncs the collections across the devices that have the same Apple ID and is quite useful in keeping things consistent across multiple devices.

- **Full Justification:** This refers to the formatting of eBooks that shows the words evenly spread across the page. Some people prefer this; others don't. It's easy to change, so pick the one you think you want and adjust if necessary.

- **Auto-Hyphenation:** This will split words to fit more on a page or line. Again, this is a personal preference, so just pick the setting you like the best.

The Settings app is also where you can set the Tap Left Margin feature to go to the previous page or to the next page.

iBooks is not the only app that allows you to sync your place and bookmarks among your other devices. If you own a Kindle and have the same books loaded on both your Kindle and your iPad's Kindle app, then the two reader tools will automatically sync to your place in the book. This means that if you read a chapter or two on the Kindle, and then switch to the iPad, the book on the iPad will automatically be set to open at the last place you reached on the Kindle. The same is true if you start reading on an iPad and continue reading on a Kindle ... or on another iPad with the Kindle app installed, as long as it has the same account info.

SHARING eBOOKS

While the nook seems to be far behind the iPad and Kindle in its capability to sync bookmarks, there is one thing that the nook app does that neither iBooks nor the Kindle does ... and it is a biggie, at least for me.

The nook app allows you to share books with other nook/ nook app users as long as you have their e-mail address and are willing to add them as a contact. That is, you can lend a book out for 14 days. But keep in mind that this doesn't mean you can lend out your books over and over again. You can lend out

Figure 5-14
The Settings panel for iBooks is located in the Settings app.

an eBook once ... and for a period of two weeks. Once you lend out a book, you can't access it—just like a real book loan—until your borrower returns it.

The recipient has seven days to accept or decline the book loan and another 14 days to finish reading it. Once (s)he is finished reading your book, you can re-download it and return it to your library.

I really wish that you could lend books in all the reader apps and share them more than once. In fact, I'd be willing to pay an extra small charge to have this functionality in iBooks. A lending fee of $0.99 would be just fine by me if it meant I could pass my books onto others. Anyone from Apple out there listening?

SELF-PUBLISHING eBOOKS

Not everyone gets a book contract, but that doesn't mean you can't write a book! Well maybe you can, maybe you can't; but while writing a book can be difficult, it is no longer as difficult to self publish that book as it used to be ... especially if you're talking about an eBook.

ePub Files

Since the iBook app and other eBook readers use the ePub format (which can be created by anyone), aspiring authors can publish a book that can be read on an iPad. This technology can also be used in other ways.

For instance, just think about a job proposal that a client (even with zero technical know-how) can read as a book on an iPad, or consider how helpful it is for student notes to be converted into a book and stored in iBooks for later reference. Find more on ideas like this for students in Chapter 18.

The easiest way to create a nicely formatted iBook is by using another Apple product:

Pages, the word-processing part of the iWork applications suite. It's only available for the Mac and iPad, but the iPad version does not create ePub files. Therefore, ePub creation through Pages is limited to the software's computer application. But the good news is that iWork has a free trial, so you can try it before you buy it. Just go to **http://www.apple.com/iwork/** and look for the free trial offer on the bottom left side of the page.

To create an ePub book in Pages, all you have to do is use the Export function and choose ePub as the format. That's it. Not tough at all—definitely the easiest way I know to create an ePub file. Yet this process is best used for text-based documents and not photo-based documents.

When creating an ePub book in Pages, the best way to format the book is to use the "ePub Best Practices" sample document from Apple. The file is available for download at **http://images.apple.com/support/pages/**

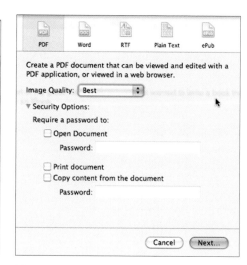

Figure 5-15
This Pages app Export menu shows the ePub settings.

Figure 5-16
This Pages app Export menu shows the PDF settings.

docs/ePub_Best_Practices_EN.zip. Open the document in Pages and use it as a template/ guide for your ePub.

PDFs

Another option for self-publishing when using Pages is to export your book content as a PDF. Since the iBooks app can read PDFs natively and Pages can export your files as a PDF, you can create PDF books from Pages. And it's not difficult. In fact, it's a one-step process: just export the file as a PDF instead of an ePub. Simple as that.

Transfer

So now that you have an eBook created as an ePub or PDF, you may be wondering how to get your book on the iPad. Just follow these steps and you'll soon be reading your very own eBooks on your iPad.

There are two ways to get your eBooks into iTunes and then onto your iPad. The first way is the easiest because iTunes does most of the work for you. Since Pages doesn't operate on a PC, this first option is only for those who are working on a Mac. And all it requires is for you to drag the ePub file onto the iTunes icon in your dock and drop it. Voila! The file is imported into the Books section of iTunes.

The second method works on a PC or Mac:

1. Open iTunes.

2. Click File > Add to Library.

TIP

It's possible to get an eBook onto your iPad by just e-mailing it to the iPad. Find more information on getting files on and off the iPad using e-mail in Chapter 8.

3. Navigate to and select the eBook file.

4. Click Choose.

5. The file is now imported into iTunes.

6. Now, just plug in the iPad and sync the eBook to the iPad.

Creating an ePub document on a PC is much more difficult, but it can be done. I suggest that you create a PDF file if you really want to create a document that can be read in iBooks. But if you really need to create an ePub document on your PC, be aware that you will need some extra software and a bit of patience. Here we go.

The basic process is to save your Word file as an HTML file ... but not a regular HTML. Rather, you need to save the Word file using the Save As Web page (filtered) option, which

---

What formats does calibre support conversion to/from?

calibre supports the conversion of many input formats to many output formats. It can convert every input format in the following list, to every output format.

Input Formats: CBZ, CBR, CBC, CHM, EPUB, FB2, HTML, LIT, LRF, MOBI, ODT, PDF, PRC**, PDB, PML, RB, RTF, SNB, TCR, TXT

Output Formats: EPUB, FB2, OEB, LIT, LRF, MOBI, PDB, PML, RB, PDF, SNB, TCR, TXT

** PRC is a generic format, calibre supports PRC files with TextRead and MOBIBook headers

Figure 5-17
At the Calibre website, you can get software to convert an HTML file to an ePub.

creates a file that a software program like Calibre can now convert to an ePub format.

Calibre is a free and open-source program that can convert files from a wide variety of formats to a different wide variety of formats, including HTML to ePub, which is our intent here. To download Calibre, visit http://calibre-ebook.com/ and follow prompts.

While this solution will work, it isn't very easy to get things just right. And when it comes to creating a book you want to sell in the iBooks Store, you might be better off using a service like Lulu.

Lulu

If you want to create an eBook, but don't want to spend the necessary time and energy to convert your file to iBooks—or, perhaps more importantly, you want your book to appear in the iBooks Store—then the Lulu option might be the best way to go. Lulu is a self-publishing option that creates physical books, but it's also an Apple-certified aggregator of content for the iBooks Store.

Lulu offers two different options. The first is a process in which you create the ePub document and Lulu submits it to the Apple iBooks Store. With the second option, Lulu does all the work; the program creates the ePub for you and submits it to Apple.

Lulu is not free, but the amount of work the service offers is well-worth the price. So, you may ask, what is the price? The breakdown is as follows: When you sell a book through the iBooks Store, Apple takes 30% of the sale. The remaining 70% is split between the publisher (author), who gets 80%, and Lulu, which gets 20%.

This means that the publisher receives 56% of the sales price. So for a $19.99 sale, the

Figure 5-18
Explore Lulu options for authors at
www.lulu.com/apple-ipad-publishing.

author gets $11.20. There is also the charge for the ePub conversion process. This total depends on how many pages the book includes. For example, right now a book that is 501 – 750 pages costs $299 to convert, while a book with 251-500 pages costs $199. A book with less than 250 pages costs $99. When you create a physical book on Lulu, you only have to pay when you actually print a book and then Lulu takes 20% of the revenue.

Movies, Television and Music

The Skim

The iPad is designed to be a media consumption device. This just means is that it's great for watching movies and television shows, and it's a great music player. To facilitate all this, the iPad comes with a Videos app and an iPod app.

The Video app allows you play movies, TV shows and other video content on your iPad, and apps from Hulu and Netflix allow for video to be streamed to the device. The iPod app makes it easy to play your music on the iPad. And there are some great options for listening to Internet radio. This chapter will cover all this and more.

If you read the previous edition of this book, some of this information will be familiar. But there is some really cool new stuff. For starters, when Apple released the iPad 2, it also released the newest version of the iPad operating system iOS4.3, which improved the AirPlay technology and finally brought Home Sharing to the iPad. This is so exciting to me because it adds a feature that I believe should have been available from the beginning ... but wasn't. The benefits of Home Sharing are covered toward the end of this chapter.

Figure 6-1
Movies look great on the iPad,
even with the black bars on the
top and bottom.

MOVIES

The iPad is a great device for watching
movies. The screen is sharp and bright, and
movies are easy-to-see. The only downside
is that the screen is not the same aspect
ratio (widescreen, or 16:9) as that of a movie
theater. So you either need to live with the
black bars on the top and bottom of the
screen or adjust the view.

To adjust, you can double tap the screen to
zoom in and fill the screen. Doing this will
obscure part of the movie, which means you
won't see the film the way the director intended.
But you don't have to see the black bars.

Watch Movies

The first thing you need to do to watch a
movie on your iPad is to find out where the
iPad actually keeps the movie player. Here's
a hint: It's in the Video app. So when you
tap on the Video app, you can access all the
movies and television shows that are available
on your iPad. This includes those you've purchased or rented on the iPad and those you've
transferred from your computer.

To play a movie, just tap on the title. This
opens up a screen that gives you info about the
movie. Two buttons on the screen let you switch
between the Info and the Chapter views.

Info View

The Info view shows the basic description
of the movie. You know, the stuff that's usually found on the back of the DVD box. This
includes a summary of the movie plot and a

Figure 6-2
The Chapters view allows you to pick your starting point for a movie.

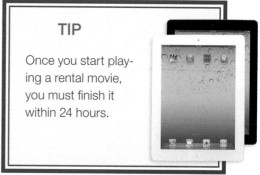

TIP

Once you start playing a rental movie, you must finish it within 24 hours.

Figure 6-3
Here is the same scene from Figure 4-1, but with the movie zoomed in to fill the screen.

list of the main actors along with the names of producers, screenwriter and director. One thing to look for here is the movie rating, which is right under the title, next to the Studio responsible for the movie and the year it was released.

Chapters View

In the Chapters view, you can scroll through the various sections in a movie and pick a place to begin watching. There is also a Play button on the top right of this screen, just below the Chapter button. This starts the movie from the last spot it was stopped. And if the movie has never been watched on your iPad before, or if it's been watched all the way through, it will start at the beginning.

The control for this feature is located in the Settings app. You can change this so the mov-

ies always start from the beginning, but I'm not sure why you'd want to do this. Seriously, if you like to always start at the beginning movie, even if you stopped watching it to take a call from your mother two hours earlier, please tell me: Why on Earth would you want to start over when you finally return to it?

Navigation Tools

When a movie has started playing, there are some options while you watch. Tap the screen once to bring up the movie controls. Across the top of the screen are:

• The Done button, which takes you back to screen you were on before starting to watch the movie. This could be the Info screen or the Chapters screen.

- Amount of time that has elapsed in the film.
- A scrubby slider bar, which allows you to use your finger to move forward and back in the movie easily.
- Time remaining in the movie.
- The full-screen button, which enables you to enlarge the video display.

Toward the bottom middle of the screen are the play controls. This is where you can skip backwards to the previous chapter, play or pause the movie, or skip to the next chapter. And if you have an AirPlay-enabled Apple TV, you will also see the AirPlay button here. There's more information on AirPlay later in this chapter.

Under the play controls is the volume control, which is adjusted by sliding your finger. Of course, you can also use the Volume button on the side of the iPad to make this adjustment.

So now that you know how to watch movies, let's get some on the iPad.

WARNING:

If you have a 3G-enabled iPad and you want to buy or rent movies, you must connect to a Wi-Fi network or use iTunes on your computer to download them. This is due to the cap on 3G data transfers.

Buy Movies

The iTunes Store is Apple's preferred source for your movie purchases. The company really wants you to shop for your movies at iTunes—and forget about buying actual DVDs or Blu-Ray movies. Fortunately, this becomes easier to do as the iTunes Store continues to evolve.

When the iTunes Movie Store first came out, you could only buy movies there. That is, none of the cool extras that come with the purchase of a physical DVD were included. But that has all changed now that iTunes has added iTunes Extras, which are bonus features that come with some movies. Just be aware that the extras are not available for every movie, and they don't come with rentals.

Figure 6-4
The iTunes Store shows what movies are available.

One more thing to know about the iTunes Extras: If you buy the movie on your iPad, the extras won't be downloaded. Only when you connect to the iTunes Store on your computer will you be able to access the extra content. So even though the extra content is available at the iTunes Store, it still cannot be viewed on the iPad.

Apple makes it very easy to get content onto your iPad. In the case of movies, all you have to do is visit the iTunes Store and tap Movies, which is located at the bottom of the screen. This brings up the Movies Store, which is set up just like the iTunes Music Store and the iTunes Television Store.

Explore the options. When you see a movie that interests you, tap on it to bring up the

information page. From here, you can see a preview of the movie and switch between Standard Definition and HD, if available, and rent or buy the movie.

If you buy a movie from your iPad, the movie file will be placed in the Download folder on the iTunes app. It will start downloading immediately if you are connected to a Wi-Fi network. Depending on your Internet connection and the speed of the Wi-Fi network you're on, movies can take awhile to download. Think: 15 minutes to an hour or more.

Once a movie is downloaded, you can start watching it by tapping on the Video app, which is where the movie will be listed. Unlike the computer iTunes Store, you can't begin watching a purchased movie on an iPad until it has finished downloading.

Figure 6-5
Here is information about the selected movie.

Figure 6-6
This download screen is showing the progress of the current download.

When the download is complete, you can transfer the movie to your computer. You'll notice a new category in your iTunes account called Purchased on the iPad. This helps you keep track of what you've purchased and where you purchased it.

You can also easily buy movies on your computer using the iTunes Store. Open iTunes and click on the iTunes Store button (located on the left side of the window) and select the Movies tab. Pick a movie and buy it. Once the movie has started to download, you can begin to watch it on the computer. That's right, you don't have to wait for it to finish downloading.

The next time you connect the iPad to the computer, make sure you add the movie to the Movies page so it loads onto your iPad during the next sync. Just select the iPad from the Device list, click on Movies at the top of the screen, and check the newly purchased movie. Now when you sync, the movie will be loaded onto the iPad.

Rent Movies

I can't actually remember the last movie I rented on DVD. Part of that is because I have an Apple TV that allows me to rent movies right on my TV; the other part is that I can also rent movies on my iPad. That, combined with Netflix and Huluplus, has ended my trips to rent—and return—movies.

There is one thing to know about renting movies on your iPad though. Here it is: You can play them on a television via the component video or VGA cable, but you can't transfer them to any other device. So if you rent a movie on the iPad, you need to watch it on the iPad (or through a projection device from the iPad).

Figure 6-7
This is the rental agreement that you see when you first play a rented movie.

You have 30 days to start watching a rented movie, and you can watch it as many times you like within the first 24 hours. (Timing begins the first time you hit Play.) When the 24 hours are over, the movie will delete itself. Poof! No need to return anything. And no late fees!

Stream Movies with Netflix

Netflix originally started as a way to get DVDs in the mail and avoid the troublesome late fees that would add up so quickly with rentals from video stores and kiosks. Basically, Netflix mails subscribers the DVDs they request ... in those now-famous red envelopes. Subscribers watch the movie and then pop the disc back in the postage-paid envelope and off it goes, back to the Netflix home base. There are never any late charges, and subscribers pay a monthly rate depending on how many DVDs they want to have out at any given time.

Well, Netflix saw the writing on the wall and realized that if the company's service didn't evolve, it would go out of business. So Netflix added a service that allows you to watch certain movies instantly via the Internet on a variety of Wi-Fi-enabled devices, including the iPad. The iPad service is controlled through the Netflix app ($FREE).

What's really amazing about the Netflix app and its content streaming though is the speed at which the movie will start to play! In my personal and very unscientific tests, it took less than a minute for a movie to begin to play after I selected it.

Here's how this works: After you install and launch the Netflix iPad app, enter your Netflix account information. If you don't have an account, you can sign up for a new account and enjoy a free one-month trial. Then you can start streaming movies and television shows immediately.

One nice feature is that you can start watching a movie on one device and finish watching it on another. Also, since your Netflix account is separate from your iTunes account, you can log in to Netflix and watch movies and television shows from any iPad or computer with Internet access. You can even watch Netflix using the 3G capability of the 3G-enabled iPad, but the quality will depend on the signal strength. And streaming video can use up your data plan quite easily.

Netflix streaming isn't free. It costs $7.99 per month for unlimited streaming. And for $2 more, you can get one DVD in the mail at a time ... along with the unlimited streaming. This isn't a huge amount of money, but it can add up over time.

Figure 6-8
This Netflix screen shows the recently watched movies and those that are available to watch now.

All this is great, but be prepared for complications when your Internet connection or Wi-Fi gets overloaded ... for whatever reason. When this happens, the movie will freeze, and this is frustrating. It happened to me when I was watching a Netflix movie on my iPad while also downloading content to iTunes on a computer using the same Internet connection. There was nothing I could do to unfreeze the movie. I just had to wait until the movie started again.

TRANSFER MOVIES

One of the questions I hear a lot is how to get the movies you own onto an iPad. These movies can be home videos you've created or (more likely) the stack of DVDs sitting on your media shelf. At some point you bought these movies—you own them—and now you want to watch them on your iPad.

With music, it's easy: Just insert a CD into the CD drive of the computer and the iTunes app will *rip*, or copy, the music right off the CD and import it into iTunes, from where it can be transferred to your iPad easily. (More on this process a little later in this chapter.) But this technique does not work when it comes to DVDs. You have to rely on an external, third-party program (e.g., Handbrake) to transfer the content.

And before I go any further with this, I need to be perfectly clear. I am not suggesting that you rent the latest Hollywood blockbuster and rip the movie to your computer. Nor am I saying that you should go to a friend's house and copy all his/ her movies. What I am saying is that there is a way to take the movies you've legally purchased and play them on your iPad.

Even this gets a little sticky, particularly when it comes to duplicating copy-protected content. But the ruling that declared it legal to jailbreak your iPhone also made it legal to copy your DVDs in Fair Use scenarios such as the one we're addressing here. (By the way, the ruling I just mentioned is based on updates to the Digital Millennium Copyright Act that happen every three years.)

Basically, it says that if you own a legal copy of a CD, DVD or movie, then you have the right to make a version of that content to play on your iPad. That's according to U.S. Copyright law, so you should be good to go. The confusion comes with another section of the law that states if there is some type of copy protection on the media, you are not allowed to break it. So part of the law says you're per-mitted to copy the material you own to a different device, but other parts of the law state that you cannot do it if you break the special encryption.

I'm not giving you legal advice here; I'm not a lawyer. I just want to show you how to watch your movies on your iPad if you want to. I believe that you should be allowed to make a copy of your legally purchased material as long as you don't turn around and sell the copies or even lend them out. Just think of the copies as being part of the original. And just as it is impossible to read the same physical copy of a book in two places at the same time, it's not a good form, in my opinion, to have the same movie playing in two places at the same time.

Alright, so with all that said, here's how to get your movies onto the iPad:

- Copy the movie from the DVD to your computer.
- Get the movie into iTunes in a form that the iPad can use.
- Transfer the movie to your iPad.

Handbrake

To get the movie from the disc, you'll need a software application. And the best program to do this is called Handbrake, which describes itself as "an open source, GPL-licensed, multi-platform, multithreaded video transcoder, available for Mac OS X, Linux and Windows." Let's look at what that means and how this program, which seems to do something that is frowned upon by the movie studios, manages to stay around.

Handbrake is an open source program … and thus *free*, meaning that no one actually owns it and no one profits from it. It's updated and maintained by a worldwide group of develop-

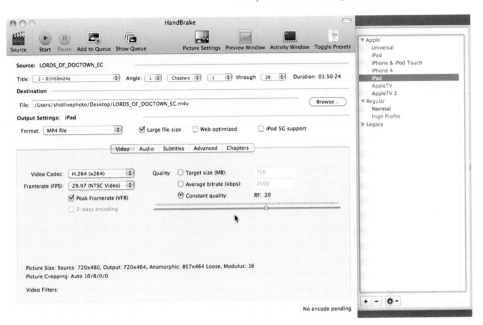

Figure 6-9
The Handbrake app's main screen shows the iPad preset.

ers that gives the movie industry no real target for a lawsuit. Now while Handbrake can rip DVDs, it cannot rip copy-protected DVDs all by itself. For that, it looks for a separate helper program, and—here is the cool part— the Handbrake application will point you to where that program is on the Internet. So, you can download a movie file and have the two programs work together to get the content you own onto your computer and then onto your iPad.

VLC (Mac)

When working on a Mac, the key to making a copy of media on a copy-protected disc is a program called VLC. This is a really powerful video player; and, when paired with Handbrake, it's awesome!

VLC contains a code library that Handbrake

Figure 6-10
The Handbrake application knows it needs VLC and will automatically tell you where to find it.

can access, and Handbrake knows to look for this code to remove the copy protection. VLC installs the components that work around a DVD's copy-protection technology onto your Mac. And when Handbrake sees that these components are present on your Mac, it can get past the disc's copy protection.

Get VLC at **www.videolan.com**. Or, if you run Handbrake with a copy-protected disc, it will ask if you want to download and install VLC automatically. It's that easy!

AnyDVD (PC)

When you want to copy a protected DVD on a PC that's running Microsoft Windows, you'll need a little extra help. The process is nearly as easy for PC users as it is for those on a Mac, but it's a little more expensive.

This is because Mac users get DVD-ripping tools for free, but PC users must pay about $52 or 41 EUR for them. By *them*, I'm talking about AnyDVD, which is the best program for the PC to get around copy protection. This program runs automatically in the background; so when you start your computer, a copy-protected DVD looks like a regular disc that can be copied. When AnyDVD is running, Handbrake can rip … well, yes, *any* DVD that you put into your computer. Find AnyDVD at **www.slysoft.com.**

Let It Rip!

At this point, let's assume that your Mac is equipped with VLC in the apps folder or your PC is running AnyDVD. It's time to run Handbrake and rip your DVD. Here's how:

1. Start Handbrake.

2. Insert the movie you want to rip into the computer's DVD player. If the DVD starts to play, press Stop and quit the DVD player application.

3. In Handbrake, set the source by clicking the Source button and selecting the DVD.

4. Click on the Toggle Presets button and then click on the little arrow next to the Apple menu choice. This will show the Apple-specific presets.

5. Now tell Handbrake what type of movie to create from your DVD by choosing the iPad preset.

6. You can now adjust what you want Handbrake to rip. The Video settings are picked for you, but you can pick the audio track, the subtitles, the advanced settings—I leave these alone—and even add chapter names to your movie file if you want them.

7. Choose a destination for your movie files. I usually pick the Desktop, because the movie will end up inside of iTunes. This is just a temporary holding spot.

8. Click Start and be prepared to wait … for a long time.

Ripping a movie can take hours. Of course, the speed and power of your computer will determine how long it actually takes. The faster and more powerful the computer, the faster Handbrake will rip your disc. Regardless, if you're thinking ahead, set up a movie to be ripped overnight. That way, you don't sacrifice time on your computer and iPad to rip your flick.

Once your movie has been ripped to the computer, all you have to do is drag it into iTunes and drop it into the Movie library. At that point, you can add the movie artwork using the same process you do for books and album covers. The process is covered later in this chapter.

Some things to know about Handbrake to help you get the best results.

- Pick the right audio track! Many movies have multiple audio tracks, and few things are as disappointing as spending hours waiting for a movie to be ripped and then finding out you have the director's comments instead of the movie's soundtrack.

This can actually be difficult … and usually comes down to an educated guess. But I've found that the best choice is usually the first one in the audio list. Many times the audio track will have a description that lets you know what language it speaks, making it easier to pick the right one.

- Get the entire movie! If you're converting a DVD that contains separate episodes or multiple versions of a movie, you can copy them all by adding chapters to the queue instead of just running the program. This way, when you run the Handbrake queue, all the chapters or episodes will be ripped. Just use the Add to Queue button on the top of the Handbrake screen

Other types of video footage you might want to transfer to your iPad are those you've shot. It is so easy to create videos these days. From the Flip® and cell phone video cameras to regular cameras with video capability and even the built-in video camera on the iPad … anyone can be a moviemaker. And it's easy to watch those on the iPad as well. So you can share footage from your last vacation or maybe even your wedding video with family and friends.

The obstacle to loading home videos on an iPad is that some movies are not in the proper format to be recognized by the iPad or iTunes. As a result, when you try to sync the movie to your iPad, you get an error message that tells you the movie is in the wrong format. Well, no worries! Handbrake can help by converting a movie from one format to another. Just follow the directions from the previous section. But instead of picking a DVD as the source, navigate instead to your movie file.

TELEVISION

Watching television on the iPad is a lot like watching movies there; it's enjoyable. The screen is bright and crisp and, with the new processing power and memory available in the iPad 2, the performance is even better than the fantastic performance of the original iPad. The controls for watching television are the same as those for watching a movie. Return to the Movies section for a refresher.

Buy Television Shows

Apple would like you to watch television on your computer, your iPod, your iPhone, your iPad and even your television (as long as it's an Apple TV). The company will gladly sell you all the TV content you can stand

Figure 6-11

Here is the TV show page where you can buy the season pass or a single episode. Sometimes you'll also have the option of renting single episodes.

to watch. And if you don't want to buy your television shows through Apple, they now allow you to rent TV shows.

Think about it. If you have a television in your house, chances are you pay for cable every month, so why would you pay Apple for TV, too? Well, the answer is convenience. Buying your TV à la carte is convenient, because you can watch a show when and where you want. Is that worth the money? It's up to you to decide.

There are three options for getting television shows from Apple. You can:

• Buy single episodes

• Buy a whole seasons

• Rent selected episodes

Apple has TV shows available in both standard and high definition, and you pay for that difference in quality. You get to pick the format when you purchase the show. The standard definition (SD) shows are priced at $1.99 per episode, while high definition (HD) versions are $2.99. But is the extra cost for HD worth it?

Here's how I see it. If you're going to watch the shows primarily on your iPad (or iPod, iPhone), then no; it's not worth it. The size and resolution of these screens won't show much of a difference between SD and HD. And since the HD versions can take up so much more space, it just seems foolish to spend the extra money. Make the HD splurge if you plan to watch your TV shows on a big screen, where the difference will be clear.

Buy Single Episodes

You can buy television shows right on the iPad or from iTunes on your computer. Apple makes it really easy to purchase TV content—both current and older shows. Let's

first cover how to buy TV content on the iPad:

1. Turn on the iPad.

2. Open the iTunes Store.

3. Tap on TV Shows at the bottom of the screen.

4. Find the TV show you want to buy.

5. Choose between HD and SD.

6. Scroll through the list of episodes and tap on the price of the one you want.

7. After you enter your password, the episode will be put into the Download area.

8. If you are connected by Wi-Fi, the show will begin to download. If you're on 3G, the show will be added to a queue that will begin downloading when you are back on a Wi-Fi network.

To buy a single episode from the iTunes Store on your computer:

1. Open iTunes.

2. Click on iTunes Store (located on the left side of the window).

3. Choose the TV Shows tab from the options at the top.

4. Find the show you want to buy.

5. Pick the HD or SD version.

6. Watch previews of episodes by clicking on the little Play button.

7. Click the Buy button.

8. The show will immediately start to download.

To sync the TV shows you've purchased on your computer with your iPad:

1. Turn on your iPad.

2. Attach the iPad to your computer with the included USB cable.

3. Open iTunes on the computer.

4. Select the iPad from the list of Devices in the left column.

5. Click on the TV Shows tab at the top.

6. Check the Sync TV Shows box.

7. You can automatically include:

   • All unwatched episode of all shows (or selected shows)

   • The newest episodes of all shows (or selected shows)

   • The newest unwatched episodes of all shows (or selected shows)

   • The oldest unwatched episodes of all shows (or selected shows)

8. Or you can pick the individual episodes you want to load onto your iPad.

9. Then click Apply which starts the sync process automatically.

If you've purchased TV episodes on the iPad itself, you can transfer those files to the computer. This will free up space on your iPad and it's a smart move, especially if you've already watched the show. The quickest and easiest way to do move episodes from your iPad to your computer is this:

1. Turn on your iPad.

2. Attach the iPad to the computer with the included USB cable.

3. Open iTunes on the computer.

4. If iTunes does not prompt you to transfer purchases automatically, click on File > Transfer purchases from iPad.

5. The content that was purchased on the iPad will be transferred to iTunes.

The above solutions allow you to buy individual episodes of television shows on the iPad or computer ... and watch them anywhere.

Buy Television Seasons

If you really like a certain television show, you can make sure you never miss an episode by buying the whole season with a single click or tap. This is the Apple Season Pass solution. And while it might sound like a waste of money—cause the show is available on television for free (or for the price of your monthly cable bill)—there are reasons to do this. The number one reason to buy a season pass is that you could actually eliminate your cable bill by buying all of your TV from iTunes or watching it on the Internet. I haven't actually managed to do that yet, but I do envision a day when my television will be completely on-demand.

The Apple Season Pass allows you to buy a whole season of a television show at one time, and you do get a price break for your bulk purchase. For example, the Season Pass for *Modern Family* Season 1 (a very funny show,

Figure 6-12
The Season Pass purchase options are available from the iTunes Store in iTunes on your computer.

Figure 6-13

Here's the e-mail that tells me that a new episode of my Season Pass is ready to download. Oops, I still get the dreaded error message when I click the link to access the new episode. It tells me that the iPad could not connect to the iTunes Store. I was hoping this would be fixed by now.

I'll add) is $39.99 for the HD version. This includes all 24 episodes. Individually, each episode of the season would cost $71.76 (24 x 2.99 = $71.76). So the Season Pass saves $31.77. The SD season pass is $29.99, which offers a savings of $17.77 compared to buying each individual episodes (24 episodes x $1.99 per episode = $47.76).

But not all the savings are that great. For example the *Smallville* Season 10 pass is $49.99 in HD and $39.99 in SD, and the *Walking Dead* Season 1 is only $15.99 for the HD episodes, but there are only six episodes. So while you can definitely save money with the season pass versus buying all the episodes individually, it can cost you a pretty penny to buy your favorite shows from Apple.

If you decide to purchase a full season of a television show, the available episodes will download immediately. All future episodes will be available for download within 24 hours of the show being broadcast—usually. Every time a new episode is available, Apple will send you an e-mail to let you know. This message will include a link for you to download the episode.

It's here that the service seems to run into problems on the iPad. I purchased a Season Pass for a show at the iTunes Store on my computer. When I received an e-mail on my iPad that said a new episode was available, I clicked on the link. The iPad's iTunes Store opened and I was asked to enter my password so that iTunes could check for new content. All good so far. But then I got an error message that stated that my iPad could not connect to the iTunes Store. *Great!*

Right now, the Season Pass does not seem to work on the iPad. You can buy a Season Pass, but new episodes need to be downloaded to the computer and synced individually to the iPad. Not ideal but do-able.

Rent Television Shows

Right now, renting TV shows on iTunes is available only in the United States. Rent TV shows from the iTunes Store inside the iTunes app on your computer or from the iTunes Store on the iPad. When you rent a television show, you have 30 days to watch it. And once you start to watch, you have 48 hours to finish it.

Keep in mind that not every television show is available to rent. In fact, there are relatively few television shows available. Hopefully Apple will grow this collection as time goes on.

Stream TV and Movies

Huluplus is an app that's available for the iPad to stream television content and movies to the device. The app is not a free service. It's $7.99 a month, which provides access to a lot of content.

Now, not everything about Huluplus is great, and there is one thing that really bothers me: I don't like paying for content and also having to watch advertisements. That's right, even though you have to pay for the Huluplus service, there are still ads during the shows. The second downside is that not all the content available on Huluplus is available on the iPad version.

When I wrote the first edition of *iPad Fully Loaded*, I mentioned that the Huluplus app kept crashing and that it was no longer worth watching. Well, I'm happy to report that the app updates have solved this problem, so I'm now back to watching it on a regular basis. Some of my favorite shows, including *Family Guy, House* and *The Daily Show* are on Huluplus. And being able to watch these programs on my iPad at my convenience is great!

Figure 6-14

The top rental list from iTunes is easy to access on the computer. Just use the drop-down menu and select TV Rentals.

Figure 6-15

This is the Huluplus main screen. It shows the newest programs available for the iPad.

Figure 6-16
The Huluplus TV Library is sorted by the most popular shows.

Now for more good news: There is a ton of content on Huluplus. The player works well most of the time, and navigation and controls are well-placed and make sense. I really love being able to grab my iPad, tap on Huluplus and, within moments, be watching one of my favorite current TV shows. There is content from a wide variety of providers; it doesn't matter if the show originally aired on Fox, NBC or ABC … or even other sources/ networks. And more content is made available here all the time.

Huluplus is a streaming solution. This means that the content you're watching through the app is available only when you're connected to the Internet. The service works with both the Wi-Fi and 3G connections, but it definitely works better when on Wi-Fi.

The stream freezes more frequently when watching on the 3G network, which gets frustrating. And the quality of the video is automatically lower on the 3G network than on a Wi-Fi connection.

Fortunately, Huluplus offers a one-week free trial, so you can try before spending any money. Here's how to access it:

1. When you install the Huluplus app and run it for the first time, it will ask you to log in if you have an account, or you can tap the Learn More button.

2. Learn More will take you to a page that, when you enter a valid e-mail address, will give a free one-week trial.

3. Or, if you click below the log-in screen, you'll be able to check out Huluplus by seeing clips from the app's library.

Now I know that some of you reading this are thinking that you'll just go to Hulu.com on the Safari browser and see the free content available there. I'm sorry to tell you that this won't work. Hulu has blocked the site on the iPad, so it is not accessible at all.

MUSIC

Apple changed the world of portable music when it released the iPod in 2001. Ten years later, the iPad has an iPod app that brings all the music playing capability to your iPad. You can access your iPod app and the music controls on the iPad at any time by double tapping the Home button. This brings up the multitasking tool bar and the iPod controls. You need to access these controls in order to listen to music while you do other things on your iPad. In other words, this enables you to enjoy background music while you read a book or check out the latest news from CNN. Let's take a look at the iPod app on the iPad.

Buy Music

The easiest way to get new music on your iPad is to buy it from the iTunes Store on the iPad. Yet this is also the most expensive way to buy music for your iPad. The iTunes Store on the computer and the iPad work the same way, and they work the same as the Movie and Television stores. Honestly, shopping in the iTunes Store for music is the same as shopping for movies or television shows, so I'm not going to cover it here again. If you want a reminder on how it works, just go back a few pages in this chapter.

iTunes Alternative

There is an alternative to the iTunes Store and it's the Amazon MP3 Store. The Amazon MP3 Store is one of the easiest music sources to use, and it has a wide variety of content. This is an offshoot of the Amazon.com online store, which has more than 12 million songs and albums. And with a little extra program (that's free), the site will add songs directly to your iTunes library. This means they can be synced to any of your devices, including the iPad.

TIP

You'll probably notice that the iPod app on your iPad will list videos along with your music. But when you tap on a video file, the iPod app will close and the video player will launch. This is great because you don't need to worry about which player to use for the different content. It's automatic.

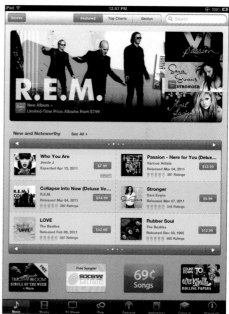

Figure 6-18
The Amazon MP3 Store has lots of music for sale.

Figure 6-17
The iTunes app on the iPad makes it really easy to buy music right on the device.

Go to **http://www.amazon.com/** and select Digital Downloads> MP3 Downloads from the list on the left to look through the huge MP3 library of music that's available on Amazon. To make life even easier, there is an MP3 downloader that will add your downloaded music to your iTunes library automatically. Just go to **http://www.amazon.com/gp/dmusic/help/amd.html/** and grab the downloader.

With the music in your computer's iTunes account, you can sync it to your iPad. The iPad has no problem playing the MP3 music files from the Amazon Store.

Transfer Music to the iPad/ Rip CDs
When my wife and I bought our first home, one of the biggest decisions was how to store all of our music. We are both music lovers and had amassed a huge CD collection. We don't buy as many actual CDs now that most of our new music is bought through iTunes or Amazon, but we still pick up a CD now and then. My car has a CD player in it, so we still use the CDs there. But with the iPod, iPhone … and now the iPad … in our lives, we play most of our music through one of Apple's portable devices. So now the question is, How do we get all the music we have on CDs into iTunes and onto our iPad?

Moving music on CDs to an iPad is actually very easy, but you need a computer that's running iTunes. Preferably this is the computer that you use to sync your iPad; but regardless, the computer just needs to have a CD drive.

There are some little things to consider in order to make the process go smoothly, especially if you have a huge CD collection to import. But the basic process is pretty simple:

1. Insert a CD into the computer's drive.

2. Answer yes when iTunes asks if you want to import the CD.

3. The music is imported into iTunes.

4. When finished importing, eject the CD.

5. Repeat with a new CD as many times as you want … or can stand. It really is a boring process.

Now, let's look at the full walkthrough and note some of the things that can trip up the transfer. The first thing to do is set your preferences in iTunes, so all your importing efforts will go as smoothly as possible.

1. Open iTunes.
   • Mac: Click on iTunes > Preferences.
   • PC: Choose Edit > Preferences from the drop-down menu.

2. In the General tab, there are some choices to the right of where it says, "When you insert a CD":
   • If you check **Show CD**, your CD will be included in the Device list on the left side of the screen.
   • Select **Begin Playing** if you use your computer as a stereo and just want the CD to play when inserted.
   • **Ask to Import CD** is the default setting and prompts the program, when you insert a new CD, to ask if you want to import the music to your iTunes library.
   • **Import CD** triggers an automatic import of the music from an inserted CD into the computer, without a separate directive from you.
   • **Import CD and Eject** is the setting to use if you are going to rip a bunch of CDs. It will automatically import the music from an inserted CD, eject it when done, and wait for the next.

3. The next box is maybe the most important; it's the Import Settings menu. This tells the program what encoder to use and how it should function. It also offers an error-correction feature it can apply when reading CDs that are giving you problems. The settings attempt to balance out file size vs. quality. Available encoders are described below.

- **AAC Encoder:** Advanced Audio Coding is the latest and greatest audio-conversion process that trades quality for space. This format does a great job of getting the best quality with the least amount of space and is the encoder I use on a regular basis. But if you want the best possible audio quality in the music files you're ripping, then look closely at the next two options.

- **AIFF Encoder:** Both the AIFF and the Apple Lossless Encoder (next) copy the CD as a perfect duplicate. This gives you the best quality available, but these files take up the most digital space of all the options.

- **Apple Lossless Encoder:** For all intents and purposes, this option is the same as the AIFF Encoder. It produces a perfect digital copy of the CD, but you pay for that in large file sizes.

- **MP3 Encoder:** This encoder imports a music file as an MP3. Skip it! MP3 is outdated. There are better options, like the AAC Encoder (above).

- **Wave Encoder:** These files usually have uncompressed audio that sounds great, but the files are huge. Therefore, I recommend skipping this option as well.

4. After you pick an Encoder, select the quality setting for your audio files by choosing

Figure 6-19
This menu shows your import settings in iTunes.

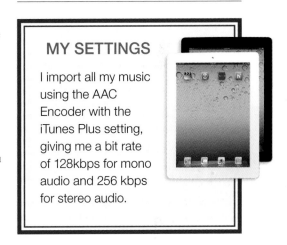

MY SETTINGS

I import all my music using the AAC Encoder with the iTunes Plus setting, giving me a bit rate of 128kbps for mono audio and 256 kbps for stereo audio.

a bit rate for your imported music. The higher the bit rate, the more information the file contains. More information means better sound and a larger file size. I use a bit rate of 256 kbps, because it gives me great quality for the required space.

5. Use error correction when reading CDs that have been scratched or damaged. This will slow down the import process, but it seems better to spend a little extra time to make sure your audio is imported correctly the first time than to deal with skipping or otherwise messed up music when you're all done.

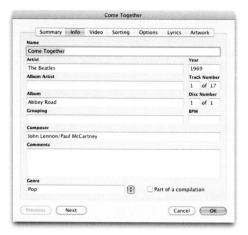

Figure 6-20
The information panel for each track
is where you can add information
and artwork.

Now you're ready to insert a disc and import
some music into iTunes.

1. Open iTunes.

2. Insert a CD into your computer's CD drive.

3. Depending on the settings you marked,
   the CD will wait to import or import
   automatically.

4. If you are prompted, go ahead and import
   the CD.

5. When the CD is done importing, it will
   automatically eject or you can eject it manually ... again, depending on the settings
   you entered earlier.

If everything went well, you should now have
a new album in your iTunes library. Each
listing should have the correct track information, and the album cover art automatically
inserted. Life isn't always perfect though,
so here is the best way to get your newly
imported music looking and acting the way
you want.

I usually import one CD at a time, so it's
easiest for me to find the new content by
sorting the music in my iTunes library by
Albums. Just click on the Music tab on the
left, and then click on the Albums tab across
the top. Each album in your iTunes library is
now shown as an album cover. The albums
that don't have any artwork are just generic
squares with big music notes on them.

To get the artwork, right click on the album
and click Get Album Artwork. This works ...
sometimes. When it doesn't, there are
other options.

The most useful of these options is the Cov-
erHunt website: **http://www.coverhunt.
com/**. Once there, type in the album name.
There's a good chance you'll find the artwork
you need. But if you don't, use any of the
music sites on the Internet, or try the band's
official website. What you're looking for is an
album cover image of the music that you just
imported into iTunes.

Once you have the artwork on the screen,
you need to take the following steps:

1. Copy the image file to your computer's
   clipboard. To do this, right click on the artwork and select Copy.

2. Back in iTunes, right click (PC) or control
   click (Mac) on the album and select
   Get Info.

3. After Apple warns you that you are about
   to edit multiple tracks, click Yes and then
   click on the Info tab.

4. You'll see a box here on the right called
   Artwork. Highlight the box and press ctrl-z
   (PC) or command-z (Mac) to paste the
   image into the box.

5. Click OK.

If all went according to plan, the album now has the correct artwork when it appears in your iTunes library.

Another problem that can occur with music files is that the album and tracks don't have the right name ... or any name. This shouldn't happen often, because iTunes will usually know the name of every album you import as well as every track on that album. It does this by looking up the info in a really big Internet database called Gracenote.

If the computer you're using isn't connected to the Internet or the album is one of the really rare ones that isn't in the Gracenote database, then you have a little work to do to get the information into iTunes. Here's what you're facing:

1. Select the first track in the album.

2. Choose File > Get Info.

3. Click the Info tab.

4. Enter all the information for the track.

5. For live albums, click on the Options tab and check the box next to Gapless Album. (This option removes any break between songs, giving you seamless playback.)

6. Click the Next button to move to the next track.

Now you have the right info for your music tracks, and the album cover is showing in iTunes. When you sync your iPad and computer, all this info will be in both places.

INTERNET RADIO
A great way to listen to music, especially music you don't have in your collection, is through Internet Radio. This is very much like traditional radio; but, instead of being transmitted over the air, it's sent over the Internet.

TIP
I have a lot of live concerts on CD from my years collecting live Grateful Dead shows. These and other live shows don't always show up on Gracenote, so entering the track info is important if you want to have an easily searchable iTunes library.

PLEASE SHARE!
If you need to enter track information for a CD, please do everyone a favor and submit the info to Gracenote. Do this by selecting all the tracks and clicking Advanced>Submit CD track names. Done. Much appreciated ...

There are lots of options for accessing this, but the best, in my opinion, is Pandora. In the first edition of this book, I also talked about last.fm, which is a great service; but there is still no real iPad app for it, so I don't use the service any more. It's too bad. But, seriously? The iPad has been out long enough now for the last.fm folks to have developed a real iPad app.

Pandora App ($FREE)

There is a reason that Pandora is so popular; it's a really good program. It's easy to use, it works great on both Wi-Fi and 3G iPad models, and the Pandora app is very slick. Plus, it's FREE. Download the Pandora app; sign in or create an account; search for an artist, song or composer; and you're good to go.

Now, since Pandora is free, there are audio ads; but you can avoid them by upgrading from inside the app to Pandora One for $36 a year—a great price if you use the service all the time. I would love to spend hours going on and on about how great Pandora is, but how 'bout you just go try it for yourself. There's no risk … except you might like it so

much that you won't be available to listen to your grouchy neighbor complain anymore.

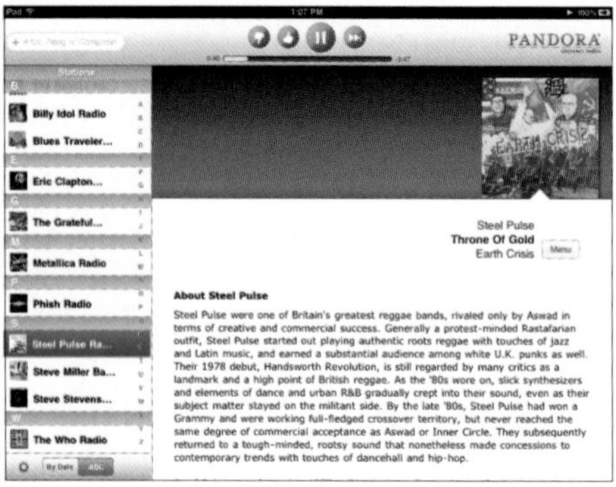

Since Pandora is one of the apps that uses the multitasking feature of the iPad, it will keep running while you do other stuff … exactly like the iPod app. But when Pandora is running and you double tap the Home button, instead of the iPod controls being visible, the Pandora controls show. A big thank you to Apple for that one!

Piracy and BitTorrent Sites

There are so many legal ways to listen to music—from ripping your CDs into iTunes to listening to Pandora—that I'm going to take a moment to cover BitTorrent and its library of music and video.

I know it's easy to go out on the Internet and get music and movies for free at numerous BitTorrent sites. But keep in mind that downloading content from the Internet— content that you know you should be paying for—is called *stealing*. I'm sure you wouldn't do that, but you might have heard others justifying it by saying it's easy … and that if you aren't supposed to take it, it wouldn't be on the Internet. Not true.

I know how easy it is to get this free content, but I also know how hard musicians work on creating their art. In my other life as a professional photographer, I spend a lot of time photographing musicians; and I've seen the change in the music business firsthand. So even though it is tempting and really easy to grab cool stuff from those dark corners of the Internet, first go and check iTunes or Amazon for the content you want. If no one pays for the music or movies or books or art, then the talented folks who create that stuff will have to do something else to buy their bread. And that would be a great loss for everyone.

Figure 6-21
The Pandora app screen shows how easy it is to find your favorite artists.

AIRPLAY

Apple's AirPlay technology allows you to stream your media from your computer or iPad to other devices seamlessly. I'm going to break this down into two different applications. The first is streaming audio; the second is streaming video.

Streaming Audio

You can use AirPlay to stream music from your computer or iPad to any AirPlay-enabled device or any Airport Express-connected speakers.

The AirPlay technology has been part of iTunes for awhile. It used to be called Air-Tunes, and it allowed audio to be streamed to Airport Express-connected speakers or Airport Express-connected audio receivers. It was really easy to use. All you had to do was pick the speakers you wanted to use from the drop-down list in iTunes. The music playing on your computer was sent to the other devices and you could really fill an entire house with the audio from your iTunes. Apple no longer calls this service AirTunes.

The service is now called AirPlay and there is a new group of devices that are AirPlay-enabled, including speakers and audio receivers that don't need the Airport Express device to work. The cool part is that the older Airport Express models still work, so you can continue to build a system with a mix of components. And AirPlay actually streams more than just music. It also streams information about the music, including the song title, album, artist and more, which all appears on AirPlay-enabled speakers or receivers with built-in displays.

Streaming Video

You can wirelessly send video from your iPad to your television using the $99 second-

Figure 6-22
The AirPlay button appears when there is an Apple TV on the network.

Figure 6-23
You get to pick the speakers that will play your music. Everything just needs to be on the same network.

TIP

The Apple Airport Express is a small Wi-Fi device that allows you to set up Wi-Fi network, add a printer to your Wi-Fi network and stream audio to any device that has an audio input.

Figure 6-24
When playing a movie over AirPlay, the iPad screen shows the generic movie icon.

generation Apple TV. And because of this, the Apple TV could really be sold as an iPad accessory. Truly, this wireless feature is one the coolest things the Apple TV can do.

Don't get me wrong, I'm a huge fan of the Apple TV and I have a first-generation unit as well as the newer second-generation unit. But up until this point, it wasn't used all the time. Now I constantly switch between watching on the iPad and the television.

The Apple TV also allows you to stream the media content from your iTunes library to your TV. And it allows you to easily stream the media that's playing on your iPad to your television with the tap of a button. This works for movies and television on your iPad, but it also now works for photos, slideshows and any other app that is AirPlay-enabled. To get this to work, the most important thing to know is that the Apple TV and the iPad need to be on the same Wi-Fi network. The iPad will automatically see the Apple TV, and the AirPlay button will appear in the controls.

So you can be watching a movie on your iPad, walk into your living room where the Apple TV is connected to your television, and—with a tap—start to stream the movie from the iPad to the television. Since AirPlay is designed with multitasking in mind, you can use the iPad to check e-mail during a movie or, in my case, check my IMDB (Internet Movie DataBase) app for information about the movie I'm watching.

iTUNES HOME SHARING

Shared libraries are a relatively new addition to iTunes and, with iTunes 10.2.1 or later and iOS 4.3, Home Sharing has come to the iPad and it is AWESOME.

The Home Sharing technology allows you to stream any media that you have in iTunes to your iPad as long as the computer and iPad are on the same network (and use the same Apple ID). In practical terms, this means I can be anywhere in my house, watching a movie (any movie I have on my main computer) on my iPad.

That's right, iTunes Home Sharing allows you to share the media that lives on your computer(s) with your iPad—and your iPhone, iPod Touch or other computers. There are some restrictions and the setup is not out in the open, but this is a really great service.

Here's a real life situation: I have an older Apple desktop computer that holds my main iTunes folder. This is on a 2 TB drive and is nearly full, because I've ripped just about every CD I have into the library and have added quite a few of my DVDs as well. Add a couple of television seasons and a few movies that were purchased from the iTunes Store.

And now there's way more media on that computer than could possibly fit on an iPad—no matter what size.

Now, that computer is on my home network and has Home Sharing turned on. This means I can open my iPad, tap on the iPod app, and navigate to my shared folders. I then tap on the main iTunes folders and access all the music that is actually located on my desktop computer. So I can listen to any of the music on my iPad without affecting what I'm doing on the desktop computer. Or if I'm watching a movie or listening to an album on the computer and my wife decides to listen to something different on her iPad, no problem. Home Sharing works just as well with movies and television shows. So let's walk through setting up Home Sharing and getting it to work on all your devices.

Set Up Home Sharing on a Computer

You need to set up iTunes Home Sharing on both the computer and the iPad to get it to work. Let's start with the computer. It's the same process for Mac and PC.

1. Open iTunes.

2. Click on the Advanced menu.

3. Click Turn on Home Sharing, and enter your Apple ID and password. Only computers sharing the same iTunes account can use Home Sharing together. So if you use multiple iTunes accounts, you'll have to choose one for Home Sharing.

4. Click Create Home Share, and Home Sharing will be activated.

5. There will now be a Shared menu on the left side of your iTunes window.

6. Click the name of an iTunes user to see a list of all the media that's available for sharing.

> ### TIP
>
> Home Sharing works with the original iPad and the iPad 2 running iOS 4.3 as well as iTunes 10.2.1 or later, so make sure you have updated both your iPad and iTunes to the latest versions.

Figure 6-25
The Home Sharing screen on the Mac is under the Advanced tab.

7. You can also click on the little arrow next to a user's name to see his/ her media in a more organized manner.

8. Double-click a song to play it, or click a playlist and the Play button to hear an entire playlist.

You can transfer content from one iTunes library to another. When you are looking at the shared iTunes library and you see something you like, select the song or album and click the Import button on the bottom right of the window.

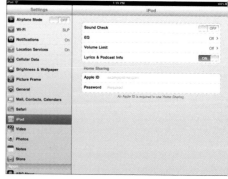

TIP

For Home Sharing to work, both machines need to be authorized under the same Apple ID. You can only authorize five computers under a single Apple ID.

Figure 6-26
The Settings menu on the iPad shows where to turn on Home Sharing.

Media Types for Sharing

There are certain types of media that can be shared; some cannot. You can share video, MP3, Apple Lossless, AIFF, WAV and AAC files as well as audiobooks purchased from the iTunes Store and shared radio station links. You can even share music that was purchased from the iTunes Store. But first you need to authorize your computer to the same iTunes account that originally purchased the music. To authorize the computer, open iTunes and click on the Store menu, and then click on Authorize this Computer. You will need to enter your Apple ID and password.

What you can't share is content from Audible.com, QuickTime sound files and QuickTime movie files. Movie rentals and television show rentals can be streamed but not transferred using Home Sharing.

Access Home Sharing with iPad

Now that iTunes Home Sharing is set up on your computer, it's time to set it up on the iPad. Don't bother going into the iPod app or the Video app yet. The place to start is in the Settings app.

1. Turn on the iPad.

2. Tap on Settings.

3. Tap on iPod from the list on the left.

4. In the Home Sharing section, enter the Apple ID and password for the Home Sharing account.

To access a shared music library from the iPad, tap on the iPod app. It will show the music that you have on your iPad. Notice that just under the volume control on the top left, there's a new button called Library. Go ahead and tap the word *Library*. A list of shared libraries will appear, and this allows you to pick any of the shared libraries. Tap on the library you want to access, and it will show up (after a minute or two, depending on the size of the library and the speed of your network). Now you can play—on your iPad ... or other Wi-Fi-enabled device—any of the audio content that lives in your computer's iTunes library.

So that's how you can listen to all the music, audiobooks and podcasts you have in your collection. But what about the movies and television shows? Guess what, once you have set up the sharing in the Settings app, it automatically allows you to view your video content using the Video app.

Just tap on the Video app to open it. Across the top of the screen, you'll see up to four buttons, depending on your content. The four buttons are Rental, Movies, TV Shows and Shared. To access the video content on your computer, tap on the Shared button and you'll see links for all the shared computers. Tap on the one you want to access and, after a few moments, it will show all your Movies, TV Shows, Podcasts and Music Videos. You can pick the category by tapping on the corresponding button at the top of the screen.

Here are some final tidbits about the iTunes Home Sharing feature:

- An unlimited number of iOS devices can access content via Home Sharing.

- If you want to use Home Sharing in a different location, just enter the new account information. This means you can use Home Sharing at home as well as in your office. You will have to change this for each location since you can only be on one account at a time.

- Remote streaming of iTunes video looked better when on the high speed 802.11n Wi-Fi network, because it has a higher data rate.

- Playback requires a Wi-Fi network, and this is limited to iOS devices that are running iOS 4.3 and iTunes 10.2.1 or later.

All in all, this alone is really worth the upgrade to iOS4.3. It's made accessing my media so much easier!

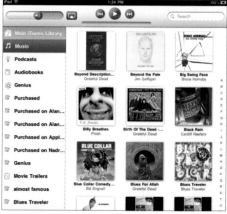

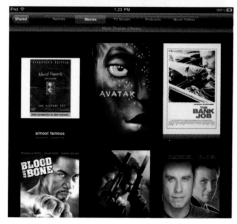

Figure 6-27
The Home Sharing option is available for the iPod and Video apps.

Magazines and News

The Skim

When the iPad was released in 2010, many people thought that it would be the savior of the magazine and newspaper industry, which seemed to be failing at the time. And when I saw some of the proposed magazine apps, I was really impressed. It seemed to me that the iPad could and would be a great platform for reading magazines and news. Let's look at magazines first.

MAGAZINES

Especially after I saw the concepts from *Sports Illustrated*, I really couldn't wait to see magazines on the iPad. I pictured an interactive publication with embedded audio and video—technology to get readers fully immersed in the magazine-reading experience.

Well, the future is here, and execution of this cool concept is not going great. I do get some magazine content on the iPad, but I still read paper magazines primarily—mostly because publications I want are not available on the iPad or because there's not yet a subscription model that works well. The other reason, and this is a big one for me, is that it's been really difficult to control magazine purchases on the iPad.

For example, the first magazine I got on the iPad was *Wired*. I love the way the magazine looks and works, even though the files are really big and take a long time to download. When the app first came out, it didn't allow much control over the issues and the way they were stored. There were even times that the app wanted me to pay for the same issue twice.

Well, that has been fixed and there is even a way now to transfer the magazines off the iPad for storage on the computer using iTunes. If you attach your iPad to the computer with the USB cable and open iTunes, you can select the iPad from the Device list on the left. Click on the Apps tab on the top and scroll down until you see the File Sharing section. Select the Wired app from the list to see the data from the app. You can now save the issues folder to your computer. More on *Wired* a little later in this chapter.

This chapter is all about magazines and magazine subscriptions … with a healthy dose of news apps. The iPad has been out for more than a year now, and while Apple has recently announced the details of subscription services, there are only two magazine/ news subscriptions available.

SUBSCRIPTIONS

There's a lot of talk in the publishing world about the Apple subscription plan. The basics are actually very simple, but the ramifications get a little complicated. See, Apple wants magazines and newspapers to sell subscriptions though their apps on the iPad. The cost of the subscription needs to be the same (or cheaper) than the cost of the subscription outside of the app. Apple takes 30% of the money and promises not to share the subscriber's name or e-mail information.

If a subscriber signs up for a subscription outside of the app, Apple gets nothing. And here is where it gets a little tricky. If the magazine or newspaper offers a subscription plan out-

Figure 7-1
The first subscription app for the iPad is The Daily.

side of the iPad app, then it has to offer the same subscription inside the app—and the app cannot link to the outside sign-up site. In Chapter 6, I mentioned that this could force apps like the Amazon Kindle or the Barnes & Noble nook off the iPad.

Here's what this means. If the Kindle app is to survive on the iPad, it will have to offer the iPad Kindle users an ability to buy books from inside the app—and not exclusively from the webpage that it uses now. This would mean that Apple would get 30% of the purchase price, and Amazon would get 70%—not the current 100%. Since Amazon would not be able to sell books through the iPad at a higher price, this would mean that Amazon would have to raise the price for all the books or make a lot less money.

THE APPLE SUBSCRIPTION PLAN

- **Plan Price and Length:** The publisher sets the price of a subscription and, like traditional subscriptions, you pay up front for the content. The subscription is managed inside of the subscriber's iTunes account. The publisher can set the length of the plan—weekly, monthly, bimonthly, quarterly, bi-yearly or yearly.

- **Billing:** Purchasing a subscription inside of an app is handled by Apple. Purchasing a subscription outside of the app—through the publisher's website, for example—is managed by the publisher.

- **Privacy:** The publisher's privacy policy, not Apple's, governs a subscription. Apple demands that the publisher give customers a choice about information sharing and that the customer is aware that the publisher's privacy policy (not Apple's) will handle their information.

- **Subscription Policy:** If you want to read the Apple press release for all the information on the subscription plan, find it here: http://www.apple.com/pr/library/2011/02/15appstore.html.

This subscription plan by Apple is a big gamble. Are content providers going to give 30% of their subscription revenue to Apple ... just for the pleasure of having their content available on the iPad? I don't know the answer, but one thing I do know is that U.S. anti-trust investigators are looking at this very closely. Of course, this doesn't mean that what Apple is doing illegal or that there will be a formal investigation, but it does mean that things might change in the future. If you do not agree with the Apple subscription model, go to the website of the company who is offering the subscription and look for alternate ways to purchase the subscription you want.

THE DAILY

The Daily is the first iPad-only "newspaper" and it's created by News Corporation. The Daily is "the industry's first daily news

Figure 7-2
The Daily gets updated every day automatically when you launch the app.

Figure 7-3
A free trial of The Daily allowed me to check it out without having to send any money upfront.

Figure 7-4
The Daily shows all the menus across the bottom.

publication created from the ground up for the iPad." The service costs $0.99 a week, or $39.99 a year. And since it works on the Apple subscription model, all transactions will be a part of your iTunes account.

Let's start with what's new and newsworthy about this app and then look to see if it's a good match for you. The Daily promises new content every day of the year, a lot like a daily newspaper. But since it only exists in digital form, it doesn't have costs related to printing, delivery and print overruns. It can use a mix of still photography and video in the same story, and it all looks great on the iPad. So it's very much like having a top-quality glossy magazine published as often as a newspaper.

I think the writing is pretty good and the stories are interesting. And an all-electronic newspaper can be updated as stories change, which brings the power of the web to the news. Seems like it the best of all worlds!

My biggest problem with this publication is the length of time it takes to start the app and get the new content. I know it may seem odd that a 45-second wait is too long; but in this day of instant news, I really have become very impatient. And I don't read the newspaper every day. It doesn't matter if that's a paper version or an electronic version. I honestly forget to tap on The Daily app for my news.

But the real problem that I see for apps like The Daily is the free alternatives, like CNN or USA Today. It's not that the app is sub-par or lacking anything, it's just that I don't understand why I'd pay for content that I could get for free. That said, I believe that more and more content that's now free will end up costing in the future. And The Daily has a giant head start in capturing iPad readers.

When you run The Daily, you'll notice two menu bars across the bottom. The first shows the sections of the news app; the second menu, accessed by tapping on the up arrow on the right side of the categories menu, gives you access to some of the more special features of the app, including:

- **Video** gives you a quick video overview about the current day's content.
- **Audio** automatically starts to play stories that have been converted.
- **Auto Scrolling** scrolls unprompted through the day's stories.
- **Randomize** jumps around through the stories, giving you a random selection.
- **Saved Pages** is the storage place for articles you've marked to read later.
- **General Settings** and **Account Info** is where you can set your specific information, such as location, so things like the weather are updated correctly. This is also the place to get your horoscope and set up breaking news notifications. It is the spot to check and update your account information as needed, too.

One important feature is the ability to save an article in the app and open it later. When you're in The Daily app and reading an article:

1. Tap the Export button. A screen will open that allows you to post the article to Facebook, post it to Twitter, or e-mail to save it for later—which is depicted with a paperclip symbol.

2. Tap on the paper clip symbol to save the page into your Saved Pages page.

3. You can also post a comment on the article that will show up for other readers.

4. When you're done, tap the small x on the top of the screen next to the paperclip.

Figure 7-5
Tapping on the Export button allows you to tap on the paperclip to save articles for later. The Saved Pages screen shows your saved pages.

WARNING:

The Daily is still one of the most unstable apps on my iPad and needs to be updated soon. It crashed four times while I was trying to read it this morning! That's just not going to cut it.

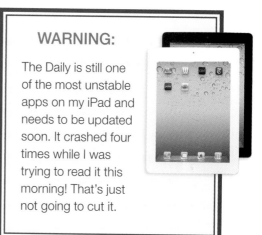

The article is now saved for later reading … as long as the app doesn't crash. And it seems to crash quite a bit. Many times, I save an article and then the app restarts, and the article is gone. So if you use this: beware. Saved items might not be there later.

Figure 7-6
The opening screen for the Wired app shows issues you can buy. It also shows you which issues are purchased and archived and which ones are ready for you to read.

Figure 7-7
Each issue of *Wired* is big … really big … and can take awhile to download.

WIRED

Reading *Wired* magazine on the iPad is great. I love everything about the navigation, the integration of video and audio, and the general look and feel of the app. I like that I can decide to buy the magazine one issue at a time (which is a good thing since there is no subscription plan) and that I can archive the past issues to free up space on the iPad.

If I go to buy a previously purchased issue, *Wired* tells me that I already purchased it and allows me to re-download it for free. *Wired* really does things right on the iPad. Now, if only there was a subscription for the magazine …

The only downside is that each issue is big— think: hundreds of MB in size. So you will need a Wi-Fi network to download an issue. This is not something you can do over 3G right before you get on an airplane. And since my iPad is set to turn off automatically after two minutes if nothing is going on, it tends to go to sleep about halfway through a download of *Wired* magazine.

CNN FOR THE iPAD

I was using the CNN app for the iPhone on the iPad until CNN released an iPad version. At that point, I switched over and haven't looked back. The first thing to know is that the CNN app is free. This means you can try it and, if you don't like, *fah-ged* about it. Checking it out doesn't cost you anything.

The main thing that I like about the CNN app on the iPhone is the push notifications. For me, it was the right balance—not too many but enough to keep me updated on the top news stories of the day. The iPad CNN app does the same thing, but it has an interface built for the bigger iPad screen.

Figure 7-8
The CNN iPad app takes advantage of the bigger screen. This is the grid view of the app.

Figure 7-9
A story on the CNN app is showing the main text in the middle of the screen. And since the app is free, there are advertisements (on the right). More headlines are positioned across the bottom of the screen.

There are three different ways to look at the current news stories on CNN:

- Grid View
- List View
- Single Story

It's easy to change the view of the front page. Just tap on one of the three view option buttons at the top of the page. No matter which view you use—I personally like the grid view—just tap on the story icon/button to read it. Stories that include video will have a little Play symbol in the middle of the story icon/button. You can also watch LIVE video or get audio Hourly Updates when you're connected to the Internet.

As mentioned, I really like the CNN app's push notifications. To set up the notifications,

Figure 7-10
The Notifications menu shows the apps that want to send notifications and those that I have allowed to do so. The only two that are turned on here are CNN and The Daily.

go to the Settings app and tap Notifications. Make sure that Notifications is turned on, and then tap CNN, which will give you the option to turn Sounds on or off and activate the Alerts and Badges. Note: *Badges* is the term apps use to send pop-up notification widows. Turning this on allows the CNN app to send you notifications on the really big news.

NEW YORK TIMES

The *New York Times* has announced a paid subscription plan for premium content in its publications that will be available on the iPad. The good news for those of us who like free stuff is that the Top News section will continue to be free on the iPad. But beginning March 28, 2011, the *New York Times* offers three different plans for subscribers to access the rest of the news. The plan for the iPad is available for purchase on the iPad per Apple's new subscription plan.

The *New York Times* offers three separate pay plans, which represent various levels of access for a four-week period:

1. Access the NYTimes.com website and receive a smart phone app for $15.

2. Access the NYTimes.com website and receive a tablet app for $20.

3. Access the website and receive a smart phone and tablet app for $35.

The *New York Times* and Apple have had a rocky past when it comes to the iPad. News stories circulated in 2010 that reported Steve Jobs' dissatisfaction with the limited amount of content available in the NYT app on the iPad. It appears that those concerns have been resolved now that the *New York Times* has become the first newspaper to adopt Apple's subscription plan.

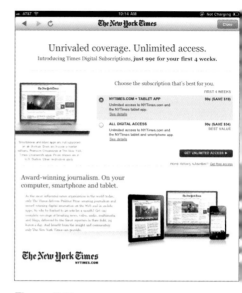

Figure 7-11
The NYT subscription page on the iPad shows the details of the plan.

NEWS AGGREGATORS

In news aggregator apps, the news doesn't come from one source; it is compiled by the reader (via settings) in real time from many different Internet sources. That is, news aggregators allow you to pick your favorite news sources and have them all show up in the same place at the same time—on your iPad.

The news aggregator apps take advantage of RSS feeds to pull information from the Internet into its results. If you want to understand how these work, learn more about RSS feeds in the sidebar on the next page.

Pulse

Pulse is my favorite news reader on the iPad. And at $3.99, I find it well worth the money. When judging my advice, one of the things you should know about me is that I'm a gadget fan, and I really like to know what's going

RSS FEEDS EXPLAINED

RSS stands for *Really Simple Syndication*. This format was created to allow users to pull information from websites automatically, especially those that are updated regularly. RSS sends updates from a website without a user having to actually go out and check the site. This is really useful when it comes to getting information from news websites and blogs.

To take advantage of this service, you need a news aggregator or feed reader that does the search-and-find work for you. Just tell the reader what feeds to explore, and it will go and get new content when it's available.

The best part about an RSS feed is that it can grab content from a variety of sources and put them in a single place for you. This means you get all the new information available from a variety of different sources in the same app, and the aggregator keeps that information up-to-date.

Most blogs and news websites now have RSS feeds that news aggregator apps can use. So take the time to build your own custom news reader on the iPad. You'll love it.

on in the tech world. I read a variety of tech-related blogs every day. So what used to take a large chunk of my morning now takes only an hour or so ... thanks to Pulse. I use Pulse to collect the RSS feeds from the tech blogs I read, so I can see at a glance what's new ... and catch up on a whole slew of articles without ever opening a web browser—without even turning on a computer.

Since the Pulse reader allows you to manage the RSS feeds that it displays, let's look at the process for adding, finding, deleting and organizing RSS feeds.

When you open the Pulse reader, you'll see an icon on the top left that looks like a gear. Tap this to bring up the Pages view, where you can add/ remove feeds and organize the feeds that are already there. You can just drag and drop

GOOGLE READER

Google Reader is a web-based news aggregator that works like the news aggregator apps on the iPad, but it lives on the web (and not on your iPad). Google Reader has been around longer than the iPad and, if you have a Google Reader account, your feeds can be transferred over to many of the news aggregator apps on the iPad.

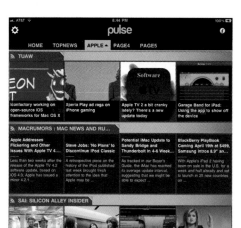

Figure 7-12
This page of Apple news on my Pulse app shows the news from TUAW, Mac-Rumors, SAI and Macworld.

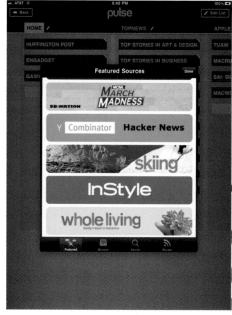

Figure 7-13
The featured sources can give you access to feeds that you might not know about.

the feeds to the various pages.

As you can see in Figure 7-12 (above left), I have a whole page of just Apple-related feeds. I also have a full page of news feeds that brings in information from sources ranging from CNN.com to the *Washington Post* print edition.

Add Feeds

To add a new feed to any of your pages, just tap on the (+) sign on the blank feed at the bottom of any of the pages.

Find Feeds

To search for an RSS feed:

1. Open Pulse.

2. Tap the gear icon on the top left.

3. The Pages view will open, showing any and all feeds.

4. Tap on the (+) sign on the blank feed at the bottom of any of the pages.

5. A pop-up menu appears, allowing you to add feeds by the following choices:

   • **Featured** gives you a list of web sources, including feeds from diverse interests (e.g., *Hacker News*, Whole Living , etc).

   • **Browse** lets you search for feeds by category—from Art and Design to Trending. This is really useful for finding new feeds that might interest you. You don't have to know about the feed; you can just look under a category and pick from the list that appears.

- **Search** is where you can enter a name or subject to ask the app to find all the feeds that include the words you enter.
- If you have a **Google Reader** account, enter your username and password here to transfer the feeds to the Pulse reader.

6. When you're done adding feeds, just tap on the Done button on the top of the menu.

7. To go back to the main screen, tap on the Home button on the top left. (The button looks like a little grid.)

Delete Feeds

To delete a feed:

1. Open Pulse.

2. Tap on the gear icon, it's on the top left.

3. The Pages view will open, showing all the feeds in columns.

4. Tap on the Edit button that's located on the top right, or just hold your finger on a feed (any feed) for a few seconds.

5. A small x will appear at the top left corner of each feed.

6. Tap on the x of that feed to delete it.

7. Tap Done.

Organize Feeds

To rearrange the order of your feeds:

1. Open Pulse.

2. Tap the gear icon on the top left.

3. The Pages view will open, showing all your feeds in columns.

4. Tap on the Edit button on the top right, or just hold your finger on a feed for a few seconds.

5. A small x will appear at the top left corner of each feed.

6. Place your finger on the feed and drag it to a new place on the screen.

7. When the feed is in the new location, lift your finger.

You can also rename the individual feeds as well as the pages that store the feeds. Both actions are handled on the Manage Feeds page. Just tap on the Manage Feeds button, and then tap on the name of the feed. The keyboard will pop up, allowing you to change the name. The same process will allow you to change the name of a page. Instead of Home, Page01, Page02, etc, you just tap on the page name and change it using the keyboard. I have renamed pages to Apple and News, so that I can easily see which page I'm on.

The main screen of the Pulse reader is divided up simply. Each of the feeds has a single line of previews, so you can either scroll through the feeds by swiping your finger up and down, or you can look through the stories from a particular feed by swiping left or right on that feed. If you see a story that you like, just tap on it to access the full content. Notice the grid icon at the top of the screen on the left side. Tap this button and the other pages of the feed will become accessible. Now you can tap on one of those to bring up its list of articles.

View Feeds

Once a story is on the screen, you have two options for viewing it: text view and web view. For a lot of stories, the text view might be the better choice, because it removes all images and just gives you the text of the page. If you want to make sure you get to see all the images, use the web view. You can change the view by tapping the Text or Web button, located on the top right.

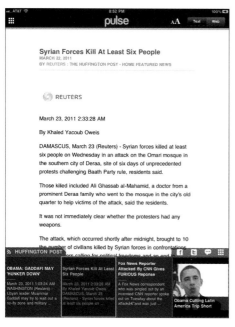

Figure 7-14

Here is the same article shown in both the text and web views. I prefer the text view.

Keep in mind that the text view saves bandwidth when on 3G. If you determine that a story is worthy of seeing in all of its graphic glory, just switch to web view.

A tap on the grid button (top left) will take you back to the list of articles from your feeds.

One last thing that makes Pulse enjoyable is the care its developers have taken to make the app behave well when rotated. I like to read a lot of things on the iPad in portrait mode. I think it's more comfortable, because it reminds me of reading a book. Many apps seem to lose my place if I rotate the device to change the orientation. Pulse does a great job of keeping the view consistent … even when the orientation is switched back and forth.

MacHash News (free)

This app is for the Apple news junkie—like me. This app combines all the Apple, Mac and iOS news into a single place. I know it's really specialized, but this app does a really nice job of bringing together information from a variety of sources.

When you first open the app, you get a black screen with a small MacHash Menu button on the top left of the page. Tap this button to open the list of current articles. Tap on any of the articles to open it on the front page of the app. Now you can either read the article or share it via Twitter, e-mail or Facebook. You can also save it to read later.

There is no way to control which feeds are being pulled into the app, but in my very unscientific exploration, it seemed like every Apple news feed was present. I know this app won't appeal to everyone, but if you want to stay up-to-date on what's going on with Apple, then this news aggregator is right up your alley.

MORE NEWS

There are two more news apps that I want to mention in closing. These are the *USA Today* app and the BBC news app for the iPad. I love the *USA Today* app if only for the crossword. In the Life section of the app, just tap on the crossword to open a new crossword … six days a week. It's awesome.

The other app I recommend is the BBC iPad app, because it tends to offer more balanced world news than other news sources. Both these apps are free, so what do you have to lose? Check 'em out.

PART 3

Internet Content

E-mail

The Skim

I can hardly remember life before e-mail. It seems like I spend more time dealing with e-mail than any other type of communication. And the iPad has become my go-to device for checking my e-mail accounts … when I'm not sitting at my laptop.

The Mail app on the iPad has always been good. And with the universal inbox, which was introduced with iOS4.2, it's even better than it was. I actually think this e-mail program is close to perfect. There are just two small blips: There's no way to select multiple e-mails to delete, and there's no way to mark e-mails as spam. Hopefully these will be fixed in the future.

Since the built-in e-mail app will be the one you use on the iPad, let's go through setting up your e-mail account.

SET UP STANDARD E-MAIL

Luckily, Apple has taken care of the setup process for most e-mail services, including Microsoft Exchange, MobileMe, Gmail, Yahoo! and AOL. So if you have any of these accounts, setting up your iPad e-mail is just a matter of following the directions.

The question is, which one provides your e-mail service? Well, this is usually pretty easy to figure out, because it's part of your e-mail address;

137

TIP

The Mail app displays messages in rich HTML format, meaning that images appear inside the e-mail messages and can be downloaded to the iPad photo library with a tap and hold. The iPad Mail app can also view and zoom attachments, including PDFs and documents created by Microsoft Word, Excel, Power-Point and the iWork suite.

Figure 8-1

From the e-mail setup screen, tap on the type of e-mail you want to access.

it's the part after the (@) symbol. For example, if your e-mail address is iPadFullyLoaded@gmail.com, then your e-mail provider is Gmail.

But there are two types of e-mail that don't follow this standard. They are addresses that show a website name after the (@) symbol, which is usually a business name. This kind of e-mail address is typical for employees or entrepreneurs. For example, the e-mail address alan@ipadfullyloaded.com is tied to the website www.ipadfullyloaded.com, making it a little more difficult to set up e-mail access on the iPad.

Microsoft Exchange

The other type of e-mail that veers from the norm are those that use Microsoft Exchange—usually businesses. Setting up the Mail program to work with Exchange servers is really easy, but you might need to get some information from your business IT

office. If you are a freelancer, entrepreneur or small business, chances are you're not using a Microsoft Exchange server. If you are, then someone set it up for you, so you might need to contact this person or look up the info they left for you.

To set up your iPad to access your Microsoft Exchange e-mail:

1. Tap Settings.

2. Tap Mail, Contacts, Calendars.

3. Tap Add Account.

4. Tap Microsoft Exchange.

5. Enter your full e-mail address.

6. You may now need to enter domain information. This can be a variety of things, but here are a few to try:

   • Leave it blank. The information is most likely going to be found by the program automatically.

   • Ask your IT department for the company domain.

   • Try the Internet domain of your company's website—both with the ".com" part and without it. Your best bet is just to ask if leaving it blank doesn't work.

7. Enter your Exchange username, which is usually the first part of your e-mail address ... the characters that come before the (@) symbol.

8. Enter your password. This is the same password you use to log in to your work computer and check your e-mail.

9. Enter a description for your account. This is especially important if you plan to have multiple e-mail accounts on your iPad.

10. Tap Next.

11. The iPad will try to verify the account information. Be patient; this can take awhile.

If your Microsoft Exchange server does not allow for auto-discovery, you'll get an error message and will need to enter the rest of the information manually. If this happens, ask your IT department for the information and enter it in the Server field. If this request confuses the techs, just ask them for the information they'd use to set up a Windows Mobile smart phone; it's the same info.

MobileMe

To set up a MobileMe e-mail account—an Apple program—on the iPad, you either need to already have a MobileMe account or sign up for a free trial. From there, you can set up access to your e-mail on the iPad by following these directions:

1. Tap on Settings.

2. Tap Mail, Contacts, Calendars.

3. Tap Add Account.

4. Tap MobileMe.

5. Enter your name.

6. Enter your full e-mail address.

7. Provide your MobileMe password.

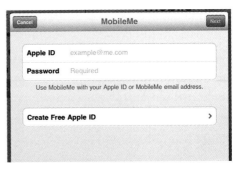

Figure 8-2
The MobileMe sign-in page is really the simplest setup on the iPad. Hey, it is an Apple product. Simple is the gig.

8. Add a description of your account. This is important if you plan to have multiple e-mail accounts on one iPad.

9. Click Save to set up the account.

A person may have as many MobileMe e-mail addresses on the same iPad as (s)he wants—but not multiple contacts, calendars and bookmarks. More on that in Chapter 9.

Gmail

Gmail, the Google e-mail solution, is free and widely used. It's a great solution for those who want a free e-mail account with lots of storage and a clean interface. To sign up for a Gmail account, just go to gmail.com and click Create an Account. To read your Gmail on the iPad, set up your e-mail as follows:

1. Tap Settings.

2. Tap Mail, Contacts, Calendars.

3. Tap Add Account if you already have a Gmail e-mail account set up.

4. Tap Gmail.

5. Enter your name.

6. Enter your full Gmail address.

7. Enter your Gmail password.

8. Add a description for your account. Again, this is helpful if you plan on having multiple e-mail accounts on your iPad.

9. Click Save.

10. You can now decide if you want to have the iPad get the Mail, Calendars and Notes associated with the account.

11. Done. It's that easy!

Now here is a little twist: If you have a Gmail account and want your e-mails pushed to the device (so that they appear in your Inbox without you asking the system to check for them), you need to add the Gmail account as if it is a Microsoft Exchange e-mail account.

1. Tap Settings.

2. Tap Mail, Contacts, Calendars.

3. Tap Add Account

4. Tap Microsoft Exchange.

5. Enter your Gmail e-mail address.

6. Enter your password and tap Next.

7. Now you have to enter the server information. Enter m.google.com and leave the domain field empty.

8. Tap Next.

9. You will now be asked which of the Google services you want on your iPad. If you select Mail, Contacts, and Calendars, then your Gmail e-mail will be pushed to the device. Moreover, your calendar(s) will be available in the iPad Calendar app and your contacts will be available in your Contacts app. We'll cover Contacts and Calendars in more detail in Chapter 9.

Yahoo!

Yahoo! is a great solution for those who want a free e-mail account. To sign up for a Yahoo! account, go to www.mail.yahoo.com and sign

up. To read your Yahoo! e-mail on the iPad, set up access as follows:

1. Tap Settings.

2. Tap Mail, Contacts, Calendars.

3. Tap Add Account.

4. Tap YAHOO!

5. Enter your name.

6. Enter your full e-mail address.

7. Enter your Yahoo! password.

8. Add a description for your account, especially if you plan to have multiple e-mail accounts on your iPad.

9. Tap Next to finish setting up the account.

AOL Mail

One of my first e-mail accounts was provided by AOL. This used to be a paid service, but it's now free. Most people who started out with AOL as an Internet service provider started with an AOL e-mail account. And there are enough of these folks still using AOL that the company developed the basic setup to work with the iPad.

Make your AOL e-mail accessible on the iPad:

1. Tap Settings.

2. Tap Mail, Contacts, Calendars.

3. Tap Add Account.

4. Tap AOL.

5. Enter your name.

6. Enter your full email address.

7. Type in your AOL password.

8. Add a description for the account, especially if you plan to have multiple e-mail accounts accessible on your iPad.

9. Tap on Next to finish the setup.

SET UP ALTERNATE E-MAIL

So we've covered the standard e-mail providers. But what about the rest of the e-mail accounts out there that don't fit into these neat presets? Yes, of course, Apple has taken them into consideration as well, and here's how to set up other kinds of e-mail accounts.

By the way, don't feel alone if your e-mail is in this category. I'm with you. My main e-mail account is not through a standard provider. But it's not difficult to set up access. You just need some information about your service.

Basically, the alternate e-mail accounts referenced here are provided by an ISP (Internet Service Provider), the phone company (e.g., AT&T), your cable company (e.g., Comcast, Cox), or as part of your own website (www.ipadfullyloaded.com). Setting up iPad access to these types of accounts just requires that you do a little research. You'll want to make sure that you have the information you need ahead of time to enter into the e-mail setup menu.

The first thing you'll notice here is that the setup looks just like the menu for any of the other e-mail accounts. When we set up the standard accounts, you tapped on Next, and the account setup was done. Well, here, you tap Next and move on to the more complicated part.

IMAP/ POP Accounts

The first choice you get after entering the basic information for setting up access for an e-mail account on an iPad is between an IMAP account and a POP account. Well, many people have no idea what these acronyms are. I know I was clueless the first time I heard these terms. So here's the deal.

IMAP Accounts

IMAP stands for Internet Message Access Protocol, and it allows an e-mail client to access e-mail messages on a remote server.

Figure 8-3
The choice between POP and IMAP is an important one; that's why it's at the top of the screen.

What this means is that the e-mail you're seeing is not actually on the device you're using; instead, the device is looking at the e-mail on an external computer. Among the advantages of this is the automated syncing you can enjoy if you have multiple devices that can access your e-mail account. If you read an e-mail on one of them, the message gets marked as Read on the server. So every other device that accesses the account will show the accurate status of your messages and activity. On the downside, if you delete a message on any device, then it is gone from all of them. Poof! Once you delete a message on the server, it's deleted on the devices as well.

POP Accounts

POP stands for Post Office Protocol. It's used by e-mail clients to get messages from the e-mail server. What usually happens is that the e-mail client goes out on the Internet to the e-mail server and downloads the new messages directly to the device. Once you

141

read the e-mail on the device and delete it, the message is deleted from the e-mail client. But ... an important distinction here ... it survives on the server. This means that when you instruct another device to go out to the server to get e-mails, that message you deleted from the other device will be sitting there waiting to be read. So if you have an e-mail account on an iPad and a laptop ... and also an iPhone and a desktop computer, then you'll get the same message four times with a POP setting. This means that you'll have to delete, file or mark it read on four separate devices.

To set up these kinds of e-mail programs on the iPad successfully, you need to know which of the two services you use. Different e-mail hosting companies choose the service format they prefer. Some offer IMAP service, and some offer POP service. The best bet is to contact the company and ask which type of service you're receiving.

Server Information

Once you know the answer, you can move onto the questions related to your incoming mail server. You'll gather information about this from the e-mail hosting company, too. Typically, it will look something like: mail.(*your domain.com*), where (*your domain.com*) is replaced with the name of your domain. For example, since the domain for the e-mail address I'd add is **www.ipadfullyloaded.com**, the incoming mail server will be: **mail.ipadfullyloaded.com**.

The next thing is to enter the username for your account, which is usually the full e-mail address. If necessary, enter your password; but it should auto-fill based on your entry on the previous page. The final step is to configure an outgoing e-mail server, because we want

to get e-mail and to send it as well. Again, all the information in this menu area is available from the company that provides your e-mail service. After you enter your outgoing mail server and the username and password, tap Save. That's when the iPad goes out to see if the account info you entered is correct.

ADVANCED FEATURES

With the e-mail account set up to send and receive messages through the iPad, it's time to access the Advanced features. Among these features is an ability to set preferences for the Sent Mail, Drafts and the Trash. To access the Advanced tab for e-mail:

1. Tap the Settings icon.

2. Tap Mail, Contacts and Calendars.

3. Tap on the e-mail account to edit.

4. Tap on the Advanced button, which is located on the bottom of the screen. Note:

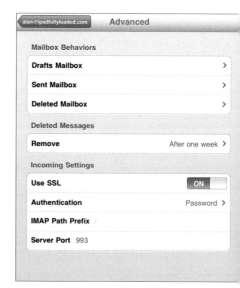

Figure 8-4

Here is a view of the Advanced settings for one of my e-mail accounts.

You might need to scroll down to access this button; sometimes the keyboard hides it.

5. You can now dictate where the Drafts mailbox, the Sent mailbox and the Trash will reside. Your options depend on the type of hosting service you're using for the account, so check with the e-mail hosting company for information.

GENERAL E-MAIL SETTINGS

Some general e-mail preferences are set up in the Settings panel.

- **Show:** Choose how many messages you want to see listed at a time. Your options are 25, 50, 75, 100 or 200 messages.

- **Preview:** Here, choose how many preview lines of a message you want to see. Pick between none to five. I like two. This provides enough info about the e-mail for me to decide if I need to open it right away, wait until later or delete it.

- **Minimum Font Size:** Pick the size of the font. Options range from small to giant. I like medium, but pick the one that looks best to you.

- **Show To/ CC Label:** Decide here if you want to see the To and CC fields when reading e-mail messages.

- **Ask Before Deleting.** This gives you the option to confirm every deletion request. I know that it's important to know that deleting e-mails means they will go away, but this just drives me crazy, so I turn it off.

- **Load Remote Images:** Decide here if you want to display images that are sent in e-mails.

- **Organize by Thread:** This is a very cool feature, because it allows your e-mail messages to be organized by the subject.

- **Always Bcc Myself:** Turn on this feature if you want to blind copy yourself on every message you send from the iPad.

- **Signature:** If you set up and activate a signature, the information you enter will automatically be included at the end of each e-mail message you send.

- **Default Account:** Whichever e-mail account you select as the default will be the one that the iPad will use to send e-mails from other apps. So if you are e-mailing a document from the Pages app, Pages will use this account automatically.

Set these options according to your personal preferences.

PUSH VS. FETCH

Now that you have your e-mail account(s) set up, it's time to instruct your iPad to go out and check for mail. If you tap on Settings and then Mail, Contacts and Calendars, a button called Fetch New Data will appear in the middle of the iPad (right side of the screen). Tap on that to bring up the Push and Fetch menus. These are the two methods that the iPad uses to go out and get mail.

Push

The first option, Push, means that e-mails are pushed from the server to the device whenever there are new e-mails present. Messages are on the iPad as soon as the e-mail server receives them. And this is great, but the real-time service comes with a price … in the form of battery life. Constantly monitoring your account to keep your mailbox current requires a lot of power.

To help users preserve battery life when enjoying push delivery, Apple provides an OFF switch. When you're running low on battery power or want to conserve your

TIP

Not all e-mail servers are compatible with the push service. To see which of your e-mail accounts offer push service, make sure Push is turned on. Do this in the Settings app by tapping Mail, Contacts, Calendars and then tapping Fetch New Data. Tap the Advanced button. This will bring up the list of e-mail accounts on your iPad, and it will show which of your accounts offer push and which do not.

Figure 8-5
The Push and Fetch settings are accessed in the Settings menu by tapping Mail, Contacts, Calendars and then tapping on Fetch New Data.

remaining power, turn off the push service. This is done in the Settings app and is covered a little later.

Fetch

The other option for receiving e-mails on your iPad is Fetch. This is usually set up to happen in regular intervals—every 15 minutes, 30 minutes, hourly—or you can fetch your messages manually. The less often you check for new messages, the longer your iPad battery will last. So this really is a matter of priority. I usually have the iPad go fetch new mail every 30 minutes.

Use the advanced fetch settings to change the way each e-mail account checks for mail. Those who can use the push method can use this area to change to fetch or manual

delivery. Those who use the fetch method can change delivery to push (if it's offered) or manual. To change your settings, just click on the account you want to change and pick the new method of e-mail retrieval.

Manual

If you change your setting from, say, a 30-minute fetch interval to manual retrieval, then the e-mail app will get new messages only when you tell it to go out and fetch your e-mail. This setting is really useful when you're running on a low battery.

The Push and Fetch settings are accessed in the Settings menu by tapping Mail, Contacts, Calendars and then tapping on Fetch New Data.

To get your e-mail when the fetch is set to manual, you have to open the mail program and tap on the Update button on the bottom of the Accounts panel. It looks like a three-quarter circle made by an arrow.

READING E-MAIL

Reading your e-mail on the iPad is as easy as tapping on the Mail app and selecting the Inbox ... if you have one account. If you have multiple e-mail accounts, there are some other options. With more than one account, you can look at the Unified Inbox, which shows all your e-mails from all your accounts ... without actually having to go into each individual account! There are also buttons for the individual inboxes, so you don't have to go all the way into each account just to get your e-mail.

If you hold the iPad in portrait orientation, all you see is the currently selected message. But when you turn it "sideways" to landscape orientation, you see not only the currently selected message but also the Inbox showing the message list with a two-line preview. This is one of the reasons I like to read my e-mail in landscape orientation on my iPad. More info!

If you have multiple e-mail accounts on your iPad, it's pretty easy to change which one you're accessing at any given time. On the top of the Inbox is a button that shows the currently selected account. It also shows how many unread e-mails are in the account ... and offers an Edit button. Let's start from the right and work toward the left.

The **Edit** button allows you to delete or move multiple e-mails at a time, but there is still no way to select multiple messages with a single tap. You have to select each e-mail individually. (I really want a Select All option here.) Instead, you need to tap Edit, and then select the e-mails you want to delete or move by tapping the message in the list. You'll know if you have selected a message, because a red circle with a white check mark will appear to

Figure 8-6
These are different e-mail accounts available on my iPad and the new All Inboxes feature.

the left of selected messages. You can then delete or move the selected messages by using the buttons on the bottom of the screen.

If you have multiple e-mail accounts and want to access a different account, it's pretty easy. Just tap on the current account name or the **Mailboxes** button located on the top left of the screen. Keep tapping on this button until you see a list of your accounts. You can then pick another Inbox or you can tap on one of the e-mail accounts to look at the folders in that account.

When you're actually reading an e-mail, there are some tools available to help you manage your mail. The most obvious is the **Trashcan** (or file box, depending on the account). By tapping the Trashcan, you send the message to the trash (or to the file box to be archived).

Tapping the **Folder** icon saves the message to that folder, but not all e-mail accounts have folders to which you can save e-mails. There's more on that a little later.

In the meantime, the last three options are to **Forward** (to send the message to another recipient), **Reply** (to respond to the sender), **Print** (if you have a compatible AirPrint printer) or **Compose** a new message.

ACCESSING ATTACHMENTS

The iPad can display images that are sent inside an e-mail message, as long as they are in the following formats: JPEG, GIF, PNG or TIFF. The iPad can also play audio attachments that are sent as MP3, AAC, WAV or

Figure 8-7
This e-mail has an embedded photo (guitarist Billy Morrison). By tapping and holding on the image, options appear to save the image or copy it.

AIFF files. These audio files will show up as attachments in the e-mail program, and once they've finished downloading to your iPad, a single tap will play them.

A simple way to get content onto your iPad is to e-mail a file to yourself. But which files are supported by the Mail app and which will just not open? The following file types are supported by the iPad Mail app and can be viewed there. And in many cases, these files can be downloaded to your iPad and opened. Some files types are even editable on the iPad.

• **PDF** files are very common e-mail attachments, and the iPad Mail app makes these files easy to deal with. When you tap on an attached PDF, it opens in a preview mode. Pinch to zoom; and if you hold your finger on the PDF part of the message, a menu pops ups to ask if you want to Quick Look at the PDF or if you would like to open it in any of the apps on the iPad that can read or edit PDFs. These apps include iBooks, GoodReader and CloudReaders.

• **DOC/DOCX** files are Microsoft Word files. And since Microsoft Word is the most commonly used word processer (most of this book was written using Word), chances are, at some point, you will get a Word document as an e-mail attachment. Now there is no Microsoft Word for the iPad, but that doesn't mean you can't read Word documents! On the contrary, Apple has built in the ability to read Word files right in the Mail app. Just tap on the Attachment icon. When you are viewing the attachment, you can also open it using a document reader app (e.g., GoodReader or CloudReaders). If you have the Pages app on your iPad, you can even edit Word files. Just know that not all of the Word functions and formatting tools are available through Pages.

- **HTM/ HTML** files are web files; and since they are actually in the same format as the e-mail program, they are easily readable here.

- **PPT/ PPTX** files are PowerPoint files. And while they can be viewed in your e-mail and edited in the Keynote app, some of the formatting and controls that are available in PowerPoint will be missing in Keynote.

- **RTF/ TXT** are rich text files and regular text files. The Mail app handles these with ease, and both can be edited in the Pages app and read by numerous other applications.

- **XLS/ XLSX** files are based on the Excel program and readable by the iPad Mail app. So if you want to check those spreadsheets or charts, it's easy. If you want to edit spreadsheets, then you have to wait to be back on a real computer. Or you can use the Numbers app. Just know that it doesn't support all the functions or formatting of Excel.

- **Numbers, Keynote** and **Pages** files are accessible through the Mail app. When you receive a Pages file, one tap will open it in a viewer or allow you to look at the file in one of the reader apps. However, since there is a Pages app for iPad, you can also open the file and edit it. The same is true for Keynote and Numbers files, but—and there is a big but—even though these files can be loaded and edited on the iPad versions of the software, some functions are missing. If you open a file created in the full version of Pages, Numbers or Keynote, and then open the same file with the iPad versions of the software, you will get a warning that certain information will be changed.

- **Image Files** are a popular kind of attachment. I love to send and receive photos by e-mail. Being a professional photographer,

I do this all the time, and I know I'm not alone. One of the really nice features of the Mail app is that images show up in the mail message; and tapping and holding on an attached image downloads it right to the image gallery of the iPad. It's that easy.

SENDING ATTACHMENTS
Sending e-mail is very straightforward when using the iPad, but adding attachments isn't so simple. Once you're ready to write a simple e-mail on the iPad, just follow these steps:

1. Tap on the Mail app.

2. At the top right of the screen, tap the New Message icon to bring up a blank message.

3. Enter the name of the recipient or tap on the (+) to bring up your iPad address book.

4. Enter any CC or BCC recipients.

5. Enter the subject and type your message.

6. When finished, tap Send.

The process for adding attachments to an e-mail when using an iPad is a little different from the one used when working on a computer. This is because you usually need to send the attachment(s) from the original program, not the e-mail program. This is because the browse and attach option that most people use on their computers is not available here. Therefore, images need to be sent from the Photos app. Similarly, Pages documents get sent from the Pages app ... and so forth. You get the idea. Details are below:

Send Photos
One of the easiest things to do is e-mail photos from your iPad. All you have to do is open the Photos app, tap on a folder or album, and then tap on the image to open it. One more tap brings up the top menu bar. Tap on the Export icon; it looks like a box with an arrow

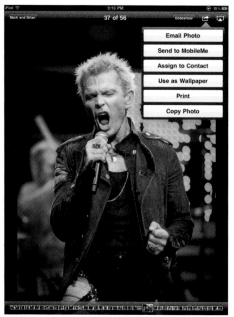

Figure 8-7

When you have an image open in the Photos app, just tap on the Export button and choose Email Photo. The e-mail program will open with the image in it.

coming out of it. This will reveal a drop-down menu that lets you choose Email Photo. Tap that choice, and the Mail app will open with the image embedded in the body of a new message. You can now type a message and send the e-mail.

Just keep in mind that many e-mail programs have a limit on the size of messages and attachments. And usually, this limit makes it necessary to reduce the file size of images being sent by e-mail. So remember that the iPad has a resolution of 1024x768 pixels at 132 ppi. This means if you're e-mailing images, you don't have to make them any bigger than that.

There is a way to add an image to an e-mail you are already writing. It's a little more complicated that starting with message with the attachment, but here's the process:

1. Open Mail.

2. Start writing a new message.

3. Press the Home button.

4. Open Photos.

5. Navigate to the photo you want to add to the message.

6. Tap on the photo and then open the Export menu on the top right.

7. Select Copy Photo.

8. Press the Home button.

9. Open Mail. Your half-written message should be on the screen.

10. Press and hold where you want to insert the photo.

11. Remove your finger from the screen. The Select | Select All | Paste menu will appear.

12. Select Paste.

13. The image that you copied will appear in your message.

Now, these methods work great for single images, but why stop there? You can e-mail multiple images in the same message. To do this:

1. Tap on the Photos app.

2. Open an album by tapping on it.

3. Before opening an individual image, tap on the Export icon in the top right corner. It looks like a box with an arrow coming out of it.

4. The heading on the top of the page will change to Select Photos.

5. Tap on the images that you want to e-mail. They will be marked by a white checkmark on a blue background. (Remember, you can only e-mail five images at a time.)

6. Once you've selected the images you want to send, look at the top left of the iPad screen. Find two buttons: Email and Copy.

7. If the Email button is grayed out, it means you've selected too many images and need to de-select a few.

8. Tap on Email and the Mail program will open with all the images you selected. They will be embedded into a message.

WHY HAVE MULTIPLE EMAIL ACCOUNTS?

I'm a firm believer in multiple e-mail accounts. I think it's a good idea to have one for work and one for private (i.e., non-work-related) correspondence. Among the many benefits of this is retaining information and messages that may be important to you, especially when you leave a job.

When you begin a new job, your employer will typically assign you an e-mail account. Something like bob@companyXYZ.com becomes the main way for your colleagues to communicate business messages to you. But when/ if you ever decide to leave the company, that e-mail address stays with your company. If you have been using it for personal e-mails, then those are lost to you as well. And your former employer retains access to those messages.

This also applies when dealing with a home e-mail. I'm not a fan of getting my e-mail from my ISP (Internet Service Provider); because if I move hosting companies, my e-mail doesn't move with me. So, if I use a cable company for my e-mail and switch provider—say I move to an area where that cable company isn't located—then I'd have to get a new ISP with a new e-mail account.

For these reasons and more, I recommend creating two (or more) separate e-mail accounts on a service like Gmail or Yahoo!. These accounts go where you go, and it's usually possible to access the e-mail from any computer that's connected to the Internet. Devices like the iPad make it easy to check all your e-mail accounts in the same place. And with the unified inbox, it's now even easier.

9. Type your e-mail message.

10. Tap Send.

Many different apps (Pages, Keynote, Numbers, Photoshop Express, Portfolio, etc.) allow you to send content as an e-mail. Check with the specific app to see how it handles this function.

Send Files from iPad Apps

When it comes to sending attachments from other apps, the app itself will have an e-mail option. For example, each of the iWork apps (Pages, Numbers and Keynote) allow you to e-mail files from inside the app. Just tap the Export button and choose Email. This opens a new message with the file embedded.

Similarly, apps like GarageBand (covered in Chapter 16) and iMovie (covered in Chapter 4) allow you to e-mail your creations from the app. It's like this across the board for the iPad. So to e-mail specific kinds of attachments from this device, go to the app where the content was created and look for its Export or Email function.

WEBMAIL

Not everything runs smoothly all the time. And while the Mail app usually works great, there are situations in which the Mail app doesn't work. But don't worry; you don't have to use the Mail app. There is an alternative. Most, if not all, e-mail providers have a way for you to access your account using an Internet browser.

On the iPad, use the Safari Internet browser to access your e-mail through webmail. Just type in the correct URL and enter your info. Your e-mail should pop up in the window. Since the iPad has a browser, this is a viable alternative, especially if you

share an iPad and don't want your e-mail to be accessible to anyone who picks up your device.

Many providers also offer a special Mobile page that might be easier to use than Safari. Since the iPad version of Safari is based on the iPhone version, many websites recognize it as a mobile device and, by default, offer the mobile version of the site, which is more limited than the full version.

Other options may be provider-specific apps. Some e-mail companies now also developing dedicated apps that will allow users to access their e-mail. An example is the mailPro app, which allows you to access your Hotmail and Windows Live e-mail accounts. Another option is the EmailPush app, which provides access to your Gmail account. These alternatives may be helpful if you want/ need to avoid the Mail app.

Calendars, Contacts and Lists

The Skim

I used to have a calendar hanging on my wall at home, and a desk calendar at work and a little pocket calendar that I carried with me. And I really tried to make sure that all my important dates were marked on all the calendars. But it never worked. Inevitably, I would miss something somewhere.

Digital calendars make it easy to keep the same information on multiple devices. So now I keep a calendar on my computer, my iPhone and my iPad. And if I do everything right, then the information will stay in sync no matter which calendar I update. The same is true for my address book, which now lives on my computer, my iPhone and iPad. And I can access the information on the Internet from any computer that is online.

Well, yes, this is all fantastic … until something goes wrong. When the calendars and contacts work right, it's great. But when they don't, it's a real pain. I get more e-mails and phone calls from friends and clients asking for help with missing calendars and contacts … and questions on why suddenly the calendars are not syncing or updating … than any other topic.

So let's get on with it. The iPad comes preloaded with two aptly named apps: Calendars and Contacts.

Figure 9-1
Here are the four views of the Calendar app: Day, Week, Month and List of Events.

CALENDARS

The very first time you tap on the Calendars app, you'll see that the iPad has created two calendars for you. One is called On my iPad. The other is a Birthday Calendar. Neither calendar has any information in them. And if you just use your iPad as a stand-alone device and don't care about syncing to any other devices, then you really don't have to do anything else. You can start entering information now. But before you do, let's look at the Calendar app and the options available.

The first thing to know is that there are four views for your calendar: Day, Week, Month and List. Each of the views offers the same information but in a different format. This versatility makes it easy to get an overview or detailed information about what's on your calendar, as needed.

- The Day view shows you the whole day by hour at a glance.
- The Week view shows your events scheduled for the week.
- The Month view offers information for the whole month on a single page.
- The List view is a line-by-line display of events on the left side and a detailed day view of events on the right.

Create an Event

Calendars are only helpful if you enter information into them. Here's how to enter an event onto your iPad calendar.

1. Open the Calendar app on the iPad by tapping on the icon.

2. Tap the (+) button at the bottom right of the screen to open the Add Event window.

3. Enter a title for the event.

TIP

While you can view and pick different calendars to view on the iPad, you can't create new calendars on the iPad.

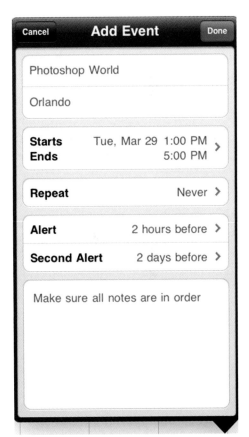

Figure 9-2
Here is the Add Event entry window.

4. If you want, add a location in the Location field or use this space as a secondary field for event info.

5. Tap the Starts/ Ends area to open the date controls.

6. Adjust the day, hour, minute and AM/PM wheels to set the start time of the event.

7. Adjust the day, hour, minute and AM/PM wheels to set the end time of the event.

8. Or, if the event lasts all day, like a birthday, turn on the All Day switch.

9. Tap Done to finish entering in the start and end times.

10. You can now set the repeat options for recurring events.

11. First, pick the frequency of the event. (Leave it as None if the event doesn't repeat.)

12. Choose Every Day, Every Week, Every 2 Weeks, Every Month or Every Year.

13. You can now set an Alert so you have a better chance of remembering your event. Alerts can be set for anywhere between five minutes before the event's start time to two days before.

14. If you set an alert, you can set a Second Alert. (Never miss an anniversary again!)

15. Click Done.

16. You can now enter any Notes you have for your event.

17. Tap Done to complete the entry.

Once an event has been entered, it will show up in your calendar and can be edited or deleted as needed. Tap on the event and you will see a little pop-up window that allows you to edit the information.

If you're using the iPad calendar all by itself, then this is the end of your functionality.

But if you already have a calendar program, you can set up the iPad to access that calendar. And the really cool part is that if you have multiple calendars, you can see them all in the same place. For example, if you have a MobileMe account with a calendar for home, and a Microsoft Exchange calendar for work … and maybe even a Google calendar, you can see them all in the same place on your iPad. Let's talk about setting up that syncing.

MobileMe

Apple really wants you to use MobileMe. According to Apple, it's the best solution for e-mail, calendars and contacts. And when it comes to keeping your information synced, MobileMe does a great job. It keeps the information in your contacts and calendars (along with e-mails and Internet bookmarks) all synced among all your computers, iPad,

Figure 9-3

In the MobileMe settings, this is where syncing is turned on or off.

the MobileMe website and your iPhone. Plus, it does so in the background automatically, if your hardware is new enough and running the latest OS.

MobileMe is a service by Apple, and it's meant to be used on Apple products. If you use a PC, this is not the product for you, and you're probably using the Microsoft Exchange server anyway. But there is a good third-party alternative to MobileMe and Microsoft Exchange, and it's from Google, which makes applications for managing your calendar and contacts. The data on the Google apps can be wirelessly synced.

But if you have MobileMe, here is a quick rundown on getting your iPad to play nice with your MobileMe calendars and contacts. More on the Google solution in a minute.

1. Turn on your iPad.

2. Tap on Settings.

3. Tap Mail, Contacts, Calendars.

4. Tap Add Account and choose MobileMe.

5. Enter your MobileMe account information.

6. Tap Next.

7. Turn on Mail, Contacts, Calendars and Bookmarks.

8. If it asks, tap on Merge with MobileMe. This tries to make sure that the contacts, calendars and bookmarks already on your device sync with MobileMe and are not duplicated.

9. On the main Settings screen, tap Mail, Contacts, Calendars and tap Fetch New Data.

10. Make sure that Push is set to wirelessly and automatically get data from the

> **TIP**
>
> Full disclosure time! I have a MobileMe account, and I've been using it since it was called a .mac account. I keep my calendars synced on a Mac laptop, a Mac desktop, the iPad and an iPhone.

server, so your MobileMe contacts and calendars will be automatically updated whenever a change is made.

Now, when you make a change to any of the Calendars on your iPad, it updates your iPhone and computers, too. The same is true in the other direction. When you update a calendar item on the computer, the iPad receives the new information and updates your calendar information.

Microsoft Exchange

If you have a Microsoft Exchange calendar set up, you can sync it with your iPad. Do this the same way you would set up the iPad to access a Microsoft Exchange server for your e-mail (covered in Chapter 8).

1. Turn on your iPad.

2. Tap on Settings.

3. Tap Mail, Contacts, Calendars.

4. Tap Add Account and choose Microsoft Exchange.

5. Enter your Exchange Server account information.

6. Tap Next.

7. Enter the server information.

8. Tap Next.

9. Turn on Mail, Contacts, Calendars.

Your Exchange Server accounts will now be synced wirelessly and automatically to your iPad, including the contacts and calendars.

Google Sync

It might seem that Google is taking over the world, because the company seems to be everywhere these days. That Map app you have on the iPad, that's from Google. And when it comes to a calendar or contact program, Google has you covered there, too.

Google Sync syncs your Google calendars and Google contacts on all of your devices, including the iPad. I know there are folks out there who don't like the idea of all their information sitting on the servers of a single company; but for those who don't mind, the Google calendar and address book are great options. Plus, they're free.

To set up your iPad with Google Sync:

1. Turn on the iPad.

2. Open the Settings app.

3. Tap on Mail, Contacts, Calendars.

4. Tap Add Account.

5. Select Microsoft Exchange. (If you already have a Microsoft Exchange account set up for your e-mail, then skip to the next section.)

6. In the e-mail field, enter your full Google account e-mail address.

7. Leave the Domain field blank.

8. Enter your full Google account e-mail address as the username.

9. Enter your Google account password in the Password field.

10. Tap Next at the top of the screen.

11. In the New Server field, enter **m.google.com**.

12. Tap Next at the top of the screen.

13. You can now select the Mail, Calendar and Contacts to sync.

If all you want to do is add the Google calendar, you can use the CalDav technology (which allows users to access scheduling information online via remote server) to set up the Google calendar. To do this:

1. Turn on the iPad.

2. Open the Settings app.

3. Tap on Mail, Contacts, Calendars.

4. Tap Add Account.

5. Select Other.

6. Select Add CalDav Account.

7. Enter the following:

   • In the Server field, enter **google.com**.

   • In the Username field, enter your full Google Account or Google app's e-mail address.

   • In the Password field, enter your Google Account or Google app's password.

   • Enter a description of the account, like *Google Calendars*.

8. Tap Next on the top of the screen.

9. You're done!

10. Now, when you open the Calendar app, your Google calendar will begin to sync wirelessly.

To get the Google contacts and calendars on your computer, go to **http://www.google.com/ sync/index.html** and follow directions for your computer.

CONTACTS

I used to be able to remember my friends' phone numbers and addresses, no problem. But not anymore! Smart phones and computers have made me really lazy, and I can't seem to remember any phone numbers anymore. Part of this is because we no longer actually dial numbers, but instead press a single button on our phones, and we so frequently use other ways to communicate, like e-mail. Plus, it's just not necessary to remember contact information. It's become so easy to keep track of all those names, numbers and e-mails on our phones, computers and iPads.

The address book on the iPad is really very nice. It has a great layout, and it's easy to navigate and edit.

Add a Contact

Adding a contact to your iPad address book is pretty easy. Just turn on the iPad, tap on the built-in Contacts app and follow these steps:

1. Tap on the (+) that's located at the bottom of the screen.

2. Enter the contact's first name, last name and company info.

3. To add a photo, tap the Add Photo button in the Contacts app. This will enable you to pick a photo for this contact. Choose from the images that are loaded on your iPad.

4. Tap on the word Mobile and pick your type of phone from the pop-up menu.

5. Enter the contact's phone number.

Figure 9-4

Here, the Contact app shows my contacts. I really love the look of this app.

6. Choose the phone type (e.g., home, work, mobile) in the field below the entry. Enter as many different phone numbers for a contact as necessary. As you start to type a new number, a new number box will appear below the existing one(s).

7. Next is e-mail. Tap on the type of e-mail (e.g., home or work) and then enter the e-mail address.

8. After you enter the first e-mail, you'll be able to enter a second, third, fourth and so on … in the same manner you did with the phone numbers.

9. You can also enter a contact's website (or two, three, four of them).

10. Next, enter a mailing address.

11. You can then add a second address or even a third, fourth or fifth address.

12. Add any Notes you want associated with this contact.

13. If needed, add custom fields, including a prefix, the phonetic spelling of the first and/or last name, middle name, suffix,

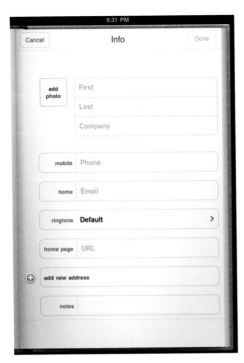

Figure 9-5
Here's how the Info window in the Contacts app looks.

nickname, job title, department, instant message information, birthday and/ or a date.

14. When all the contact's information has been entered, tap Done on the top right.

You now have a contact in your address book. I know, you're thinking that there must be a faster way. And what about the contacts that are already on your computer?

Well, the good news is that if you have a MobileMe address book or a Microsoft Exchange address book or a Google address book and have already synced the calendars, then you also synced the address book. If this is your situation, just follow of the instructions on adding your e-mail account that's provided in Chapter 8.

Yet there is another type of address book in use on computer systems today; it's a LDAP address book.

LDAP Address Book

If you have a LDAP (Lightweight Directory Access Protocol) address book and you know your account information, then you can access that address book from the iPad as well. (If you do not know your account information, you can get it from your System Administrator / IT person.) Just follow these steps to set up this access:

1. Turn on the iPad.

2. Open the Settings app.

3. Tap on Mail, Contacts, Calendars.

4. Tap Add Account.

5. Tap Other.

6. Select Add LDAP Account.

7. Enter the following:
   - The LDAP server
   - The username (optional)
   - The password (optional)
   - Description

8. Tap Next on the top of the screen.

9. That's it; you're done.

vCards

The default file format for address book data is called a *vCard*. This format is basically an electronic business card and can contain a name, phone number, e-mail and address information as well as a profile photo in the vCard format.

vCards can be exchanged over the Internet or even on a disc or jump drive, and they can be sent in e-mails. Since the iPad doesn't have a USB port, the only good way to get a vCard in iPad Contacts is by e-mail. But vCards that are sent as e-mail attachments can be instantly loaded into the iPad's Contacts.

Sharing Contacts

Here is something that Apple definitely did right when it comes to the iPad address book. They made it really easy for you to share your contacts with others. You can share any of the contacts in your address book with a simple click. Just:

1. Open the Contacts app on the iPad.

2. Tap on the contact you want to share.

3. On the bottom of the screen, tap Share.

4. This opens an e-mail with the contact's .vcf file attached.

5. Send the e-mail.

The .vcf file extension is a version of the vCard, so it is compatible with all address book / contact programs that can use vCards.

CALENDAR AND CONTACT PREFERENCES

Setting preferences for the calendar and contacts apps is done in the iPad's Settings app. Tap on Settings and then tap Mail, Contacts, Calendars. Scroll to the bottom on the right side. There, you'll find the few settings options for the Calendars and Contacts.

Calendar Settings
- **New Invitation Alerts:** You can turn this on and off.
- **Sync:** This keeps track of how long to keep syncing events. The choices are "Events 2 Weeks Back," "Events 1 Month Back," "Events 3 Months Back," "Events 6 Months Back" and "All Events."
- **Time Zone Support:** Turning this on allows you to pick a time zone for your events. When it's turned off, the calendar

TIP

I like to sort my contacts by their last name, the way I used to do it in a real paper address book. But it's easier to find who I'm looking for if they're displayed with the first name first—just the way I like it.

will display the events in the current time zone using the iPad's location.

- **Default Calendar:** This might be the most important setting, especially if you have multiple calendars. It allows you to designate a default calendar so that when you enter a new event and forget to note which calendar it belongs to, it goes to the default.

Contacts Settings
- Sort Order sets the sequence of contact listings by the different types of information: Last, First (default) or First, Last.
- Display Order establishes the format of your contact listings; the choices are First, Last (Default) or Last, First.

I have become quite reliant on having my calendars and contacts available to me at the touch of a button no matter where I am. So if I could to ask for anything of Apple, it'd be the ability to have two (or more) MobileMe accounts on the same iPad. This would mean that my wife and I could both have our MobileMe address books and calendars on the same iPad. Then ... total bliss.

NOTES AND TODO LISTS

The iPad was built for lists, and app developers have been quick to create a slew of Todo list apps. Apps in this category range in price from free to $39.99. So the main downside to using the iPad as a big electronic todo list is picking just one app for the job!

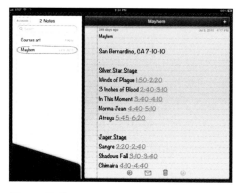

Figure 9-6
This page of my Notes app shows the bands and set times for a shoot I did last year.

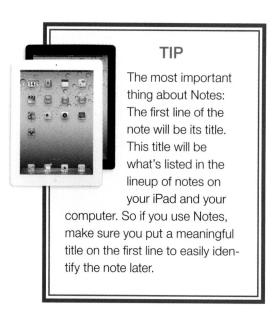

TIP

The most important thing about Notes: The first line of the note will be its title. This title will be what's listed in the lineup of notes on your iPad and your computer. So if you use Notes, make sure you put a meaningful title on the first line to easily identify the note later.

Notes App

Before I get to the cool todo list apps, I want to cover one more of the free preloaded apps from Apple: the Notes app. I'm not a huge fan of the Notes app, but it can be useful. And, since it's free and you can't delete it, you might as well know what it does, when to use it and when to avoid it.

The biggest mistake you can make here is thinking that the Notes app is a word processor; it isn't and never will be. It's just a place to jot down a quick note. The Notes app is a one-trick pony.

Notes opens to the last note you wrote or, if you haven't written a note, a blank page. This is one of the apps that has a different look depending on how you're holding the iPad—in portrait or landscape orientation. In the portrait view, all you get is a yellow-lined notebook page. In landscape mode, the screen is split. A list of notes is on the left and the notebook page is on the right. So there you are, staring at a blank piece of electronic paper. From here, just tap on the page and start typing your note(s).

When you're done typing a note, you have some (although not many) options.

- Create another note by pressing the (+) button on the top right.

- Delete a note by tapping on the trashcan icon at the bottom of the screen.

- E-mail a note by tapping on the envelope on the bottom. If the keyboard is covering it, just tap on the Hide Keyboard button. (It's on the very bottom, to the right of the keyboard, and it looks like a keyboard with a down arrow.)

- If you have multiple notes, you can use the arrow keys on the bottom of the screen to scroll through your collection.

• If you're in the portrait mode, tap the Notes button at the top left to bring up your Notes library.

The Notes app is nice, but I could have achieved the same thing with a little paper notebook and pen. The only real benefit to electronic notes, in my opinion, is the sync function that supposedly puts the notes on multiple devices automatically. So theoretically, I should be able to make a note on my iPad at home and rely on it to sync to my other devices (e.g., home computer, iPhone, etc).

Well, Notes isn't reliable in this way. Its sync function just does not work the way my Calendars and Contacts do. And I'll be frank; it is really, really frustrating! This simple task takes a very long time and only works occasionally. I often long for the little notebook I used to carry.

So the bottom line on the Notes app is that it's fine for taking quick notes. But unless you have your iPad with you all the time, it falls short on the practical level. Good thing there are other options.

Evernote App ($FREE)

Evernote is one of those services that is just really cool, and I'd be willing to pay for it … but I don't have to; it's free. The Evernote app allows you to make notes on your iPad and store them on the Evernote server. So, through a web browser, you can also access notes you took on your computer or smart phone that's running the Evernote app. This means you can get your notes from whatever device happens to be handy. Your notes go with you everywhere … as long as you have an Internet connection.

If you're a very heavy note taker, you'll soon realize that the basic (read: *free*) Evernote

Figure 9-7
The Evernote app doesn't have the slickest-looking interface, but the program really does a great job.

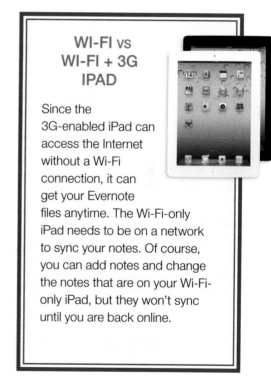

WI-FI VS WI-FI + 3G IPAD

Since the 3G-enabled iPad can access the Internet without a Wi-Fi connection, it can get your Evernote files anytime. The Wi-Fi-only iPad needs to be on a network to sync your notes. Of course, you can add notes and change the notes that are on your Wi-Fi-only iPad, but they won't sync until you are back online.

package has some limitations. The free account has a monthly usage limit of 40MB. This is plenty for basic note takers, but perhaps not for the highly industrious. For these folks, there is a Premium Evernote service that currently costs $4.99 a month or $44.99 a year (which gives you two months free).

The premium account offers 500MB of monthly uploads and allows a user to sync all types of files, including Microsoft Office documents. The premium package is also good for users who want to give others the ability to read and edit their notes. You can even search within the text in PDFs with this service.

Sign up for the premium service right from inside the Evernote app on the iPad; it couldn't be easier. When you tap the Synchronize button, an option to Go Premium appears. Just tap on this to bring up the sign-up page for the upgrade.

OnmiFocus for iPad ($39.99)

This one's for the Mac users out there; Omni-Focus is only for the Mac, iPad and iPhone. And this is one of the more expensive note-type apps available on the iPad. But it's really only worth it if you already use the OmniFocus app for the iPhone ($19.99) and/ or Mac OmniFocus desktop application ($79.99). The OmniFocus app has a great user interface that allows you to enter information easily and quickly. More importantly, you can sync the information to your other devices.

If you have OmniFocus for Mac or OmniFocus for iPhone, you can sync to those devices using the following methods:

- Use MobileMe to create and store a sync database on your iDisk, which is part of the MobileMe service from Apple.

- Sync over Wi-Fi to create and store a sync database on your Mac. (If you sync over Wi-Fi, you must be on the same network as the Mac running OmniFocus.)

- Use the work-in-progress Omni Sync Server.

- Use your own WebDAV server.

OmniFocus automatically syncs hourly (when the application is open) or one minute after you make a change. If you'd like to trigger a manual sync, you can always tap the Sync button in the sidebar.

If you already use the OmniFocus product, then this might be a great way to go. But if you don't, there are much cheaper options.

WunderList HD ($FREE)

This is an app used to create todo lists and notes that are then available on your devices and computers. The concept is the same as the other list and todo apps, but the whole thing costs $0. That's right, it's free. It works on your iPad, iPhone, Android phone, Mac and Windows computers … and it can be set up and used in seconds.

To get WunderList set up using your iPad:

1. Download the WunderList HD app.

2. Tap on the icon to start.

3. If you have an account, you can sign in. If you don't, tap Register Now.

4. Enter your e-mail address and password.

5. Tap Register.

That's all there is to it. You're immediately taken to the Inbox, where a list of tasks is waiting, including a short tutorial. To get WunderList on your computer, just go to **http://www.6wunderkinder.com/wunderlist/** and download the program you need.

To have WunderList sync your information, you'll need to be connected to the Internet either by Wi-Fi or by 3G. The app automatically syncs when you open the app, every fifteen minutes after that, and when you close the app. It's also possible to sync anytime by tapping on the Sync button at the top of the Show Lists menu.

PRODUCTIVITY APPS

The apps described here are just the tip of the iceberg. Everyone uses lists and notes in a different ways, and the way I do things might not be the same way you do things. So it's nice that there are tons of apps out there to choose from. Just look through the productivity category in the Apps Store. Chances are, you'll find tons of tools that meet your organizational needs.

10

Social Media

The Skim

Facebook • Twitter • Flipboard

Based on the number of new friend requests I get every day, it seems that everyone is now using some form of social media to stay in touch. A movie about the founder of Facebook was a huge hit at the box office and won four Golden Globes. The film was nominated for eight Oscars and won three. With more than 600 million people using Facebook, it's clear that social networking is no longer something for teenagers and college students. It is now mainstream and here to stay.

Many companies believe that social networking will replace traditional search engines for people looking for products and services. Here's a hypothetical: Say I want to find a good mechanic or I'm looking for a new Chinese restaurant. Do I go on Google or Bing or Yahoo and search for *San Diego Mechanic*, or do I ask my social network for recommendations?

I'm thinking I'd use the social network, because the opinion of people I'm connected to on my networks mean more to me than the results from a search engine. So while social media might seem like just a good way to keep in touch with people, it is also really big business.

This chapter is about using Facebook and Twitter—the two biggest social media services available—on your iPad.

FACEBOOK

The most popular social media website right now is Facebook.com. And while it seems that the iPad would be a perfect device for staying current, there is no official Facebook app for the iPad. I know, it's hard to believe. But it's true. Do a search in the iTunes Store for *Facebook*, and you'll find an official app for the iPhone but not for the iPad.

The good news is that you don't really need an app, because the Facebook website looks okay on the iPad's web browser. And while there are some problems with the layout, it's more than useable. But better yet: there are two apps—one free and one that costs a whopping $0.99—that also bring Facebook to the iPad. More on these apps a little later. First, let's explore the browser option.

Facebook on Safari

The iPad comes with a web browser built in. Since the browser is a full version and not a mobile version, the Facebook website runs perfectly on it. If you don't have a Facebook account and want one, you can sign up right

from your iPad. It's easy. And according to the Facebook sign up page, "It's free and always will be."

To sign up for Facebook:

1. Turn on the iPad.

2. Open Safari by tapping on its icon.

3. Type **www.facebook.com** into the web browser's address bar.

4. Tap Go.

5. Here is the sign-up screen. Enter the following info: first name, last name, your e-mail address (twice), a password, your gender and birthday. Facebook needs your date of birth, so that it can provide only age-appropriate access to content.

6. Tap the Sign Up button.

7. The page will change to a security check, and you'll need to enter the words in the box. I know this is a pain, but it just takes a moment. Make sure that the iPad doesn't auto-correct your entry though. That happened to me, and I had to go through the entire process again.

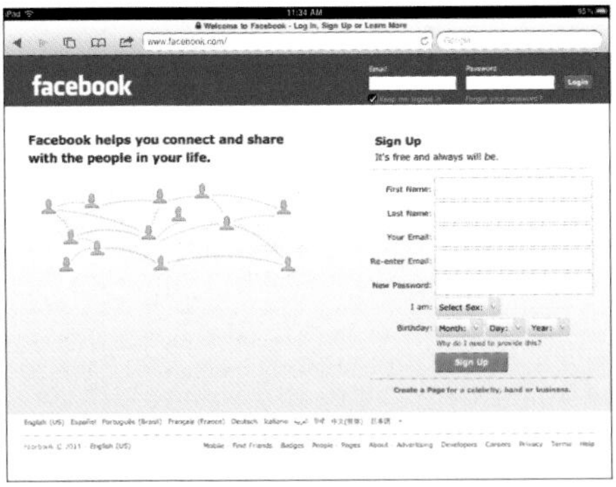

Figure 10-1
The Facebook login page on the iPad is available by using the Safari web browser.

Figure 10-2
Signing up for a Facebook account will require you to go through the security check.

8. You now have a Facebook account and can start adding friends, entering your profile information and adding your profile picture.

9. Have fun with Facebook!

Create a Business Page

If you already have a personal Facebook page, you might be interested in creating a business page. Many of the biggest companies in the world have a Facebook page, and it should be part of your business plan.

To sign up for a business Facebook page, go to **www.facebook.com** and look for the link: Create a Page for a Celebrity, Band or Business. This will be under the Sign Up button.

You can set up a Facebook page for a local business or:

- Place
- Company
- Organization
- Institution
- Brand or Product
- Artist
- Band
- Public Figure
- Entertainment
- Cause
- Community

Just tap on your category selection and follow the sign-up instructions.

Sign In via iPad

If you already have a Facebook account, signing in on the iPad is as easy as signing in on your computer. Just open Safari on the iPad and type in **www.facebook.com** into the address bar. Tap Go. When the sign-in page appears, enter your e-mail address and

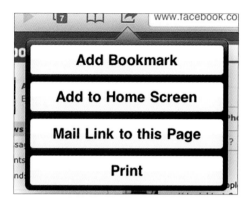

Figure 10-3
Take three easy steps to create a Facebook icon on your homepage that will open Safari and load your Facebook page.

password into the fields on the top right of the page.

If your iPad is used in a public place or more than one person uses the device, make sure that the check box for Keep Me Logged In is unchecked. If you are the only one who uses your iPad and you feel safe having your Facebook info accessible to anyone who picks it up, then consider checking the box.

Even though there is no official Facebook app for the iPad, you can still make it a one-step process to get to the Facebook website from your iPad Home screen.

1. With Facebook up and running in Safari, tap the Add Bookmark button.

2. Choose Add to Home Screen.

3. Name the shortcut (idea: *Facebook*).

4. The Facebook icon will be added automatically.

5. Now, just tap Add to create an icon on the Home page of your iPad that will take you to Facebook on Safari.

All this said, it is really evident that the Facebook code is not optimized to run on the iPad. While the pages all appear, they don't look just right ... mostly because the page width isn't right. But the bigger problem is that the pop-up windows in Facebook don't let you scroll properly. If a window pops up when on Facebook, and you use a single finger, it doesn't scroll the window; it scrolls the whole screen.

Figure 10-4

Here is the same page in the two Friendly apps. The left image shows the free version, and the right one shows the paid version. The paid version doesn't have the ad on the bottom of the page.

Nowhere does it tell you to use two fingers to scroll in the pop-up window. And while scrolling inside pop-up windows works with two fingers, it's awkward. Scrolling everywhere else works with one finger, so this technique is not intuitive.

Friendly Apps

If you search in the iPad App store for *Facebook*, the top two apps are from the same company: Oecoway. One is Friendly Plus for Facebook which costs $0.99; the other is Friendly Facebook for iPad, which is free. So which one is better and what does $0.99 get you that the free version doesn't offer? Here it is: The free version has small ads. If that's going to bother you, then pay the $0.99 to avoid them.

The Friendly apps give you access to all your Facebook information in an easy and intuitive way. When looking at the Friendly screen, notice that all the navigation tools are on the top. The first button is the most important. It's where you can upload photos, write a note, edit your profile, edit your friends, change your account settings and customize Friendly. It's also where you can send feedback to Friendly and share it with friends.

Everything you need to Facebook is available in this app, so until Facebook comes out with an official iPad application, I'll be a *Friendly* guy.

TWITTER

Twitter was recently in the news because some Hollywood actor had more than a million people following him on the program in less than 48 hours. Just for the record, I was not one of those people. And while Twitter might seem like a joke or a waste of time to some, I've found it to be a really useful tool.

It's true; many people still are unsure about what Twitter is—a service that allows you to send out short (140 character) messages that are called *tweets*. These can be read by anyone who is following you. Likewise, Twitter users can read the tweets of anyone they're following. You can reply to an individual or send a private message, called a *Direct Message*. Twitter also uses the hash tag (#) in a very cool way, but more on that in a minute. First, let's get Twitter set up on your iPad.

Search for *Twitter* in the iPad Store on the iPad, and you'll see quite a few free apps, including an official Twitter app.

Twitter App

In March 2011, Twitter updated the iPad app and finally made it worth using on the

Figure 10-5
Here is the Twitter interface. Either sign up or sign in to start your Twitter experience on your iPad.

iPad. Previously, the app would keep showing messages that I'd already read as new. Not a terrible problem … but annoying enough to make the app much less enjoyable.

To get started, the first thing to do is create a Twitter account … either on the Twitter website (**www.twitter.com**) or in the Twitter app. Since this is an iPad book, let's go with the iPad solution.

1. Turn on your iPad and tap on the App Store.

2. Search for Twitter and download the Twitter app from Twitter, Inc.

3. Tap on the app to open it.

4. If you have an account, you can sign in here. If you don't, you can sign up for an account from this page by tapping the Sign Up button.

5. The Sign Up page requires your name, your e-mail address, a username and a password. Note: When it comes to picking a username, remember that this is how you will be known as on Twitter. You have 15 characters or less, so be creative. My user-

name is ShotLivePhoto, which is also the name of my concert photography business.

6. If you have an account, just sign in using your username and password.

The Twitter app screen is divided into two parts. On the left are your navigation choices

- **Timeline** shows you all the tweets from the people you follow.

- Tapping **Mentions** shows all the tweets that mention you, even if they are from people you don't follow.

- Twitter allows you to send private messages to people who you are following. **Messages** is really handy for when you want to send someone a message and don't want everyone to see it.

- **Lists** is where the lists you've created will appear.

- Tap **Profile** to see the information you provided about yourself. Here, you'll also see the number of folks following your tweets and the number of people that you follow. It also gives you a list of users that Twitter

Figure 10-6
The Sign Up menu in the Twitter app requires your username and password.

Figure 10-7
Pick your username carefully; it's how you will be known on Twitter.

thinks are similar to you. This window lets you look at your latest tweets, mentions and the tweets you've marked as Favorites.

Search is where you can explore the Twitter universe. It shows the top tweets and what subjects are trending now. It also shows saved searches.

On the right is the main viewing area, where the information requested by your choice on the left is shown. So, for example, if you want to see the tweets from the people you follow, just tap on Timeline and the list of tweets will show up on the right. It's really easy to see when there are updates. Just look over at the navigation side of the app. If there's a blue dot next to the choices, then there are updates to see.

Get Updates

To get updates, use your finger to pull down the list of tweets. This will update the list. Want to look at an individual's tweets a little closer? Just tap on his/ her name from the list. In fact, this is where the app interface really shines. The windows all slide to the left, and the new information appears on the right side. The same interface look and feel works when you want to send a tweet, too.

Send a Tweet

To send a tweet, tap on the New Tweet button that's located on the bottom left of the screen. The keyboard will slide up into view as the New Tweet window slides down from the top of the screen.

Figure 10-8
The Twitter interface shows the recent tweets on the right.

Figure 10-9
The new tweet window opens from the top, while the keyboard slides in from the bottom.

The New Tweet window has a few options you need to notice. These options are located across the bottom of the window.

- The first is the (@) sign, which allows you to add a person to your tweet by bringing up the list of people you follow. Just tap on his/ her name and (s)he'll be added to your tweet.

- The second option is the hash tag (#). I'll cover the hash tag a little later.

- Next is the camera icon, which allows you to add a photo to your tweet.

- The final icon, an arrow, allows you to add your location to the tweet.

TweetDeck

Before I started using the official Twitter app for the iPad, I used the TweetDeck app. This is mostly because I use the TweetDeck app on the computer. TweetDeck is a Twitter application that runs on the desktop, iPhone, iPad, Android and Chrome. If you register for a TweetDeck account, you can sync the data across every platform and use the advanced features on the TweetDeck website.

The TweetDeck interface looks better in landscape mode, because it shows multiple columns at the same time.

The nice part of the TweetDeck interface is

Figure 10-10
The hash tag (#) is a simple way to search for, or tag, a tweet with a common topic. For example, if you post a tweet about the iPad, you could add "#iPad" to the tweet, so that people looking for tweets about the iPad can find them. These two examples show both the tweet I wrote and the search results for that same hash tag.

Figure 10-11
The TweetDeck interface looks better in landscape mode, because it shows multiple columns at the same time.

that it shows a lot of information all at once. It starts with columns of information:

- Timeline
- Mentions
- Direct Messages

And you can add other columns. That way, you can keep track of posts with hash tags that interest you.

FLIPBOARD APP ($FREE)

One of the coolest ways to read your tweets and other social media messages is by using the Flipboard app—a social media magazine. It's one of those apps that I downloaded the minute I found out about it. And I've never stopped using it.

I really believe that this is the future of social media. Flipboard allows you to look through the messages and photos that are being shared by your friends and contacts on Facebook *and* Twitter—in one place. Plus, it's easy to set up and use. And it looks fantastic.

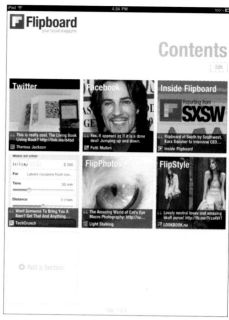

Figure 10-12
The main page shows the feeds that I've added to my Flipboard app.

Set Up

When you open Flipboard for the first time, there are six pre-formatted sections and an area to add a new section. The first two sections allow you to add your Twitter and Facebook feeds; the other four sections contain Flipboard content:

- Inside Flipboard
- FlipTech
- FlipPhotos
- FlipStyle

To add your Twitter and/or Facebook feeds to Flipboard, tap on the respective button and enter your account info. I've also added a feed from my Flickr account.

Figure 10-13
The tweets of people I'm following look much cooler in Flipboard than they do in Twitter.

Rearrange the feed buttons by pressing and holding a finger on the panel to be moved until the small white x in a black background appears on the top left. Or, just tap the Edit button under the Contents header. Now just slide it to a new spot on the screen. All the other panels will automatically adjust. Delete a feed by tapping on the small white x. Once the panels are in the order you want, tap the Done button (under the Contents header).

Navigate

When flipping through the pages, take a look at the bottom of the screen. There is a little red scrubby square that allows you to scroll through the pages easily. There is also a drop-down menu (located at the top of the screen,

right next to the Headline) that can be used to modify the feed and make your Flipboard experience unique.

For example, if you're looking at your Twitter feed, you can change the feed to see only your favorite tweets, your searches or your own tweets. If you're using Flipboard to look through your Facebook feed, you can pick the News Feed, Your Wall or even Photos of You.

The most amazing thing about this app is that it shows you your social media feeds in a new way. Go ahead and try it. It's free, so what do you have to lose?

Web Browsing

The Skim

Surfing the Internet on your iPad can be really easy and fun. It can also be an exercise in frustration. The iPad screen is a great size for looking at web pages, both in portrait and landscape views. And the Safari web browser works well. Plus, since it comes preloaded, you can access this browser right from the start. The frustrating part of using the iPad to browse the Internet is that it doesn't always render web pages correctly, and Flash and Flash components won't work at all.

There are some big differences between browsing the web with the original iPad and the iPad 2. The original iPad came with only 256MB of RAM; the iPad 2 offers 512MB. The relatively low amount of RAM in the original iPad causes the web browser to completely reload pages when a user moves from one page to another. But with twice the RAM, the iPad 2 is able to cache the pages, making it easy to jump between web pages without waiting for the device to reload each one, each time.

The interesting part for me about using the iPad to go online is that there are apps that give me better content and more functionality than their corresponding websites. For example, I find the Kayak HD app easier to use on the iPad than the Kayak website on Safari. Want to know what Kayak is? You're going to have to check out Chapter 15!

Here, let's start exploring iPad web surfing with the traditional method: a web browser.

WI-FI VS 3G

A fundamental advantage of the 3G iPad over a laptop is its ability to surf the Internet anywhere with a cell phone signal—not just in places where there is Wi-Fi.

SAFARI

Apple has preloaded each iPad with its Safari web browser, making it the most-used web browser on the iPad. Hey, it's there; it's free; you can't delete it; and it works well, so why not? With the release of the iPad 2 and iOS 3.4, Apple increased the speed of page loads of the browser by integrating the new Nitro JavaScript engine. According to Apple, this upgrade is twice as fast as the previous version of Safari for the iPad.

Create Bookmarks

Adding a bookmark in Safari is really easy, and you can store your bookmarks on the Home screen of the iPad. This makes it a one-tap operation to visit your favorite sites.

A bookmarked web page will look like an app icon on the Home screen; and when you tap it, Safari launches and the bookmarked site opens. Here's how you do it:

1. Open Safari by tapping on its icon.

2. Navigate to the page you want to bookmark.

3. Tap on the Export button in the menu bar.

4. Choose Add to Home Screen.

Figure 11-1
You have to be connected by either Wi-Fi or a 3G network to access the Internet with the iPad.

5. Name the icon and tap Add, a button located at the top right of the window.

This creates an icon that looks like an app or your iPad. One tap and you're back to your selected website. As you might have noticed, you can also add a regular bookmark within Safari and send the website URL in the body of an e-mail.

Remove Bookmarks

My list of bookmarked websites seems to grow every day, and they're rarely deleted. The problem with this is that too many bookmark can actually defeat the purpose of this feature, because it ends up being quicker to do a Google search than to sort through a huge collection of bookmarks.

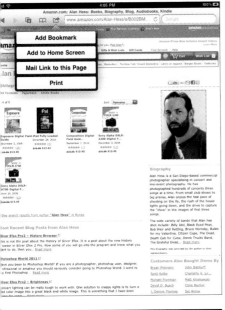

Figure 11-2
Creating a bookmark on the Home
screen is just a matter of tapping the
Export button and picking Add to
Home Screen.

SAFARI PREFERENCES

To access the Safari
Preferences menu,
tap on the Settings
icon. Once inside,
look for the Safari
tab on the left side
of the screen. Tap
the Safari icon to bring up the
Settings menu. This is where you
can choose the default search
engine, set up auto fill, show
the Bookmark bar and edit your
security settings.

THE iOS4 ADVANTAGE

The ability to create
folders for apps on
the iPad using iOS4
allows users to make
folders of shortcuts
that appear on the
main screen of the
device. This means you can have
a folder of your favorite personal
shortcuts and a folder of business shortcuts. You can even
mix shortcuts and apps in the
same folder.

Part 3: **Internet Content**

Fortunately, there are three ways to remove bookmarks on the iPad.

- The first relates to bookmarks that appear as icons on your Home screen. Delete these just like you would remove an app. Hold your finger on the icon until it wiggles and a small x appears in the top left corner. Tap on the x to delete the bookmark.

- To delete the bookmarks inside the Safari app one at a time:

  1. Open Safari.
  2. Tap on the Bookmarks button.
  3. Swipe your finger across the bookmark horizontally.
  4. Tap on the red Delete button that appears next to the bookmark.
  5. Poof. The bookmark is gone.

- You can delete bookmarks inside of Safari using the group-cuts approach.

  1. Open Safari.
  2. Tap on the Bookmarks button.
  3. Tap the Edit button at the top right of the window, which turns into the Done button.
  4. Each bookmark will sit next to a red circle with a line through it.
  5. Tap on the red circle of the bookmark you want to delete.
  6. The word *Delete* will appear to the right of the bookmark.
  7. Tap Delete to remove the bookmark.
  8. Tap Done when you're finished deleting bookmarks.

I try to go through my bookmarks about every three or four weeks and remove the ones that are no longer valid or interesting. This keeps the number of bookmarks down to a reasonably useful list.

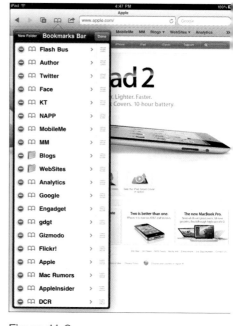

Figure 11-3
You can delete multiple bookmarks all at once using the Edit menu.

Sync Bookmarks

There is one other really good reason to use Safari, especially if you have the Apple MobileMe account. It's that you can sync the Safari bookmarks to appear on all your devices.

Just find a website that you like and bookmark it on the iPad. Then, that same bookmark will appear on your iPhone and on your computer … as long as you have syncing turned on and the devices are under the same account. This only works for the MobileMe users though. To activate this function on your iPad:

1. Tap on the Settings app.

2. Tap on Mail, Contacts, Calendars.

Figure 11-4

This menu panel allows you to turn on the Bookmarks Sharing feature.

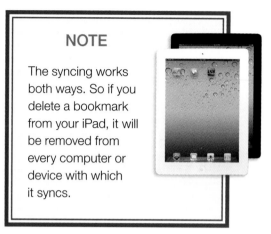

NOTE

The syncing works both ways. So if you delete a bookmark from your iPad, it will be removed from every computer or device with which it syncs.

3. Tap on your MobileMe account setup. Tap on it from the list or follow the instructions to add your MobileMe account. Then, make sure that you turn on the Bookmarks setting.

4. Now your bookmarks will be synced among all the devices where this feature is enabled.

If you use the Bookmarks bar in the desktop version of Safari, then you can have that bar visible on your iPad version as well. Here's how to set this up:

1. Tap on Settings.

2. Tap on Safari from the app list on the left.

3. Turn on Always Show Bookmarks Bar.

4. Now, when you use Safari, it will have a Bookmarks bar ... just like your desktop version.

These bookmark options are probably the reason that I end up using Safari at all. It's nice to know that the same sites are book-marked on my different machines.

OPTIONS

iPad users have some options regarding how they navigate the Internet. Although there are default programs, it's easy to switch to one that better meets your needs.

Default Search Engine

Google has been the default search engine for Safari since it was released on the iPad. But you don't have to use Google. There are two other options: Yahoo! and Bing from Micro-soft. So, if you don't like Google, you have other choices. To change the default search engine used in Safari:

1. Tap on the Settings icon.

2. Tap Safari in the column on the left.

3. Tap Search Engine.

4. Tap on whichever search engine you want as your default. The selected search engine will have a check mark next to it.

5. That's it! Now, when you open Safari and use the built-in search function, it will use the search engine you chose.

183

Browser Alternatives

Safari is not the only browser available on the iPad. A search in the App Store for "web browser" reveals more than 200 apps that have the term *web browser* in the description. The prices range from free to about $4.99, but is it worth paying for something that you can get for free? Again, it depends on what you need.

In the previous edition of this book, I covered the Atomic Web Browser, Mercury and iCab Mobile. This time, I want to talk about the PERFECT Web Browser.

Actually the full name of the app is PER-FECT Web Browser – EXTRAORDINARY Browser w/ REAL-Tabs, TOUCH Scroll & VGA. Seriously, that's its name, but I'll call it the PERFECT Web Browser for short. When it is on your iPad, the name under the icon is just Browser.

TIP

Every time you install a web browser on the iPad, you'll get a warning that the app contains age-restricted material. You have to tap OK to continue. This is Apple's way of letting folks know that the web browser can be used to go to websites that have questionable content. The app itself doesn't have age-restricted content. Tap OK, and the app will download.

At the end of this chapter is information on another option: Skyfire Web Browser, which has some very cool functions built in. But more on that later.

The PERFECT web browser ($2.99) is a really slick web browser that includes some great options. What I really like about it is that the very first time the app runs, it walks you through the Preferences settings and explains how the browser deals with the following features:

- **Startup Behavior:** The PERFECT browser can open using Saved Tabs, which loads the tabs from the previous session. Or you can start with just the Homepage. The default setting is to have the Tabs enabled.

- **History:** You can enable the browser to record the URLs you visit, so that the next time you go to the same page, the browser will try to auto complete the URL. The default is to have this turned on.

- **Enable Pop-Up Blocker:** The default setting is to have the browser block pop ups, but you can enable them here.

Once you have the PERFECT browser up and running, there are a whole lot of other preferences you can set up just by tapping the Settings button. One that is especially useful is a feature that lets you tell the browser how to render the page. This is important because different web browsers can render websites differently, which can cause layout issues.

This is most apparent when dealing a mobile version of a browser which will look very different from a desktop version of the same browser. The difference is programmed into the version, because the browser believes you're looking at the website on a small smart phone screen. The settings in the PERFECT include:

- Mobile Safari
- Safari iPad (default)
- Safari iPhone
- Safari Mac
- Firefox 3.6
- Internet Explorer 6
- Internet Explorer 7
- Internet Explorer 8
- Opera 10.5
- Google Chrome

Another thing that this browser has going for it is how fast it seems to run. Now, I haven't run any scientific tests, but it seems run really fast—even on the original iPad. The only thing that I don't really like is the full name: PERFECT Web Browser - EXTRAORDI-NARY Browser w/ REAL-Tabs, TOUCH Scroll & VGA. That is a cumbersome name to reference during a conversation.

ADOBE FLASH

The iPad is not the only tablet on the market, and more competitors are arriving daily. One of the biggest dividing points among the tablet options is an ability to run Adobe Flash player and Adobe Flash content. The iPad does not have the ability to run Flash player or view Flash content, which is unfortunate.

The feud between the pro-Flash (Adobe) crowd and the anti-Flash (Apple) crew became all too public when Steve Jobs released an open letter describing why Flash was not … and would likely never be … on the iOS devices. You can read this letter at **http://www.apple.com/hotnews/thoughts-on-flash/** and decide whether you agree or disagree with Steve.

Either way, it's probably a good idea to forget about Flash ever being supported on the iPad.

Figure 11-5

These options can be set according to your preferences in the PERFECT browser Settings panel.

The original Apple iPad and the iPad 2 will not run Flash, and if you take Steve Jobs at his word, nor will future versions. Does this matter? Actually, it might.

If you've ever watched a video on the Internet, you were likely watching it with the Adobe Flash plug-in architecture. That means that you need to have a Flash player in your web browser to view these videos. Many websites have also incorporated flash elements into their design, usually for navigation purposes or for showing embedded images or videos. Sometimes, entire sites are created with Flash, which means that without Flash player availability, the whole site is unusable/un-viewable on the iPad.

However, there is an alternative that's starting to replace some of the Flash functionality. It's HTML5, and Steve Jobs is hoping that HTML5 will replace Flash entirely. I believe that the adoption of HTML5 has been a lot slower than Apple would like, and many people still like (and use) Flash on their websites.

They don't feel the need to change platforms just to make Apple happy.

So as other tablets make their way to the market and run Flash, Apple might have to capitulate and finally become Flash-friendly. Or perhaps that's just me wishing for something that isn't likely to happen.

SKYFIRE FOR iPAD ($4.99)

The Skyfire web browser for the iPad allows you to watch Flash videos on your iPad. This browser translates the Flash content into a form that the iPad can view (HTML5). It's not perfect and there are a few extra steps you have to take to enable this conversion, but it is a solution.

When you use the Skyfire app to browse the Internet on your iPad and you come across

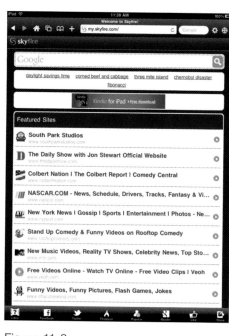

> ### TIP
>
> In my opinion, I think that the lack of Flash on the iPad is a serious detriment to web browsing there. Many sites I want to use on a regular basis have Flash components, and it's quite frustrating to have to put down the iPad and switch to my computer to explore these websites.

Figure 11-6
This is the home screen of the Skyfire web browser.

a page that has Flash video, you get an error message. It says, "Video Requires the Latest Flash Player." In other browsers on the iPad, this would be the end of it. But in Skyfire, there's a button that checks to see if Skyfire can translate the movie and play it. This works for lots of Flash content, but it still doesn't help if the Flash content you're trying to view is for the website's navigation.

The Skyfire browser has some other cool features that make it a solid competitor to Safari. The top features for me are:

- Skyfire's ability to browse privately with no data trail; neither cookies nor the browsing history is saved.

- I also like the very cool integration to social media sites like Facebook and Twitter. When you run Skyfire, the screen

is divided into three parts. The navigation controls are across the top of the screen; the actual browser window is in the middle; and the Function menu is at the bottom.

The navigation controls across the top of the screen are pretty standard. You can:

- Go back to the previous page.

- Go forward to the next page.

- Tap on the Home button to get to the homepage.

- Tap on the New Window button to open new window.

The Bookmarks menu is next, followed by the Add to Bookmarks (+) symbol. Then comes the URL field and the Google search field. The Settings button and the Full Screen button are the last two on the top of the page.

The Settings button may need a little more explanation. When you tap on Settings, there are three options:

- **Load Page as iPad/ Desktop** switches the view from the iPad-specific view to the regular desktop view. This is a decision on whether to view the page on a mobile browser or full desktop version of the browser. I have it set to iPad view, but if a page looks wrong, I'll switch to Desktop view and hope for a better layout.

- **Private Browsing** is where you can turn the privacy function on or off. The default is set for off.

- More Settings:

  - **Start** page: The default here is set to Skyfire, but you can change it to anything you want.

  - **Accept Cookies**: You can set this to Never, Always or, my choice: From

Figure 11-7
The navigation controls in the Skyfire browser show the Settings menu.

Visited, which means that the cookies stored on the iPad are only from sites that I purposely visit.

- **Clear History** is straightforward; it clears the browser history.

- **Clear Cookies** ... yep, you guessed it, clears cookies from the iPad.

- **Clear Cache** clears the stored data on your iPad.

- **Log Out of Sharing Sites**, as the name implies, logs you out of all the sharing sites. So if you are logged into Facebook or Twitter and are sharing websites you've visited, then here is where you can log out of all of them at the same time. This is useful if you share an iPad with other users.

- **Turn Off Auto-Share** turns off the auto-share function. If you have enabled this function to share your Favorites with your social media network, you can turn it off here. I always keep this turned off, because I don't really like to automatically share anything.

- **Share Skyfire** creates an e-mail that lets you tell others about Skyfire.

- Tap **Help/FAQs** to open a new browser page that loads this info for the Skyfire browser on the iPad.

- **Feedback & Suggestions** opens a new browser page with the contact form already open, so you can send feedback about the browser to developers.

- **Version number:** As I write this, the current version is 2.2.0 (22260).

The main browser window is where content is shown, and the real power of the Skyfire browser is in the Function menu across the bottom. It contains the features that are described below.

- **Video:** This is the button to press if you see a spot on the screen that shows the "Video Requires the Latest Flash Player" message. When it finds video, a small window will open right above the button and load the Flash video. When it is ready to watch, tapping the Play button will open a video-playback window and allow you to watch your video.

- **Facebook:** You can connect to your Facebook account from Skyfire. So you can check your News Feed and update your Status right here. It also gives you two new features: the Fireplace and Popular pages (described below). To set up Facebook access, just sign in using your Facebook info. You can sign up for an account here, too.

- **Twitter:** If you have a Twitter account, you can sign in here and get the latest tweets from the people you follow.

- **Fireplace:** This is where the links from your Facebook feed show up. So if you want to see what your friends are sharing, this is a very cool way to do it.

- **Popular:** This shows a list of links to the most popular pages from whatever website you're on. The program looks at what links have been shared on Facebook and generates a list.

Figure 11-8
The Skyfire Function menu is shown here.

- **Reader:** Sign in here to access the Google Reader. Google Reader is a news aggregator service that allows you to constantly check your favorite news sites and blogs for content. Google Reader is covered in Chapter 7. Sign up for the service at http://www.google.com/reader.

- **Like:** If you sign in with Facebook, you can see what your friends like.

- **Share:** From here, share anything on the current website with a variety of services, including Facebook, Twitter, E-mail a friend, Delicious, Google Reader, Read It Later, Instapaper, Pinboard and Tumblr.

Skyfire is a really great web browser. The added Flash video transcode and social media integration makes it a winner for me. There is more on social media and the iPad back in Chapter 10.

Figure 11-9
The video Transcode button will look for video and give you the option of playing it.

PART 4

Business Content

12

Office Apps

The Skim

iWork • Moving Files • Google Docs
Documents To Go Premium • AirPrint

C an the iPad be used as a laptop replacement for students, business people and those who need to do some word processing, number crunching or presentation-making? Good question ...

iWORK ON THE iPAD

While Apple insists that the iPad is not a computer or a netbook, the first iPad apps that the company released were iPad versions of the iWork application suite, which allows the iPad to be used for basic business. These three apps:

- **Pages** (word processing)
- **Numbers** (spreadsheets)
- **Keynote** (presentations)

Pages App ($9.99)

I like the Apple Pages application on my computer and use it for most of my word processing needs. On my iPad, I use the Pages app, and it does a good job most of the time. But if you're one of those Microsoft Word power users—those folks who can make Word jump through hoops and use it for everything from a single page document to a fully formatted multipage document with embedded images and graphs ... well, you get the point—then you might find the Pages app a little underwhelming. But since there is no Word app, you might need to learn to live with it.

Figure 12-1
A variety of templates are available when you tap on the New Document button in Pages.

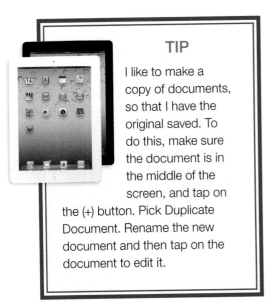

TIP

I like to make a copy of documents, so that I have the original saved. To do this, make sure the document is in the middle of the screen, and tap on the (+) button. Pick Duplicate Document. Rename the new document and then tap on the document to edit it.

Pages comes with a set of built-in templates that many users find useful. These include everything from letters to term papers. To start a new document in Pages using the templates:

1. Open Pages on the iPad.

2. Make sure you are in the My Documents view.

3. Tap on New Document at the top left of the screen, or tap on the (+) icon at the bottom of the screen.

4. Scroll up and down to find the template you want to use.

5. Tap the template to open a new document.

6. Begin writing.

After you pick a template, it will immediately open a new document with the chosen format loaded. It takes a little time to get used to navigating with your fingers, so don't get discouraged. Just keep in mind that you need to tap on various areas to edit, and the keyboard will take up half the screen. Stick with it; it can be enjoyable to work this way. Alright, maybe not *enjoyable*, but you can get work done.

One feature that is slightly hidden is the ability to rename a document right in the My Documents view. All you have to do is tap the file name, and then enter a new one. Since files are saved automatically and there is no Save As command, be careful of the changes you make. There is no way to undo them after the file has been closed, because you can't go back to an earlier version.

Numbers App ($9.99)

I have never been good with numbers or spreadsheets or any of that number-crunching stuff that some people do so well. But that's not to say I don't know my way around a spreadsheet. I've needed to use them since the first version of Lotus 123 came out. But if given a choice, I'll let someone else work with the numbers.

The Numbers app is an everyman's spreadsheet, because of the built-in templates that Apple created for this app. Numbers has fifteen built-in templates that cover a wide variety of spreadsheet types—from budgets to loan comparisons and even a travel planner. To use one of the built-in templates:

1. Tap Numbers.

2. Tap New Spreadsheet.

3. Select a template and tap on it.

4. Enter your information.

That's it… Simple. These templates make it easy to use the power of spreadsheets in an easy and useful way for people like me, but that doesn't mean that Numbers doesn't work for business applications, too. You can import Excel files and use them in Numbers.

When working on a spreadsheet, there's one really important feature … that you won't find. There is no Save button. Instead, the Numbers document is saved constantly, just like Pages files. So if you want to save an earlier version, you have to think ahead. That is, once you've entered the basic information for whatever spreadsheet you're creating, tap the My Spreadsheets button on the top of the screen. In the My Spreadsheets view, tap the (+) sign at the bottom of the screen and create a Duplicate Spreadsheet.

From here, you can add different data to the file, while retaining a previous version. Just remember to rename the different versions of the spreadsheets to differentiate them. To

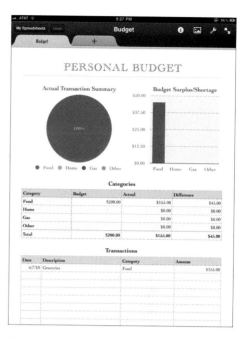

Figure 12-2
When working in the Budget template in Numbers, just tap on a cell to change the data.

rename a document in Numbers, tap your finger on the document name in the My Spreadsheet view and enter the new name. When finished, just tap Done in the top right hand corner.

Keynote App ($9.99)

This is the most specialized of the iWork apps. Many people use word processors and the Numbers app, but it's the templates here that make this program work for lots of regular folks. Not everyone gives presentations on a regular basis.

Keynote functions a little differently from the other apps. For starters, it can only be used in landscape mode. This means that it can't be used easily in the Apple Dock, which only

Figure 12-3
The Keynote app is showing the opening slide to my concert presentation.

works in portrait mode. Another really big difference is that for Keynote to work effectively, you have to attach it to an external monitor. It's tough to show a presentation on the iPad—unless you have a small group clustered around the device.

So while most of this book is about getting content onto the iPad, this section covers how to get it off … so you can properly display a presentation through the Keynote app. But first, the bad news: It's going to cost you. There's just no way to attach the iPad to a projector or monitor without some extra gear. Here are your options:

• **Apple Digital AV Adapter ($39):** This new adaptor allows you to mirror the content on your iPad onto an HDMI-enabled display. Connect the Apple Digital AV Adapter to your iPad using the 30-pin dock connector … and to your HDMI-compatible display using an HDMI cable. (You'll need to buy the HDMI cable separately.) The adapter has a second 30-pin connector built in, so you can charge and sync your device while it's connected to your

HDMI-compatible display. This is important if you're giving presentations, because running out of power would be a very bad ending to your presentation.

• **Apple iPad Dock Connector to VGA Adapter ($29):** This accessory from Apple allows you to connect your iPad to a TV with a VGA connection. You can also connect to a computer monitor, a projector or any other type of LCD display that uses a VGA connector. The output is available only in landscape orientation, but that's perfect for presentations … and Keynote only works in landscape orientation anyhow. This accessory from Apple doesn't have great reviews, but if you're going to give presentations from your iPad, it's the only way to get VGA output from the device.

With the iPad plugged into a projector or display device using one of the aforementioned accessories, the iPad becomes your presentation controller. When the Keynote presentation is in Edit mode, nothing will appear on the external display. When you press Play and the presentation begins on the external display, the iPad goes into controller mode.

The controls are simple—basic buttons to move forward and backward through your presentation. There are two other features as well, and one of them makes this a presenter's dream.

• **Thumbnails:** Displaying thumbnails of your slides on the left side of the screen helps you jump to any slide instantly. Once you've picked a new slide, in former versions, the thumbnails disappeared. Now they don't.

Figure 12-4
This is a view on the iPad when it's attached to a projector. The thumbnails are visible along the left side.

Figure 12-5
The iTunes window shows where data can be transferred onto your iPad.

• **Pointer:** The iPad's built-in laser pointer is probably one of the coolest things about presenting using the iPad. That's right, you can make a red dot appear on the screen, and you can control it with your finger! It's so very simple to use, like most of the things on the iPad. So when you're running a presentation on the iPad, just hold your finger on the screen until a laser dot appears on the display. You can move it around by moving your finger around. Take your finger off the screen and the dot disappears. I love this...

MOVING iWORK DOCUMENTS WITH iTUNES

When working with the three iWork apps (Pages, Numbers and Keynote), it's important to know how to get files from your computer to your iPad. All three apps work the same way.

A popular way to transfer files back and forth between your computer and iPad is to use iTunes. Files created in iWork and Microsoft Office can be transferred from the computer to the iPad and edited using the iWork apps.

This works the same for all three apps, so instead of going through the process three times, just follow these instructions for all of these apps.

Import a File
To import a document to your iPad for editing on the iPad:

1. Connect your iPad to a computer and start iTunes.

2. In iTunes, click on your iPad and then select Apps.

3. Scroll to the bottom of the Apps window until you see the File Sharing part of the page.

4. Select the app you want to use:

   • Pages for word processing (similar to Word)

   • Numbers for spreadsheets (similar to Excel)

   • Keynote for presentations (similar to PowerPoint)

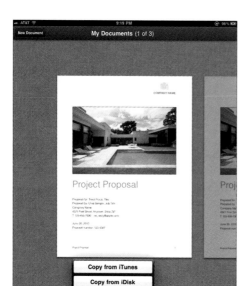

Figure 12-6
Tap the Import button in the app, and pick Copy from iTunes to open up the list of available apps.

5. Click Add and then navigate to the file's location.

6. Select the file you want to import and click Open.

7. The file is immediately transferred to the iPad.

The first time I did this, I could not find the document because the process was only half done. The imported documents don't actually go to the My Documents section of the app right away; you need to import the file into the app. To do this, just click on the icon in the bottom middle of the screen. It looks like an arrow going into a tray on the My Documents screen. Tap on the Copy from iTunes button. This will reveal a list of available

files in the middle of the screen. Click on the document you want to open, and the app will import it.

Export a File

To export a file from Pages and transfer it to your computer using iTunes:

1. Open the app (Pages, Numbers or Keynote) and make sure all the documents are closed.

2. Scroll until you see the document you want to export.

3. Tap the button with the square and arrow, and then tap Send to iTunes.

4. Choose the document format you want for the export:
   - For Pages, this will be Pages, PDF or Word.
   - For Numbers, the format will be Numbers, PDF or Excel.
   - For Keynote, it will be Keynote, PDF or PowerPoint.

5. Connect your iPad to the computer and launch iTunes.

6. Select the iPad in the Devices area of iTunes

7. Click Apps.

8. Scroll down to the File Sharing section of the window.

9. Select Pages in the apps list of the File Sharing section.

10. From the list on the right, select the name of the document you want to export.

11. Click Save To.

12. A window will open that allows you to navigate to a location for storing the file.

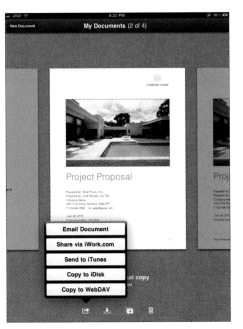

COMPANY NAME

Project Proposal

Proj

Email Document

Share via iWork.com

Send to iTunes

Copy to iDisk

Copy to WebDAV

Figure 12-7
Make sure that the document you want
to transfer is in the center of the screen,
and then tap on the Export button and
pick Send to iTunes.

13. Click Choose to transfer the file from the
iPad to the computer.

14. The file will immediately transfer to
the computer.

These methods are great for when you are
sitting at your desk, but there are other ways
of transferring files. Some of the alternatives
are easier and more efficient that those
described above, especially when you're away
from home base.

TRANSFER FILES WITH E-MAIL

One of the easiest ways to share a document
is to just e-mail it. The iPad allows you to
e-mail documents right from inside its iWork

applications. Actually it's the first choice
under the Export button. Find more on iPad's
e-mail capabilities in Chapter 8.

To send a document from any of the iWork
apps by e-mail, just:

1. Open the iWork app.

2. In the My Documents view, navigate so
that the document you want to send out is
in the middle of the screen.

3. Tap the Export button.

4. Tap one of the following options:
   - E-mail Document in Pages.
   - E-mail Spreadsheet in Numbers.
   - E-mail Presentation in Keynote.

5. Choose the document format you want for
the export:
   - For Pages, the format will be Pages, PDF
or Word.
   - For Numbers, it will be Numbers, PDF
or Excel.
   - For Keynote, it will be Keynote, PDF
or PowerPoint.

6. An e-mail message will appear with your
file as an attachment. Complete the rest
of the fields and tap Send.

To open a file you receive in an
e-mail message:

1. Open Mail on the iPad.

2. Open the message that has the attached
document.

3. Tap and hold on the icon of the attached
file in the e-mail. (If you just tap on it, but
don't hold, you'll get a Quick Look version
of the file.)
   - If it's a word processing document, tap
Open in Pages. If the attachment can be

opened in any other app, first tap Open In and then tap Pages.

- If it's a spreadsheet file, tap Open in Numbers. If the attachment can be opened in any other app, first tap Open In and then tap Numbers.

- If it's a presentation file, then tap Open in Keynote. If the attachment can be opened in any other app, first tap Open In and then tap Keynote.

4. Mail will close and Pages (or Numbers or Keynote, depending on what you selected) will open.

5. When the document is finished downloading, the new document will open and be ready for editing in the program you chose.

6. You are now ready to edit.

This method of sharing documents is nothing new. In fact, it used to be my go-to method for transferring documents. But the problem with this process is that you end up with a lot of different copies of the same document. To help manage this, and increase your confidence in knowing that you're dealing with the correct and most current version of a particular document, take a few extra steps to name the file. I like using -01, -02, or RevA, RevB at the end of the file to keep track of different versions. You could also use a date (e.g., _110311 to indicate a file is the version created on November 3, 2011.)

SHARE DOCUMENTS VIA iWORK.COM

I can't believe that parts of iWork are still in Beta, but they are. I'm talking about the iWork.com cloud-based approach to sharing documents. I've been using this service without a problem since I got the original iPad.

iWork.com allows users to share documents using a dedicated website to avoid having to attach the iPad to a computer. But this only works if you have Internet access, either through Wi-Fi or 3G.

To send a document to **iWork.com** from your iPad:

1. Open the Pages, Numbers or Keynote app.

2. Scroll to the document you want to upload.

3. Tap the Export button.

4. Tap Share via iWork.com.

5. If you are not signed in, the app will ask you to sign in using your Apple ID (or tap Create a new Apple ID). If you have an Apple ID but have not used iWork.com before, you'll be asked if Apple can send you a verification e-mail. You must respond to this question.

6. A blank e-mail will open, allowing you to add the e-mail address of anyone who will receive the document. Type a message if needed. If you don't want to share the document with anyone else, then leave this field blank.

7. Tap the (i) button (on the right side of the screen) to open the Sharing Options menu. Here, you can:

- Change the name of the file.

- Password-protect the file.

- Allow readers to leave comments.

- Allow the document to be downloaded as a Pages, PDF or Word for Pages document; a Numbers, PDF or Excel for Numbers file; or a Keynote, PDF or PowerPoint for Keynote document.

- Sign out of iWork.com.

8. To close the Sharing Options, tap outside of the box.

9. Tap Share.

10. You can now view the document via Safari at iWork.com.

To download a file from iWork.com and open it in one of the iWork apps:

1. Open Safari on your iPad.

2. Navigate to iWork.com and sign in.

3. Tap on the download arrow next to the document you want to edit in the list of shared documents.

4. A preview of the document will open. Tap Open in Pages (or Numbers or Keynote, depending on the type of document). If the document can be opened in any other app, you will instead tap Open In and pick Pages/ Numbers/ Keynote from the menu choices. (If this menu is not present, just tap on the screen.)

5. Safari will automatically close, and the app will open. The selected document will download to Pages/ Numbers/ Keynote, and it will appear as the first document in the My Documents view.

OTHER TRANSFER OPTIONS

When you tap on the Export button (looks like a box with an arrow coming out of it), Pages will allow you to send the file as an e-mail, or you can share it via iWork. But there are also some other choices. These allow you to send the file by Copy to iDisk or copy to WebDAV. Let's look at what these do:

- Copy to/ from **iDisk**—a paid service from Apple that is part of a MobileMe account. Once you tap Copy to iDisk, a menu opens that allows you to sign into your account.

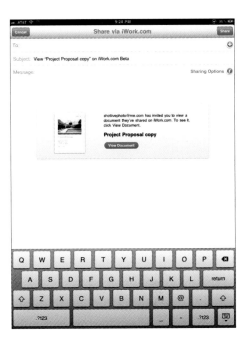

Figure 12-8

This e-mail message shows the shared document and the sharing options that are available through **iWork.com**.

Then you can pick the format to use when you copy the file to your iDisk account. You can also load documents that are saved on your iDisk. Just tap on the Import menu from inside any of the iWork apps and pick Copy from iDisk. Navigate to the document that you want and import it into the app.

- Copy to/ from **WebDAV**, which stands for Web-based Distributed Authoring and Versioning. It's a way to edit and deal with files that exist on a remote computer (called a server), if you have access to one at work,

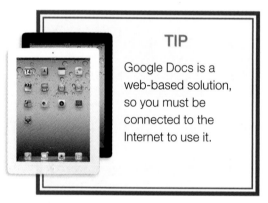

TIP

Google Docs is a web-based solution, so you must be connected to the Internet to use it.

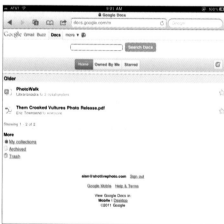

Figure 12-9
This Google Docs page has the desktop and mobile options at the bottom.

for example. Once you tap on the File button and choose Copy to WebDAV, a menu appears that asks for the server address, username and password. Once these are entered, you can send a copy of the file to the server. You can also copy files from a WebDAV server by tapping on the Import button and choosing Copy from WebDAV. Navigate to the file you want, and import it into the app.

GOOGLE DOCS

Google Docs is a free web-based service offered by Google. It's a word processor, spreadsheet, presentation application, drawing application, forms application and data storage service that allows users to create, edit and share documents online. The Google Docs service allows you to collaborate with others in real time on documents.

There is no official Google Docs app for the iPad; but in late 2010, Google released a new documents editor that supports editing on mobile browsers. This means that you can edit your Google Docs on your iPad in the Safari browser.

It's simple to get started. Just go to docs. google.com where you will be asked to either sign in to your account. (If you have Gmail, you can use the same account information.) If you don't have an account, you'll need to use your computer to set up one.

Once you log into your Google Docs account, you'll see a list of your documents. At the bottom of the screen is the key to editing on your iPad: it's a choice to view Google Docs in a Mobile version or Desktop version.

The mobile version works with the iPad better than the desktop version. While you can witch between the two, Google will warn you hat not everything is supported in the Safari version on the iPad. There are times you may want to switch between the mobile and desk-op views, but be aware that there are func-ions not available on the mobile view (e.g., ability to change fonts and colors). When working on your iPad, you can't right-click, oom, or copy and paste between Google Docs and other applications.

Some of these problems might be fixed by the time you read this, but it's likely that there will still be some issues.

DOCUMENTS TO GO PREMIUM

Google Docs doesn't have an app, but there are other solutions when it comes to editing your Google Docs. One of the best is an app called Documents To Go. This app allows you to edit, create and manage Microsoft Word, Excel and PowerPoint files as well as read PDFs, Apple iWork files and other attachments.

Enter your information in this menu so the app can sync with your desktop.

Set Up
When you first run Documents To Go, a Get-ting Started Wizard will appear. This gives you the basics.

- **Local Files** are the documents created on your device which are not synchronized with a desktop version. To sync a local file with your computer, you'll need to save the file into the Desktop Files location.

- **Desktop Files** are synced with a docu-ment on your computer. When changes are made on the mobile document, they are automatically updated on the desktop ver-sion when the files sync.

- **Online Files** (only available with the pre-mium version of the app) are stored on the web and can be downloaded, edited and synced directly inside of the app.

- **Recents** are the most recently used files.

To get the app to sync your documents from your computer to your iPad, the computer needs to have an application that lets the computer and the iPad communicate. To get this application on the computer:

1. Tap on the Desktop button at the bottom of the screen.

2. Enter your name and e-mail so that the download link can be sent to you.

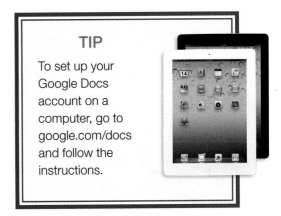

TIP

To set up your Google Docs account on a computer, go to google.com/docs and follow the instructions.

Figure 12-10
Enter your information in this menu so the app can sync with your desktop.

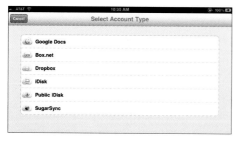

Figure 12-11
The Documents To Go Premium service can access files from any of these cloud-based servers.

3. After the installer has been downloaded, run the application and follow the instructions on how to pair the iPad with the computer over Wi-Fi.

Here's the part that's crucial for the Google Docs user: setting up the online file access. This is only available in the premium package ($16.99). So if you are a Google Docs user, you'll want to get the premium package. But even if you don't use Google Docs, this is still a great app.

1. Tap the Online button at the bottom of the screen.

2. Select the online service you want to use. You'll see Google Docs right on top. (Other online services include Dropbox, iDisk, Box.net, Public iDisk and SugarSync.)

3. Enter the login details for your account.

That's it. You can now edit your Google Docs in Documents To Go Premium. The really nice thing is that you can have multiple online accounts. So I have my Google Docs and Dropbox accounts accessible from inside Documents To Go Premium. (More on Dropbox in Chapter 13.)

The Settings menu, which is available on the bottom right of the screen, offers access to your Desktop and Online Accounts in the same place. It also lets you pick the file format for the new documents.

Create New Document

To create a new document in your Google Docs account using Documents to Go Premium:

1. Tap the Online button at the bottom of the page.

2. Tap Google Docs.

3. Tap the New Document button at the bottom right. (It looks like a piece of paper.)

4. Tap on the type of document you want to create.

5. When the document is done, tap on the arrow at the top left of the page.

6. Tap Discard Changes or Save As.

7. Enter the filename of the document.

8. The location will show the Google Docs address.

9. Tap Save, located at the top right of the screen.

10. Tap the Sync button at the bottom left of the page. (The button is two arrows making a circle.)

11. The file will now be available in your Google Docs.

AIRPRINT

I still have high hopes for this function on the iPad, but right now it's very limited. The main problem is that it's only supported on a handful of HP printers. That means that the Epson

printer I have in my office doesn't work with
AirPrint. So to enable AirPrint, I'd have to
buy a new printer.

Is it worth buying a new printer just to be able
to print from the iPad? That depends how
many documents you need to print from your
device. An easier and cheaper way to print is
to use Documents To Go and print from your
computer.

If you do have one of the AirPrint-compatible
printers—the list is on Apple's website,
**http://www.apple.com/ipad/features/air-
print.html**—then you'll have an AirPrint
icon in your multitask bar. And when you
have something that you want to print, just
double tap the Home button on your iPad
and tap the AirPrint icon. This will open up
the Print menu and allow you to print the
current document. Very convenient!

13

Document Apps

The Skim

The ability to read, annotate and fill in PDF forms on the iPad is changing the way I use this device. It makes my iPad a viable option for doing real work—not just for games. Don't misunderstand, I play plenty of games on my iPad. I call it *research*, even though this book doesn't cover games. I also spend a lot of time looking at PDF files, especially in the book editing process.

Speaking of ... here's a little peek into the book development process: Toward the end of a project, I start to receive PDF files from my editors, so I can see the book layout. Well, I used to check these files on my computer, but I've found it much easier to just read these files on the iPad. It actually gives me a better idea of how the book will really look.

In the past, when I read these PDFs in iBooks, if I needed to make a note on the file, I had to go back to the computer, open the file and make my note in the document. I can now mark up a PDF file on the iPad with an app like iAnnotate, which is covered in this chapter.

But before going any further into this, let me tell you about Dropbox—one of the easiest ways to keep the files on your computers and iPad synced. Then we'll go through the apps used for reading, annotating PDF files and even one that allows you to fill in PDF forms right on the iPad. Finally, I'll tell you about SneakPeak, an app used to view Illustrator and InDesign files for those of us who need to see design files that the iPad doesn't support natively.

DROPBOX

The more I use Dropbox, the more I wonder how I functioned without it. It offers one of the easiest ways I've found to transfer documents between a computer and iPad.

Dropbox is a web-based service used to store, access and transfer files really easily. It can be used just about anywhere. You can get 2GB of storage space for free. And if that's not enough, you can purchase more at a good price. Dropbox is one of those great apps that does its job really well. It's easy to use and simple to set up.

Set Up Dropbox

For Dropbox to work properly, you need to set up the web-based services and download the

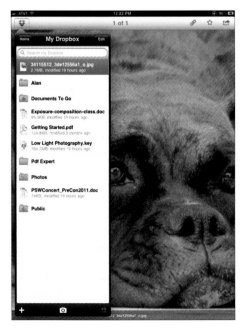

Figure 13-1

Once Dropbox is set up, you can use the device to see the files and folders that are in your Dropbox account.

Mac or PC version to your computer. Then, set up the iPad Dropbox app.

Go to **www.dropbox.com** and download the correct version of the Dropbox application (Mac or PC) for your computer. Just click on the Download Dropbox button right in the middle of the page. The correct version for the computer you're using will automatically start to download. Follow the screen instructions to install Dropbox on your computer(s). Once it's installed, you'll need to sign in to your account or sign up for a free account. I find it easiest to do this right in the Dropbox computer application.

The first time you run the application on your computer, you'll be asked if you have a Dropbox account or not. If you have an account, then it will ask for your e-mail address and password. If you don't have an account, it will ask for your name and e-mail along with a password.

Be sure to remember your e-mail and password combination; that's how you'll get into the service. And this is why you should not share this information with anyone … unless, of course, you want to offer access to all of your Dropbox files.

Once you sign in or set up a new account, you can decide to stick with the free 2GB account or upgrade to the 50GB or 100GB accounts. I still use the free 2GB account and haven't needed to upgrade yet. You'll also need to decide if you want a typical or custom setup. I recommend the typical setup unless you really need to have the location in a different spot than the default Home Folder (Mac) or My Documents folder (PC).

I have the same Dropbox account for my desktop computer, laptop, PC and Mac, and iPad. So I can transfer files among all my devices using Dropbox, and I can access the files on m

Pad at any time ... as long as I'm connected to the Internet. Since this service is web-based, the files are updated and synced only when you're online. So if I create a new document and put it in my Dropbox on my computer, it will not become accessible on the iPad until the iPad goes online and recognizes the new document. Once it's on the iPad, the document can be read and edited offline.

Loading Dropbox on your iPad is easy:

Download the app.

When you run Dropbox for the first time, enter the e-mail and password that you used to set up your account.

Tap the Login button.

If you haven't set up an account yet, you can do it here as well: Tap on New to Dropbox? Create an Account. This is located below the Login button.

Use Dropbox

Using Dropbox is very simple; just tap on the Dropbox icon at the top left of the screen to access your account. A list of all the folders and files in your Dropbox will appear. To view any of the files, just tap to open.

Once a file is opened in Dropbox, you can then open the document in any of the apps on your iPad that support that type of document. Tap the Open In menu by tapping the icon that looks like a box with an arrow coming out of it (top right). You'll find that Dropbox is accessible from other applications as well, including the PDF Expert app, which is covered in this chapter.

Share documents from your Dropbox with others by e-mailing them a link to the file. To share a link, open the Dropbox app on your iPad, open the file you want to share, and tap on the link button. (It looks like two links of

chain and is located at the top of the screen.) This offers you two sharing options: Email Link or Copy Link to Clipboard. Pick one and share.

Since this chapter is all about documents, let's look at how Dropbox deals with Word documents, Pages files and PDFs. Turns out it handles these documents seamlessly. To access files in Dropbox, simply tap on the folder that contains the file you want to read or edit. Tapping on any of the documents in your Dropbox will give you a preview of that document ... right in the Dropbox app.

Right now there is no way to edit files in the iWork apps and upload revised documents back into your Dropbox. So if you have a file in your Dropbox and you open it in Pages ... and then edit the file ... you can't put it back in your Dropbox. You have to export it using one of the Pages export methods.

I really wish it was possible to export to Dropbox. But there is an option to two-way sync using PDF Export, and this is covered a little later in this chapter.

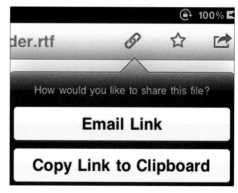

Figure 13-2
You can e-mail a link to a file in your Dropbox Public Folder or copy the link so it can be pasted elsewhere.

GOODREADER ($4.99)

I use iBooks to read a lot of PDFs. But if you want to do more than just read PDFs, you'll want something more powerful than iBooks—something like GoodReader.

GoodReader is one of the most versatile document readers available, and it allows you to annotate PDFs and manage your files. GoodReader also allows you to transfer files on and off your iPad in a variety of ways.

Right off the bat, it's important to know that GoodReader is not an editor. It's a reader app ... even though it can annotate PDF files. It natively supports the following file types:

- Microsoft Office
- Text
- Pages
- PDF
- PowerPoint
- Keynote
- Excel
- Numbers
- HTML
- Safari Web archives
- image files
- audio files
- video files

This means that whatever file you want to read on the iPad, chances are good that GoodReader can help. That said, since the app is dependent on the underlying iOS, some file types are not supported, and this might make a difference to some users (see list below). But in my practical use of the app, I've found GoodReader to work great and I haven't come across any files that the app failed to show. And since the iOS and the app are being updated all time, I expect even more file types to be supported in the future.

As I write this, the following files and file types are not supported by GoodReader.

- DRM-protected PDFs are not supported, but password-protected regular PDFs are.
- PDF portfolios must be extracted into separate PDF files in order to be viewed via GoodReader.
- Microsoft Office files that are password-protected are not supported.
- PDFs with 3D, audio and/ or video content are not supported.
- iWork 08/ 09 files must be saved with the Include Preview option.

The GoodReader interface is very intuitive and easy to navigate. The first view divides the screen into two sections. My Documents is on the left, and a series of menus are on the right. These menus:

- **Preview** makes it easy to see what file is selected. Especially when a file name is unclear or misleading, this feature lets you see if it's what you want to open. There's also an option to open the file in another app on the iPad. So if you have downloaded a PDF to check out, you can

Figure 13-3
This GoodReader interface shows the Preview turned on.

choose to open the file in iBooks instead of GoodReader.

The **Find Files** menu allows you to search the files in your My Documents area.

Manage Files is jam packed with options, ranging from placing new files in certain areas to creating new folders. It also allows you to compress or de-compress files.

The **Web Downloads** menu allows you to browse the Internet for files. It shows downloads in progress as well as recently downloaded files.

Connect to Servers shows the list of servers you've set up to access, and it allows you to add more servers by tapping the Add button. You can edit this list of servers easily.

Across the bottom of the screen is a group of icons. They're listed below with a description of the tools they offer:

Use the **Camera** to import images from the photo albums on your iPad.

The **Wi-Fi Transfer** window allows you to transfer files wirelessly online.

The **Settings** menu records your preferences for GoodReader.

Use the **Help Menu** to get information and problem-solving tips for GoodReader.

You can use an **External Display** with GoodReader, and this menu controls those options.

Lock the Orientation applies only to the GoodReader app, not the full iPad.

Figure 13-4
Here is the menu that's positioned across the bottom of the GoodReader app.

You can actually create new text documents right inside of GoodReader. In the Manage Files menu, just tap the New File button. A new text file will appear in the My Documents folder or whatever subfolder you happen to be in. And that's not all …

One of the real advantages of using GoodReader is that there are a variety of ways to transfer files into and out of the app. This alone makes it a viable choice for reading documents online. To get instructions on the multiple ways to get your files into GoodReader, visit this website for instructions: **http://www.goodreader.net/gr-man-howto.html**

iANNOTATE PDF ($9.99)

This is the most powerful PDF annotator app that I've come across. It allows you to fully annotate PDF files, so they can be read in standard PDF readers like Adobe Acrobat and Preview. This capability allows you to receive PDFs by e-mail, Dropbox or through an iTunes sync.

Once received, you can mark up files and send them back out from your iPad. You can

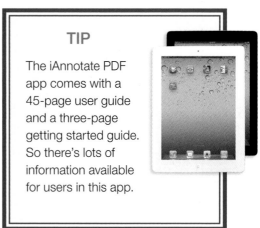

TIP

The iAnnotate PDF app comes with a 45-page user guide and a three-page getting started guide. So there's lots of information available for users in this app.

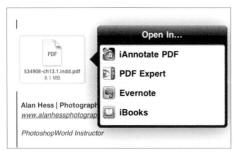

Figure 13-5
Choose which app to use to open a PDF that you receive in an e-mail.

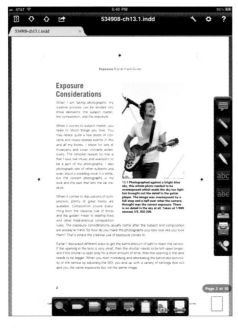

Figure 13-6
The basic annotation tools in the standard layout are available when the app launches for the first time.

also customize the tool bars so that you only see the tools you use regularly. To demonstrate these functions, let's get a file into the iAnnotate PDF app.

One of the most common ways to get PDFs into the app is by e-mail. So when you get an e-mail with an embedded PDF, just hold your finger on the PDF icon in the e-mail. From here, a menu opens with options. Tap Open In and then tap iAnnotate PDF. This tells the iPad to open the file in the iAnnotate app.

To e-mail a PDF out of the app, tap the Export button at the top of the app when the document you want to export is shown. This will give you the option to Mail Document, Print or Open In. Tap on Mail Document to save the file and embed it in an e-mail.

iAnnotate has a lot of annotating tools in two toolbars. One of them is on the right side of the screen; the other is at the bottom. First, on the right:

- **Note:** Tap on the location where you want to leave a note. Then, just type.

- **Pencil:** Draw freehand on your document with this tool.

- **Ruler:** This gives you a straight-line tool. Click on the starting point and then hold your finger on the screen to place the line.

- **Highlight:** Mark any text in your document by moving your finger over the text you want to select. When done, remove your finger. You'll see trim handles that allow you to adjust the selection. (This is great for those of us with fat fingers.)

- **Underline:** Use this tool in the same way as the highlight tool.

- **Strike Through:** This tool works just like the underline and highlight tools.

- **Stamp:** Pre-formatted stamps are available for your document. They include everything from exclamation points (in five different colors) to grades (from A+ to F-) ... as well as those very useful Sign Here tabs

Typewriter: Use this to type notes directly onto a PDF document. Tap the location for your note, and the built-in keyboard will appear.

Freehand Highlighter: This tool allows you to highlight any and every thing you want. Just draw on the document.

The toolbar at the bottom of the screen gives you the following tools (from left to right).

Tap **Search** to enter a query for exploring the document. This will search the PDF for the text you entered.

Set a **Bookmark**. You can create a bookmark to easily return to a particular spot later. The bookmark can have custom text, and it can have different colors. You can also move the location of the bookmark on the page to make it easier to see.

Tap **Find Bookmark** to bring up the bookmark list. When you find the one you want, tap it to go to that specific spot in the document.

Previous takes you to the previous annotation.

Next goes to the next annotation.

Clipboard allows you to copy the PDF into the iPad's memory, so it can be used in another application. This is a great way to grab some text you want to e-mail or paste into another document.

Zoom Lock/ Unlock turns the zoom lock on or off. When it's on, the icon shows a locked padlock; you can't zoom in or out. If zoom lock is turned off, then the icon is an unlocked padlock. This indicates that you can zoom in or out on the document using the standard iPad pinch-to-zoom technique.

If you tap **Zoom to Fit**, the app will zoom in to fit the width of the iPad.

Figure 13-7

There are tons of other annotation tools available in the iAnnotate PDF app. Definitely take some time to explore this.

One of the more powerful features of this app is the ability it gives users to customize the toolbars. Tap on the wrench icon at the top of the screen to bring up the controls. Here, you can configure the toolbars to your liking by adding functions that are not part of the standard toolbars and removing those that are. If you only use a certain set of tools, then those are the ones you'd keep in the tool bars. This can save a ton of time if you're a big PDF annotator. I know of no other PDF app that offers this many tools and gives you so much control over where (and if) the tools are positioned.

PDF EXPERT ($9.99)

Use the PDF Expert app to read and annotate PDF documents; it also lets you actually fill out PDF forms! If filling out forms is important to you, then this is definitely an app you should check out. And since the app can annotate as well, it might just be the only PDF app you need on your iPad.

When you open PDF Expert, four choices appear on the left.

- Tap on **Documents** and find two preloaded PDF files. There's a PDF Expert Guide and a What's New file for Version 2.2.

- The **Recents** tab shows a list of files that've been opened recently. This is very useful when you have a ton of files loaded and need to find one quickly.

Figure 13-8
Cloud services are accessible from inside the PDF Expert app.

- The **Network** tab allows you to transfer files to the app without having to connect by USB cable or send yourself an e-mail. Tap on the Navigate button to access two options. The first is the address of the iPad on the network, and the second is a button that tells the app to look for nearby servers, including WebDAV servers. On the top left of the Network menu is the Add button. Tap this to access your cloud-based storage (e.g., MobileMe, Google Docs, Dropbox). To set the PDF Expert app to use Dropbox, tap on the Dropbox button on this menu. Now enter your name and password for the account. The Dropbox account will then be listed under Favorite Servers in the Network list.

- Tap the **Settings** tab to get the following options:

  - **Passkey Lock:** If you activate this option, then a passkey is required to open the app—every time. This is nice if you use the iPad for business and also let your kids play with it. It means other people can't get into your files in this app and delete important stuff. Be careful you don't lose the passkey though. There's no way to recover it.

  - **Wi-Fi Drive:** The PDF Expert app allows you to share data with computers on the network using WebDAV protocol. There are detailed instructions to set this up right here.

  - **PDF Viewer:** The settings here allow you to turn Highlight Links on and off and to highlight form fields. This is also where you can scroll pages horizontally or vertically, and you can adjust the lowest page zoom to page width or whole page.

- **Auto-Open:** Turn on this option so the document will open after it downloads.

- **Support:** Send feedback to the app team from here.

- **Legal Notes:** Find all the legal stuff here that no one ever reads.

Now, to give you an idea of how powerful and easy it is to use this app, here's a quick walk-through with a real-life example of getting a PDF, filling it out and returning the form. (I'd like to thank Terry White for the idea to use an IRS PDF form. Tax forms are available from the Internal Revenue Service.)

1. Download the 1040 form onto the computer.

2. Open Dropbox on the computer.

3. Create a new folder in Dropbox and call it PDF Expert.

4. Put the 1040 PDF file into the PDF Expert folder in Dropbox.

5. Open the PDF Expert app on the iPad.

6. Tap on Network.

7. If you haven't added your Dropbox account, do so now. (Instruction is pro-vided above.)

8. Open your Dropbox account and tap on the PDF Expert folder.

9. Tap Sync. This will enable two-way syn-chronization. The folder is added to the Documents list and the Sync button will appear in the bottom left corner.

10. Tap Sync this Folder.

11. Tap on the file you want to edit. (In this case, it's the 1040 tax file.)

12. All the fields that can be entered are highlighted.

13. Start entering information into the form.

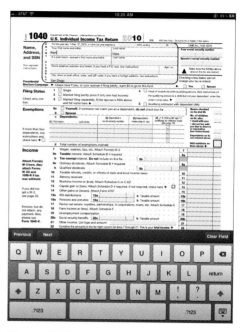

Figure 13-9
You can fill in a PDF tax form on the iPad with the PDF Expert app.

14. When you're done, tap the Back button (top left of the screen).

15. A list of your documents will appear.

16. Tap the Sync button (bottom left).

17. Pick either Push Changes or Full Sync, and tap it. The difference is that the Push Changes option only changes the docu-ments you've worked on since the last sync, while the Full Sync makes sure the whole folder is the same on your synced machines.

18. This will sync the PDF Expert folder with Dropbox, so the same file is now updated back on the computer.

If you need to fill out PDF forms, then this is the app to use. You can even add a

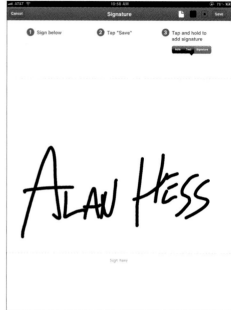

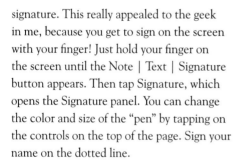

Figure 13-10
Tap the Sync button to decide whether you want to Push Changes or do a Full Sync.

Figure 13-11
The signature panel in PDF Expert is very cool!

signature. This really appealed to the geek in me, because you get to sign on the screen with your finger! Just hold your finger on the screen until the Note | Text | Signature button appears. Then tap Signature, which opens the Signature panel. You can change the color and size of the "pen" by tapping on the controls on the top of the page. Sign your name on the dotted line.

It might take a try or two to get through all this, because using your finger as a pen can be a little difficult. To start over, tap the New button at the top of the page. (It looks like a blank page.)

Once you have the signature done, tap Save. Your signature will appear in the PDF. Re-

position and re-size it as needed. You can reuse your signature over and over again. But if you want to change the signature—or just want to experiment with using your finger to sign stuff—tap on the Pen tool at the top of the screen to open the signature panel.

While I like the ease of GoodReader and the annotation ability of iAnnotate, this PDF app is the one I find myself using more and more ... especially due to the two-way sync with Dropbox.

SNEAKPEEK APP ($9.99)

I have lots of friends in the design business, and once in awhile I need to look at Adobe Illustrator CS5 files (.ai) and InDesign CS5 files (.indd) on my iPad. This is the app that allows me to do it.

But for this app to work, you need to make a few changes to how the Illustrator and InDesign files are saved. That is, the File Handling preferences in InDesign need the following settings:

- Turn on Always Save Preview Images with Documents.

- Set the page's drop-down menu choice to "All Pages."

- Change the Preview Size to "Extra Large 1024x1024." This makes the files bigger, but it allows you to view them properly on your iPad.

For Illustrator, it's a little easier. All you have to do is make sure PDF Compatible File is enabled in the Save dialog box.

While SneakPeek doesn't let you edit these design files, it does give you more information about the them than just a visual peek. You can view the fonts used in the document and see the colors and swatches that were used. You can also see which images are linked. This is easily done by tapping on the icons at the bottom of the page.

If you need or want to see Illustrator or InDesign documents on your iPad, then this is the way to go.

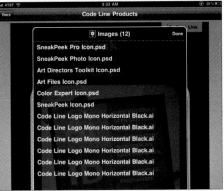

Figure 13-12

In SneakPeek, you can see the Fonts, Images and Swatches that were used in the file ... just by tapping on the corresponding icon on the bottom of the page.

Remote Desktops

The Skim

Accessing my desktop (or laptop) computer remotely is one of the coolest things you can do with an iPad. And I use this feature all the time. See, my main desktop computer is in my home office, and I have a couple of laptops on which I do most of my writing work. So with the iPad's remote desktop feature, if I have an idea or want to check something on any of these machines, I can do it from my couch!

Remote desktop apps allow users to control various computers with an iPad. The idea is pretty simple: Load and run a program on your computer, and run a remote desktop app on your iPad to control the computer via the iPad over the Wi-Fi network.

SCREENS ($19.99)

The remote desktop app that I like the best and use the most is called Screens (from a company called Edovia Inc). It's squarely on the expensive side of to iPad apps, but I think it is worth every penny. One of the reasons I really like this one so much is its ease of use. I'm getting used to downloading apps onto my iPad and having them work right away, and I prefer it that way. I don't want to spend a ton of time setting up apps. If they don't work when I download them, then I usually just delete and forget about them.

Set Up Inter-Network Access

The easiest way to use Screens is to have the iPad and computer on the same network. In this scenario, you don't have to deal with Internet settings.

Figure 14-1
The Screens welcome app has a very polished look and is easy to use … right away.

Figure 14-2
The sharing setting in the Apple System Preferences.

(We'll cover how to run these apps over the Internet a little later.) For now, here's how to set up the machines to interact when they're on the same network. Note that setup is easier for Mac users than PCs, but we'll go through both.

Mac

1. Download the Screens app … either in iTunes or through the App Store on the iPad.

2. Open the app and notice the welcome screen.

3. On the Mac computer you want to use for remote desktop access, open System Preferences and click Sharing.

4. Enable Screen Sharing.

5. Click on Computer Settings. (On older versions of the Mac OS, this could be referenced as Access Privileges.)

6. Enable VNC, so viewers may control screen with password. Enter a password of your choice.

7. Click OK.

8. Back on the iPad in the Screens app, tap New Screen (top left).

9. When the New Screen menu appears, tap the Nearby Computers button.

10. This reveals a list of computers that are on the same network and have screen sharing turned on.

11. Tap on the computer you want to control with your iPad.

12. Tap Save on the Screen Details window.

13. Tap the Screen icon to access the VNC password menu. Type in the password that you entered in Step 6.

14. Your iPad can now control your computer.

There are other cool controls that Screens uses to help you navigate. More on these is coming up later.

PC

This setup is a little more complicated. It requires you to download a separate program onto your PC. Screens recommends that you use TightVNC, and that's what I use. Visit **http://www.tightvnc.com/download.php,** and download the TightVNC program for the PC.

1. Install the TightVNC application, and click on the icon in the system tray to run the program.

2. The TightVNC Service Configuration menu will open. Make a note of the Main server port. You'll need this later.

3. Click OK.

4. Hover your mouse over the TightVNC icon in the system tray. Note the IP address that appears. Write it down; you'll need it to set up Screens.

5. In the iPad app, tap New Screen.

6. In the Name field, enter the name of the computer.

7. In the Address field, enter the IP address from Step 4.

8. In the Port field, enter the port number from Step 2.

9. Tap Save.

Done. You can now access the PC on your iPad … as long as everything is on the same network.

Set Up Internet Access

Running Screens over the Internet to access and take control of your computer(s) is a little more difficult than when the machines are on the same network, but it's not prohibitively difficult.

Mac

If you're trying to connect to a Mac, your best bet is to use the optional and free application from Edovia called Screens Connect. Download it from **http://edovia.com/screens**.

The following specifications are required to run Screens Connect: Mac OS X 10.6 or

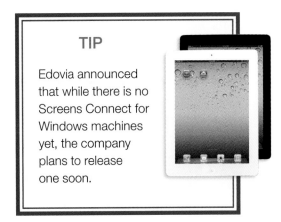

TIP

Edovia announced that while there is no Screens Connect for Windows machines yet, the company plans to release one soon.

Figure 14-3
Loading the Screens Connect application is a one-click process.

later and a UPnP or NAT-PMP enabled on your router. (See your router user manual for details on this.) Once you have Screens Connect installed on your computer, you can access the application in the System Preferences pane on your Mac.

In the Screens Connect program, type in a unique name for your computer. Then, when you go to the Screens app on the iPad:

1. Tap the New Screen button on the top left.

2. In the Screen details, scroll down to the

Screens Connect field and enter the computer name that you entered in the Screens Connect field on your Mac.

3. Tap Save.

Now you can connect to your computer through your iPad using 3G connections ... if it has 3G capabilities.

PC

To set up this access on a Windows machine, until Edovia releases the Windows-compatible Screen Connect software, follow the directions below. Keep in mind that the idea is to make your computer accessible to your iPad, so you can connect when not on the local network.

1. Download and install a VNC server. The instructions for downloading TightVNC are provided above.

2. Get a static IP. Go to http://portforward. com/networking/staticip.htm and select your Operating System.

3. Now, open a public port on your computer. Go to **http://portforward.com/ cports.htm** and select the VNC server

that's installed on your computer. Follow the instructions.

4. Use DynDNS, a utility that allows the remote software to reach your computer: **http://www.dyndns.com/support/kb/ dyndns.html.** Or you can install a free Updater app, such as http://www.dyndns. com/support/clients/windows.html. But there's a chance that your router already provides this functionality, so check your router documentation.

5. Open the iPad Screens app.

6. Tap New Screen (top left).

7. Enter a new name for the computer.

8. Enter your DynDNS address in the address field.

9. Enter the public VNC port you've configured.

10. If you're using SSH, enable it and enter the required information.

11. You can now open and control your PC with your iPad over 3G when you're not on the local network.

Run Screens

When you run Screens, you'll be asked to pick a computer to access (among those you've set up). If you haven't already entered the password in the description of the machine, then you'll need to enter the password now.

Note: If your iPad is used by multiple people or is out of your control at any time, you will want to make sure that you require a password here. Otherwise, anyone using your iPad can gain complete control over your computer ... as if they are sitting in front of it.

TIP

If you have an SSH server installed (e.g., freeSSHD), you'll need to open a port for it at **http:// portforward.com/ english/pplications/ port_forwarding/ SSH/SSHindex.htm**.

Screens Controls

Controlling your computer from your iPad can be a little frustrating at first, because you don't have a mouse or keyboard. You have to control everything with your fingers. So it's a good thing that Screens supports a lot of different commands or finger movements.

These basic gestures let you mimic the mouse.

- **Click** by tapping on the screen.
- **Double Click** by tapping twice on the screen in quick succession.
- To **Right Click**, press two fingers on the desired element. If you need to drill down into a contextual menu, such as *Open with*, then:

    a. Tap with one finger and hold until you see the blue fading circle.

    b. Drag your finger over the desired menu item.

    c. Release your finger to select the menu item.

- **Scroll** by brushing two fingers over the desired elements … either vertically or horizontally.
- **Drag an Item** by tapping with one finger and holding the item until you see the blue fading circle. Then, just move the element.

There are some other controls that you'll need to know to get the most out of the Screens app. These are visible on the screen. The first are the modifier keys, which are positioned across the bottom of the screen.

Figure 14-4
Screens will ask for the VNC password so it can connect to your computer.

At the top of the screen is the button that brings up the keyboard with one tap … and hides it with another tap. Next to that is the shortcut view, which brings up a series of shortcut buttons.

I really love the ease of this app. I use it way more than I probably should and have therefore become quite lazy. It is so much easier to just log onto my computer from my iPad than actually getting up and walking into my office to use my computers.

JUMP DESKTOP ($19.99)

This app is another great solution for those who want to control a computer remotely from an iPad. To do so, Jump Desktop users need a desktop server application that communicates with the iPad app. The directions are pretty easy, but you'll have to download the iPad app as well as a separate program onto your computer.

Figure 14-5
The Screen controls are Escape, Tab, Shift, Control, Alt, and Command (the Windows key on Windows computers). There are also four arrow keys for navigation.

Figure 14-6
Here are the keyboard and shortcut menus.

Figure 14-7
See the mouse control of the Jump Desktop app. Place you finger in the circle under the mouse pointer and move it around.

To set up Jump Desktop on your PC:

1. Go to **http://jumpdesktop.com/quick-start-on-windows**.

2. Follow the directions:

   • Download and install Jump Desktop.

   • Run the Jump Desktop Configuration Wizard.

   • Enter your Gmail username and password.

3. Click Finish.

To set up Jump Desktop on your Mac:

1. Go to **http://jumpdesktop.com/quick-start-on-mac-os-x**.

2. Follow the directions:

   • Download and install Jump Desktop.

   • Click on the Jump Desktop icon in the toolbar at the top of the screen.

   • Sign in using your Gmail e-mail login information.

3. If screen sharing is turned off, you will be asked to turn it on. Screen sharing has to be on for this to work.

On your iPad, start the Jump Desktop app and enter the Gmail account information you used to set up the desktop version. Then connect your iPad to the computer and use the iPad to control your computer.

When you open the Jump Desktop app, tap on the gear icon (top left of the screen), and tap on Account. Enter your Gmail account information. Tap Done.

You can also change the way the app deals with mouse input, the controls and even the appearance of the app. Tap on the Jump button (top left) to return to the list of computers available through this app. Tap to select a computer to access.

The Jump Desktop app does a really great job with mouse control. When you have control over your screen, notice the pointer. Under it is a circle. Put your finger in the circle and move it around as if are moving the mouse. Tap in the circle to simulate clicking the mouse. This makes click-through menus a snap to navigate.

Tap on the Keyboard button (top left or right) to open the keyboard. In this layout, you can change between the regular keyboard, the number pad and the function keyboard by tapping on the corresponding buttons on the top left of the keyboard. This interface doesn't move anything out of the way. Instead, users see an overlay keyboard as shown in Figure

Tap on the X to disconnect. If you want to see the whole screen at once, tap on the Full Screen icon. You can also change the settings by tapping on the little wrench.

This app even allows you to use Photoshop on the iPad. It's not perfect, but it means you can check work and e-mail files while on the couch. Ahh ... such leisure.

This functionality of the iPad is getting better all the time, and the advances in the last year are really amazing. Remote desktop access is one of those functions that turn the iPad into a very useful tool, especially for those who are a more technically minded than the average computer user.

Many IT specialists have been doing this type of remote desktop computing for a long time, but this is really the first time it's been available and easy for the rest of us. The iPad brings it home. Try it!

Figure 14-8
There are three different keyboard layouts for the Jump Desktop app.

Figure 14-9
It's possible to run Photoshop on my computer and access it through the Jump Desktop app.

PART 5

Lifestyle Content

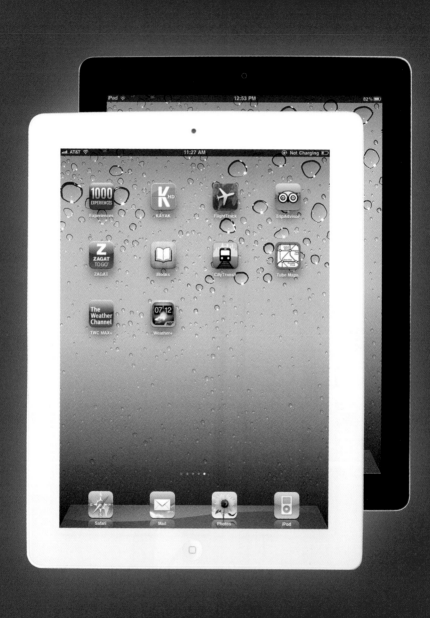

15

Travel

The Skim

The iPad is the perfect device to take on the road. For starters, it can hold a whole slew of entertainment media for long flights. Load a few movies or the last couple episodes of your favorite television show along with the novel you're reading and all the other books you've been trying to get around to reading … and even a magazine or ten.

Plus, the iPad can add so much to your travel planning. There are iPad apps and uses for just about every part of your travel plan—from finding the best deals on flights and lodging to recommendations on the best places to eat … and even quick access to subway maps. The iPad can keep you updated on flight times, check the weather and give you advice on what to do when you're at your destination.

The iPad can be a vacation lifesaver. I know this from experience. My wife and I were in Florida for a few days of rest and relaxation last year. We were heading down the west coast of Florida in our rental car when I realized that I'd left the charger cable for the GPS at home. And I hadn't bothered to print any of the maps or directions.

Enter the iPad: I used the built-in Google Maps app to get directions, and I was able to use the web browser to get information on areas of interest along our route. We even managed to score a great online deal for a hotel while on the road.

But now a word of warning: To use the iPad on the road like this, you will need a Wi-Fi + 3G-enabled iPad. Otherwise, you're limited to updates at Wi-Fi hotspots only.

1000 ULTIMATE EXPERIENCES ($4.99)

The 1000 Ultimate Experiences app by Lonely Planet profiles the top 1000 travel destinations. But instead of being sorted by location, the trips are sorted by topic. Here's the deal. When you first launch the app, you get an introduction by the founder of the Lonely Planet travel guides, explaining that the app is basically a set of lists that are offered to help you pick a place to go … based on what you want to see and/or do.

The lists include "Best beaches to swing in a hammock," "World's happiest places" and "Top travel boasts, myths & legends."

When you tap on a list, such as "Best way to eke out your holiday money," you're likely to get ten tips on how to get the most vacation for the least amount of coin. This will probably include a tip on house swapping or house sitting.

What takes this app a step further than others is that each tip comes with relevant links. And an easy way to share the vacation idea by e-mail is available through the app. Plus, this app has some of the best travel photographs that I've seen, and it uses them to make destinations look really great.

Figure 15-1

The lists in the 1000 Ultimate Experiences app are easy to navigate. Just use your finger to scroll up and down until you find a category that interests you. Then tap on the cards to open that list.

There are just three things that I'd add to this app's functions. And hopefully they'll be added to future versions.

- **Bookmarks:** My first wish is for users to be able to bookmark the cards. Right now if you want to save a card to look at later, you need to either remember how you found it in the first place or e-mail it to yourself.

- **Custom Lists:** I also think users should be able to create their own list(s). That is, it'd be great to have a few personal lists ... to help me keep track of the places I've been

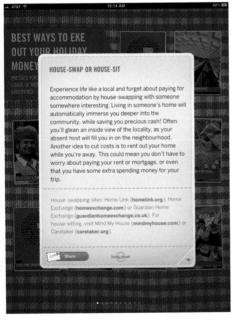

Figure 15-2
The location cards in the 1000 Ultimate Experiences app show the trip information and offer links to more details, if available, along with a link to e-mail the card to yourself or others who may be interested.

or the places I really want to go. It'd make this app a lot more practical ... for me anyway.

- **Search:** And it'd be nice to have a search function built into this app. While the navigation and method for looking at the places are very cool, a master list that could be searched would be a great addition.

AIRLINES AND HOTELS

Before your travel begins, the iPad can be used really effectively to plan a trip and get you the lowest price on all aspects of your travel. The app that I find myself using for this more than any other is Kayak.

Kayak HD ($FREE)

Kayak HD is the free travel-planning app for the iPad, and it is really easy to use. Since most people start planning travel by looking for flights, the app is designed to begin there.

To get started, enter the relevant locations and your travel dates, and tap on the search bar. Kayak will return a list of flights that match the search parameters. For flight details, simply tap on any of the listings. You can even book your flights right then and there.

But if you need a bit more time to pull the trigger, just e-mail yourself the links to the search or the search results. Tapping the back arrow (top left of the screen) will take you back to the main page. Your searches are preserved in the Search History panel, which makes it easy to keep track of multiple searches.

Booking hotels follows the same pattern. Just tap on the Hotels tab at the bottom of the screen, and the app will bring up the last airline search as a location for the hotels

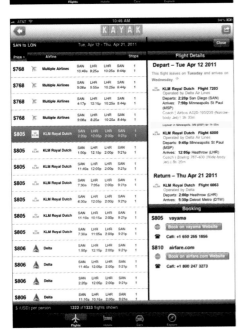

Figure 15-3

The Kayak HD interface makes it easy to enter your travel needs and find results.

search. But, if you want to switch things around, it's really easy to adjust any of the parameters.

Once you've got a list (which will appear on the right), pick a hotel and tap Get Rates. Or you can tap the Get Rates button without picking a hotel. This will give you the basic rates for all the hotels. Either way it's simple to see a ton of choices to help you make an informed choice. And each hotel listing in this app has a tab that provides an overview of the hotel as well as photos, reviews and important booking information.

When you decide on a hotel, just tap the Booking tab and pick the price you like. Tap the Book Online button. Kayak will load the relevant booking page, allowing you to purchase a hotel room reservation.

The Hotel search page in Kayak HD gives you lots of options … and even includes reviews!

The Kayak HD app has one more neat feature; it's the Explore option. This is a cool way to see what trips are available from your current location. The app opens a page that shows a world map with your current location marked with a red pin and the available destinations marked with orange circles. You can change your current location by tapping the Change Location button on the top left. And use the Price Slider to adjust how many and what kind of destinations are shown. That way, you can control the results based on your expectations and budget for your trip listings.

You can also control the when, what and flight details using the three pop-up menus that are available across the bottom of the screen. Once you've filtered the choices, just tap on one of the orange dots to bring up that location info.

Figure 15-4
The Hotel search page in Kayak HD gives you lots of options ... and even includes reviews!

FlightTracker

I live in one of the most popular tourist destinations in the United States: San Diego California. And it really is a very beautiful place to live ... and visit. So the thing about living here is that I get a lot of friends and family visiting all year long. And it usually falls to me to provide them ground transportation to and from the airport. Well, the FlightTracker app has become my friend, because it helps me monitor any flight quite easily.

When the app opens, a world map appears ... along with a button to add flights to your tracking queue. Your search options are:

• By Flight Number

• By Route

• By Airport

Figure 15-5
The Explore option in Kayak HD is a great way to find out where you can go and for how much ... without having a real destination in mind. Just keep adjusting the variables to get the perfect location.

Tapping on the By Airport option brings up an offer to purchase the Flight board for $3.99. This tool shows the arrival and departure information for thousands of airports and is updated every five minutes. While I'm not sure I actually need this, I think it's very cool that I can access this information that easily. So I bought the in-app upgrade, but you don't need this to get the information for a couple of flights.

233

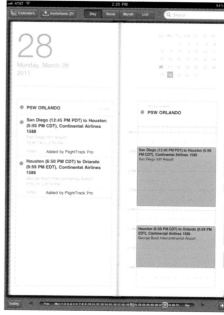

Figure 15-7
Selected flight info from the
FlightTracker app is automatically added
and updated in my iPad calendar.

Figure 15-6
The interface for the FlightTracker app
is great, and the addition of the Flight
board makes it fun to see what's going
on at any airport.

There are actually two versions of
FlightTracker. The regular version costs $4.99
and the pro version costs $9.99. Both have
the in-app purchase ability to add Flight
board, and the regular version can be updated
to the pro version for $4.99 at any time.

To access the Settings menu in FlightTracker,
tap on the (i) at the bottom of the
FlightTracker screen. In the regular version,
this is where you can update to FlightTracker
Pro, which offers extra service/ information,
such as:

- push alerts for flights

- ability to auto import flights from TripIt

- airport terminal maps

- weather info for airports

One of the neatest and, in my mind, most
useful features of this app is that it allows you
to add events to your calendar for flights.
FlightTracker will update the info if needed.

READ REVIEWS

There are also apps that will help you pick the best spots to stay and eat. Many of these use customer reviews, so I urge you to read more than one review to get a full understanding of the lodging or restaurant you're considering. Sometimes people have a bad day at a great place, so their review is skewed. Other times, a person may give a great review for a not-so-great place.

Trip Advisor ($FREE)

Trip Advisor can help you find the cheapest airfare, and it can provide great insight to venues and activities that you may (or may not) want to check out. The combination of the app's location service and reviews makes it easier for travelers to make informed decisions about how to spend vacation time ... and money.

As I write this, I'm planning another trip to Florida. So I entered Orlando as the location and tapped the Stay button. This brought up a list of Orlando hotels ranked from the best reviews to the worst. On the right side of the screen, a map with the locations of the hotels is shown, and I can navigate around this by using my fingers. It makes it easy to see what's around a certain location and where you're actually located in relation to where you may want to go.

I highly recommend spending some time with this app if you're planning a trip to someplace you've never been—or want to experience it differently. The reviews alone make it so much more likely that you'll pick a place for dinner that leads to a great night out instead of a night you prefer to forget.

One of the best things about this app is the Near Me Now button. One tap and the app uses the iPad's location to find rated

Figure 15-8
This Trip Advisor interface shows my lodging choices in Orlando on the map on the right side of the app.

restaurants, hotels and attractions nearby. Just tap on the Menu button (on the top right), and tap on Near Me Now. The iPad will want to use your location and therefore needs to access the Internet for this app to work right. This means you'll need to be in a Wi-Fi hotspot or using a 3G-enabled iPad with an active data plan.

Zagat To Go ($9.99)

I like to eat out, especially on vacation. And no other restaurant guide is as complete or has as much name recognition as the Zagat guide. The Zagat To Go app is a single app with reviews from 45 of the Zagat restaurant guides—all for less than the cost of a single guide. This app is $9.99, which is a lot of money considering that most of the apps I use are free or less than $4.99. But I think it's worth it. There's a lot of info and, because the app works for both the iPad and the iPhone, you can always access the guide.

Open the Zagat guide and enter a city, or allow the iPad to use your current location. Either way, a map will open with the Zagat-reviewed restaurants shown by little pins with a Z.

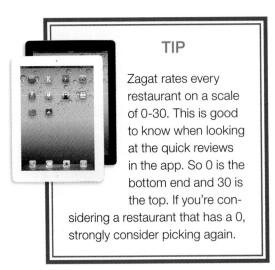

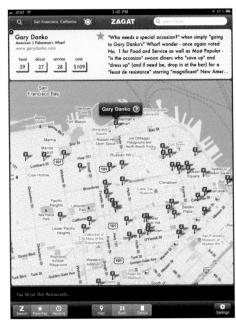

> ## TIP
>
> Zagat rates every restaurant on a scale of 0-30. This is good to know when looking at the quick reviews in the app. So 0 is the bottom end and 30 is the top. If you're considering a restaurant that has a 0, strongly consider picking again.

- Tap on a pin to see info about that specific restaurant. The information will appear at the top of the screen.
- Tap on the description to bring up the full restaurant listing. This includes an ability to mark it as a favorite. Just tap on the star next to the business name, and it will be available in the Favorites tab on the bottom.

There are seven buttons across the bottom of the app that allow you to search, access your previously marked favorites or recently visited. This is also where you can change the display from Map to Book, which gives you the same information but in a more traditional guidebook style (versus a map view). One of the buttons offers the details of your chosen restaurants.

A great feature of this app is the ability to use the Zagat guide offline. Download the offline database in the Settings screen, accessible through the Settings button on the bottom of the main page. This is great for times when you don't want to have to go searching for a Wi-Fi spot, and you don't want to use the 3G capability of the iPad.

Figure 15-9
Here's a search for places to eat in the San Francisco area. Just tap on a flag to get that restaurant's info.

If you use the printed Zagat guide, then this will be a great addition to your iPad. If the printed Zagat guide is something you'd never reference—because you prefer to be surprised and develop your opinions independently—then you might want to skip this app. For me though, I've found that it comes in very handy when trying to pick a restaurant in a somewhat informed manner.

And this app is better than the print version, because it includes Nightlife, Hotels and Shopping guides as well. Just tap on the icon in the middle of the top bar to change the category.

One last thing here: The search function is located at the top left of the screen. It offers options to filter your search. This is a great

Or, even better, gather a variety of PDF documents about your trip and load them into iBooks to read while on vacation. I have found that searching Google, but limiting the results to PDF files only, really helps.

1. Go to **www.google.com.**

2. Click on Advanced search. (It's at the end of the text-entry box.)

3. Type in your search term(s).

4. Change the file type in the drop-down box from Any Format to Adobe Acrobat PDF (.pdf).

5. Click Advanced search.

You can append file type .pdf to the end of the search string in the regular Google page to get the same results.

6. Now all you have to do is save the PDF file(s) to your computer and add them to iTunes.

Figure 15-10
The Zagat search function allows you to narrow your choices in a number of different ways.

way to find exactly what you're looking for. You can pick by cuisine, neighborhood, food rating or price, which is very useful!

LOAD IT

So you've picked a spot to visit, booked your flights and hotels … and planned a dream vacation. Don't put away your iPad just yet. It can be a really useful tool when you're *on* vacation as well. Here are just a few uses for the iPad that you may or may not have considered:

Guidebooks

Get the latest tour guides from the electronic bookstore of your choice—iBooks, Kindle or Nook—and load them onto your iPad!

Contacts App

Add hotels, restaurants and attractions to your iPad address book and create a group for the vacation. This will allow you to find trip-related addresses and numbers easily. It also makes it quicker to use the Maps app to find places while on vacation. More on map apps coming up.

GETTING AROUND

The iPad comes standard with a Map app that gives you directions and shows the current traffic volume. And it's really useful … all by itself. But there are places it doesn't cover and times that it can't be used. Good thing there are other options. Let's start with the freebie that comes preloaded on the iPad.

Maps App

You can look up any address in the iPad's Maps app to see where it is ... and get there! Even better, you can use the addresses in your address book to access this info without having to type it in on the fly. Just tap on the Address Book icon on the top of the Maps app, and tap on Groups. Pick the vacation group (described in the previous section), and then tap on any of the locations to see on the map. You can also use the addresses to get directions, including a walking route.

1. Open the Maps app.

2. Tap on Directions (top left).

3. Tap in the first direction box, and then tap on the Address Book icon.

4. Tap on the Starting Address field.

5. Tap Directions From Here.

6. Tap on the second direction box, and then tap on the Address Book icon.

7. Pick the Destination location and tap Directions To Here.

8. Across the bottom of the screen is a blue directions bar which prompts you to select your mode of transportation: car, public transit or walk. There's also a Start button here. Tap the type of directions you need and hit Start.

9. You will now get step-by-step directions for reaching your destination.

Or perhaps you prefer to leave the wayfinding to someone else. There are also apps available to help guide users through city transit system.

City Transit – Official NYC Subway Guide ($2.99)

This app will help you navigate the New York City subway system, which can be very

intimidating to those of us who are not from New York City. The app includes the official MTA subway map, the Manhattan Bus Map and the Metro North Map.

London Tube Maps for iPad ($1.99)

There are quite a few apps that are designed to help people get around the London Tubes, but I really like this one the best. I've visited London quite a few times and this app would have really helped. One of the best things about this app is that it doesn't need 3G or Wi-Fi connection to run! Convenient ...

You will need an Internet connection, either Wi-Fi or 3G, to get any updates on the Tube service, but that's not needed for the app to run. It works offline, so you can actually view the maps while riding the tube. There have

Figure 15-11

The London Tubes app allows you to see the tube station on a real map right inside the app.

een talks about outfitting the Tube system ith 3G or Wi-Fi, but for now you'll need to ork offline when on the Tube.

nother other useful feature is the tegration with Google maps. This helps you ·e where the stations are located, which is a g help.

·ountry Maps ($FREE, $5.99)
he iPad developer Dubbele has created ore than 170 apps that give you iPad maps cities that work when you have no Wi-Fi or G. These are priced anywhere between free id $5.99, and they're great for travelers who on't want to deal with the Internet or cell one data plans when they're out and about.

n entire map is stored on your iPad. And nce this can take up a lot of space (and xceed the 3G cap), be sure to download the ap you want before leaving a Wi-Fi spot. For xample, the San Diego Map is 173 MB, and e New Delhi map is 55.3 MB. Just search e iTunes store for Dubbele when in the iPad p listings, and click See All. This will open e page of all available maps.

VEATHER
eing able to check the weather forecast hen you travel can be important. The ·llowing apps take advantage of the ·ad's big screen and offer a ton of weather formation.

he Weather Channel Max App ($FREE)
·he Weather Channel (TWC) created 1ax for the iPad. And given that the sole ·cus of the channel is weather, this app ·as a lot going for it. It can show you radar ·iews; local, regional and national weather; ·nd even Twitter feeds from TWC's on-air

personalities. On the downside, this app also shows ads for shows on The Weather Channel, but I guess that's the price for a free … and awesome … weather app.

AccuWeather App ($FREE, $0.99)
The AccuWeather app comes in two flavors: a free version and a $0.99 version. The difference is that the $0.99 version is ad-free. That's the one I use. This app gives really quick access to relevant weather information, including current temperature, humidity, sunrise and sunset times, and notification of severe weather warnings.

Warnings are shown by a red exclamation point. Tapping on it will bring up any important information for your current location. The interface is friendly and the buttons are … well, they just look cool.

Tap on the location field to change it, and then tap on the menu button (located on the right side about three quarters down the side). The menu brings up your choices:

- **Forecast:** The main display gives the current weather information and a forecast for the next 15 days.

- **Hourly:** This shows the forecast for the day by the hour. Just tap on the time, and the icon will change to reveal the forecasted weather.

- **Videos:** You can watch a selection of current weather videos right on the app.

- **Maps:** This shows weather maps centered on your current location.

- **Lifestyle:** This is one of the more unique features of this app. It lets you know if the weather is going to affect activities like Dog Walking, Sailing, Jogging and many more. Each activity is rated Poor to Excellent.

Figure 15-12

These two views of the AccuWeather app show how much more information you get in the portrait view.

- **Hurricane:** This shows the current hurricane maps around the world.

- **Settings:** You can adjust the stored locations and change the measurement units from English to Metric here.

This app looks and works better in portrait mode, because the current weather

conditions are always present at the top of the screen in that view; they are missing in the landscape view.

Weather + App ($1.99)

If I could use only one weather app, this would be it. For starters, I love this app's interface, which is stunning. It's very enjoyable to look at. The developers took advantage of the iPad's display with terrific images and very detailed backdrops. But this app is more than beautiful. It's also very easy to use, and it can be customized to give users the information they want.

When you first run Weather +, it asks permission to use your current location (as do all the weather apps). I allow it to do so, because this enables the app to show the local weather. This is kind of the point, right?

The app provides the basics on the front page:

- Location
- Current Time
- Current Date
- Current Weather Conditions
- Five-Day Forecast
- Five-Day Forecast in Three-Hour Intervals

Across the bottom of the screen is information on the humidity, precipitation, pressure and visibility along with wind direction and speed readout.

To add a city, tap on the (i) located at the bottom right of the page. This brings up the Settings menus, where you can add, delete and edit the locations list as well as change the layout and settings. So tap on the (+) sign at the top left of the menu window and start typing in a city name. The app will offer you choices based on your input. Select the

Figure 15-13
The layout of Weather + offers clear and easy-to-read information.

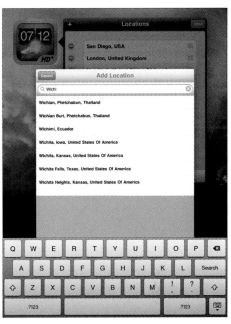

Figure 15-14
You can easily add new locations in the Weather + app.

city you want to add and it will appear in your Locations list.

To delete a city, tap on the (–) sign (to the left of the listing) and then tap on the Delete button that appears next to the city's name.

If you want to move cities around the list, there's a button located to the right of the city name that looks like three horizontal bars. Just hold your finger on this button and move the city up or down the list.

To switch locations, open your locations list, swipe sideways to scroll, and select the location for which you want to know the weather.

To change the layout of the information you see when using the app, tap on the Layout button. This reveals eight choices for the information shown. I like to have information

at a glance, so I keep the layout set to All Widgets; but you can decide which layout works for you.

The last menu is the Settings menu, which controls:

• Brightness of Foreground and Background

• Temperature and Distance Metrics

• Autolock Feature (on and off switch)

• App Orientation (horizontal or vertical)

• Weather Refresh Rate

This app looks so good that sometimes I just have it playing on my iPad when my iPad is on my desk. The images it offers are really a treat.

16

Hobbies

The Skim

Cooking • The Photo Cookbook • Epicurious App • Drawing and Painting
Brushes App • Inkpad App • Music • GarageBand App • djay App

This chapter is all about having some fun. It describes some ways to use your iPad to enjoy a hobby or area of interest. Some of these apps are right up my alley, like those that focus on great cooking and music. Then there are some that I really love, like the ones used for drawing and painting ... even though I can barely draw a stick figure.

There are so many fun things to do with an iPad. This chapter can get you started, but it just scratches the surface. Definitely take some time to browse the App Store for more fun.

COOKING APPS

I really enjoy cooking. Actually I really enjoy *eating*, and I've found that the best way to get healthy meals on my table is to cook them myself. Plus, I enjoy being in the kitchen. And if there's one place that has more gadgets available than an Apple Store, it's a good cookware store. I'm such a sucker for gadgets!

iBooks as a Cookbook

Before getting into the official cookbook apps on the iPad, I want to share what I did with those folders of old recipes I've kept around for so many years. Ready? I turned them into PDF files and loaded them into my iPad as a recipes collection! Here's how to do this.

TIP

Be sure to keep your iPad safely away from any water, and protect it while you work in the kitchen.

Figure 16-1
The main page of the Photo Cookbook app lets you quickly and easily find a recipe. The recipe pages are laid out beautifully and make it a breeze to follow along.

1. Type the recipes using a word processor.

2. Export the file as a PDF.

3. Import the PDF into iTunes.

4. Sync the PDF onto your iPad in the book tab.

5. In iBooks, create a collection and move the recipes into it.

If you want to get a little fancier, create an ePub book of recipes that can be read in iBooks. Check out the directions for creating an ePub in Chapter 5.

The Photo Cookbook – Quick and Easy ($4.99)

This app is just plain fun. It's loaded with lots of tasty recipes, which can all be prepared in 30 minutes or less. Each recipe starts with a tempting photo. Just tap on this photo and you'll be presented with all the steps to create the pictured meal.

This app is not aimed at the culinary expert, but instead for the cook that's just starting out … or preparing quick meals for a family. It walks you through each of the preparation steps with clear and concise instructions and photos of each step.

E-mail yourself (or your spouse) the list of ingredients needed for the recipe by tapping on the Export button on the top right.

Epicurious Recipes & Shopping List ($FREE)

This is one of the first apps I ever downloaded for the iPad. And it really has come a long way. The first thing you may notice about the app is that you can now sync recipes between the iPad and iPhone versions of the app. There's also a personal recipe box on epicurious.com that you can sync with your iPad app for the in-app purchase price of $1.99.

Figure 16-3
Searching through the recipes in
Epicurious app is fun and easy.

Figure 16-2
The main menu in the Epicurious app
gives you a ton of choices for meals,
including those that are Quick and
Easy and some that are tied to the
current time of year … like Passover or
Thanksgiving meals.

If you have an Epicurious account, sign in; if
you don't have an account, it just takes a few
seconds to set one up. When you're signed
into your account, you can access your own
recipe box and sync it among your iDevices
and the Epicurious website (**http://www.epi-
curious.com/**).

The most important button in this app is the
Control Panel button (top left). Tap it to see
the list of featured recipe categories. Pick a
category and start looking at the recipes. I
picked Spring Dinners and received 238 recipes. Picking just one was tough.

Tap on a listing to bring up the ingredients
and directions. There are three buttons on
the top right of this recipe window:

• The first is a star that, when tapped, marks
the menu as a Favorite and adds the recipe
to your recipe box.

• The second button adds the ingredients
for the recipe to the shopping list. (This
list can be edited later.)

• The third button allows you to export the
recipe by e-mail, Twitter, Facebook and
whole lot more, including Tumblr and a
Google Reader.

There is a button on the top of the page that
looks like two capital As next to each other.
This button allows you to change the size of
the text. I only wish it could be made even
bigger than the largest option. That would
make it more convenient to set the iPad in a
book stand in the kitchen … and keep it safe
and sound—out of the way of my cooking—
and still be able to read the directions.

You can also search for food or drink by a
variety of criteria, including main ingredient,
dietary considerations and season. Every one

of the search criterion is added to the search box and can be removed by tapping the corresponding button.

The app also has a great shopping list built in. It automatically adds all the ingredients of the selected recipes to the shopping list. E-mail the shopping list with the tap of the finger.

DRAWING AND PAINTING APPS

These apps are great … and a lot of fun to use. As I mentioned earlier in the chapter, I'm no Picasso; but I have artist friends who can create amazing images on the iPad by using these apps. I just like to play around with them.

To keep this chapter at a manageable length, this section assumes a general knowledge of how art programs, like Photoshop and Illustrator, work. After reading it, you should have a working knowledge of the apps to get started on your own creative iPad pursuit. But if you need help with any of the terms or concepts, a quick Internet search should offer the explanations you need.

Brushes ($7.99)

The Brushes app is electronic finger painting at its finest. This app has been used to create four different covers of the *New Yorker* weekly magazine! Obviously, the artist who did those covers has a lot more talent than I do, but it's amazing to think that a $7.99 app—that's finger-operated—can create work of such high caliber. When you open the app for the first time, you are presented with a blank canvas that can be a little intimidating. Just tap to open it and get to creating your masterpiece.

The first thing to know is that there are nineteen different brushes and nineteen different erasers in this app. Each has adjustable

Figure 16-4
This brush control shows the spacing, size and opacity.

spacing, size and opacity. Switching between the paintbrush and the eraser is just a matter of tapping on the tool icons in the bottom middle of the screen. The paint brush tool looks just a little paintbrush and the eraser looks like … you got it, a small eraser.

Between these two icons is the Settings menu for both tools. It looks like a curving paint stroke with a number below, which shows the size of the brush. Here, you can change the brush type, spacing, size and opacity of the stoke. You can even turn on (or off) the ability to change the brush size and stroke opacity based on the speed of your finger.

You can undo and redo multiple times, and the app has a great color picker and paint bucket. These controls are positioned along the bottom of the screen, and a single tap will bring up the controls. Yet the real power of this app is in the layers menu, where you can create up to six layers. Each layer can have its own blend mode; there are five different blend modes.

Each of the paintings in the Brushes app is made up of layers. Think of each layer as a transparent sheet with ink on it. When these are stacked together you can see the final painting. You can only work with one layer at a time. For example, one layer can be the background, one can be the main subject, and another could be a special effect. In the layers menu, each of the layers is shown as a box with the active layer surrounded with blue. To access this, tap on the layers menu at the bottom far right of the screen.

Across the top of the layer menu are the layer controls. These are:

- **Transform the active layer** allows you to move a selected layer around.
- **Flip horizontally** flips the layer horizontally.
- **Flip vertically** flips the layer vertically.
- **Eraser** removes content from the layer.
- **Merge** combines the layer with the one below it.
- **Duplicate** copies the current layer.
- **Delete** removes the current layer.
- **Add Layer** creates a new layer.

When you open the layers palette, you can add a new layer, select which layer to draw on, and change the way the layer interacts with those below it. This is known as blend modes in the computer arts, and each mode does something different. You can apply one of the following five blend modes to any of the layers:

Figure 16-5
The Layer menu shows the blend modes and menu choices.

- **Normal** is the default mode and has no effect on the layers below it.
- Choose **Multiply** to make the colors on the lower layer get darker based on the darkness of the art in the Multiplying layer. This is used to darken the painting or parts of the painting.
- **Screen** brightens (lightens) the colors of the underlying layer.
- **Overlay** is a combination of Multiply and Screen. It brightens the lighter colors and darkens the darker colors. This increases the contrast of the artwork.
- **Color** is used to set the hue and saturation of the lower level to the color of the coloring layer. This works great for colorizing artwork.

Each of the layers can have only one blend mode applied at a time.

There is one more feature that I really like. It's that you can place any of your photos into the app as a starting place for your paintings. To import a photo, find the Photo Album button at the top of the screen; it looks like two squares crossing over each other. Tap it and a list of the Photo Albums on your iPad opens. Now just find the image you want in your painting and tap on it.

You can resize and adjust the placement of the photo in your artwork. And each image is placed on a new layer so you can keep adding images until all six layers are used. Then, you can merge the layers and add more photos. My next project is to use this to create a great photo collage.

Inkpad ($4.99)

This app was created by the same geniuses who created the Brushes app. But Inkpad is a vector-based drawing program that's designed specifically for the iPad. It offers users a wide variety of vector drawing tools, including paths, compound paths, images, masks, text and an unlimited number of layers.

Now, since I am not an artist and don't do much vector drawing, I had to ask some artist friends of mine to explain this. But basically, when you draw with vectors, you create paths and then you fill those paths. This is the way that Adobe Illustrator works, and this app does a very nice job.

Start a new drawing by tapping on the (+) sign at the top right corner of the screen. This opens the New Drawing menu, which allows you to pick the size and orientation of your drawing. Then tap the Create button.

When you have opened a new document, the following options appear across the top of the screen.

Figure 16-6
The New Document menu offers size and orientation options for your drawing.

- Tap **Gallery** to get back to the main storage area for your images.

- The **Reset Screen** button resizes the screen to show the full artwork. This is a great way to get back to the full-screen view.

- The **Place an Image** button looks like a little painting. It allows you to put images that are on your iPad into the drawing. Tap this button to access a list of your images. Tap the image you want to place into your drawing, and it will appear in the center of the page. Move the image around the page with one finger. You can use the scale tool to change its size if needed.

- The **Settings** menu icon looks like a little gear. This is where you can set up a grid on your page and turn it on and off. You can also turn on (or off) the ability to Snap to Points, Snap to Edges, and Snap to Grid. You can adjust the size of the grid from 1pt to 100pt. You can also isolate the active layer and run it in outline mode.

- The **Sharing Options** menu looks like a arrow coming out of a box. With this, you can Add (a drawing) to Photo Album, Copy Drawing, Duplicate the Drawing, Print Drawing and Email Drawing. Note that the printing function is only available if you have AirPrint.

To zoom in or out on your drawing, use the standard iOS pinch zooming gestures. This allows you to get in closer to see details or back up for an overall view. You can zoom all the way in to 3200% and out to 10%. Move the image around the screen using two fingers.

Across the bottom of the screen are more tools:

- The **Edit** menu allows you to Select All, Select All on Layer, Deselect All, Cut, Copy, Paste, Duplicate, Duplicate In Place (the copy is placed over the original), and Delete.

- **Arrange** lets you decide the order of the selected items. You can Bring Forward, Bring to Front, Send Backwards, Send to Back, Flip Horizontally, Flip Vertically, Group, Ungroup, Align Left, Align Center, Align Right, Align Top, Align Middle and Align Bottom.

- The **Path** menu allows you to edit the selected path. (Paths are the building blocks of vector artwork.) You can Add Anchor Points, Delete Anchor Points, Join Paths, Combine Paths, Separate Paths, Reverse Path, Direction, Mask and Unmask.

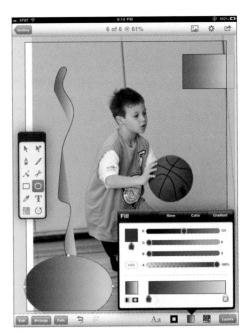

Figure 16-7
The Fill menu shows the gradient options.

- **Undo** removes the most recent change. Your drawing goes back a step each time this is tapped.

- **Redo** re-creates a step that you previously deleted.

- **Font** is where you can change the text treatment used in the drawing, including the size and justification.

- Use the **Stroke** menu to adjust the formatting of the stroke, including the color and transparency. It also allows you to adjust the end points and size (from 1pt to 100pt).

- **Fill** is where you can adjust the color, transparency and type of fill in your artwork. Use this menu to set the color or gradient and the transparency level.

- The **Swatch** panel is used to save colors and gradients that you want to reuse. Tap

249

the (+) sign to save the current stroke and fill as a swatch.

- **Layers** are the transparent sheets on which your art is created. You can add a new layer, select a layer to use, and turn off a layer's visibility by tapping the icon that looks like an eye (next to the layer). This hides the selected layer. Anyone who works with Adobe products on the computer will feel really comfortable with these layers.

I know, this is a cool app, right? Well, the best features were saved for last. It's the Tool Palette. This is where you'll find the actual tools you can use to create your artwork. Anyone who's used Photoshop or Illustrator will recognize these tools.

The first thing to know is that you can move the Tool Palette just by holding your finger on the black bar at the top and sliding it around the screen. Put it in a place on the screen that doesn't interfere with your work.

The Tool Palette

The twelve tools available here are used to create your artwork.

Figure 16-8

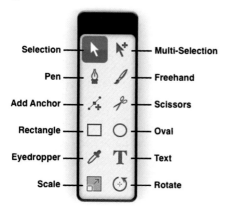

Selection — Multi-Selection
Pen — Freehand
Add Anchor — Scissors
Rectangle — Oval
Eyedropper — Text
Scale — Rotate

- The **Selection** tool activates a single object when you tap on it in the drawing. Anything that's already selected is de-selected when a new selection is made.

- **Multi-Selection** is used to select multiple objects at the same time. When you use this and tap on the drawing, it will select an object but not de-select the previously selected object. And if you tap on a selected object, it will de-select it.

- The **Pen Tool** is the main way to make paths. Tap once on your drawing to add a point; multiple taps will create a polygon with sharp corners. To make a curve, just tap and drag. Control handles appear on curves. By moving these, you can control the size and shape of the curve.

- Use the **Freehand Tool** (looks like a small paintbrush) to draw freeform paths.

- **Add Anchor Point** allows you to add points to any path after it has been created. These points allow you to adjust the shape of the object. First select the path and then tap Add Anchor Point.

- The **Scissors Tool** cuts existing paths, splitting them into separate paths, which allows you to edit the separate parts individually.

- Use the **Rectangle Tool** to easily create rectangles in your drawing. Just tap and hold on the screen, and then drag your finger to create the rectangle.

- The **Oval Tool** makes it easy to create ovals in your drawing. Just tap and hold on the screen and then drag your finger to create the oval.

- Tap the **Eyedropper** anywhere on the drawing, and it samples the style of the area you picked. This allows you to use that same style on other objects, so you can recreate elements in your drawing.

- Use the **Text Tool** to place words in your drawing. Just tap and drag to create a text field. You can now use the keyboard to enter the text you want in your drawing

- The **Scale Tool** can transform an object in your drawing but retain relative dimensions. This allows you to create different elements that look the same but are different sizes.

- Tap the **Rotate Tool** to place a pivot point on which you can swivel an object. You can move your pivot point to gain greater control over an object.

Check out the four examples of artwork that this app comes with to see what can be done. It's very impressive.

MUSIC APPS

I know a lot of great musicians—many through my job as a concert photographer—but I have no musical ability myself. You'd think that after listening to so much music and watching so many shows that I might have picked up a sliver of timing and rhythm. But sadly, I haven't. That doesn't mean I can't create music though! And with the iPad, I can do it without spending a fortune on instruments and sound equipment.

There are apps, like GarageBand and djay, that are great for creating music or music mixes on your iPad.

GarageBand ($4.99)

When Steve Jobs took the stage on March 2, 2011, to announce the iPad 2, he also announced two new apps. One of these is the iPad version of GarageBand. (The other is the updated iMovie for iPad 2 and iPhone, which is covered in Chapter 4.) The GarageBand app is the most fun I've had with my iPad … even though I truly have no musical ability.

It's also one of those apps that really shows off what the iPad can do.

Smart Instruments
The stuff that makes GarageBand usable for those of us with limited (or no) musical talent are the Smart Instruments: drums, bass, keyboards and guitar. Each of these four instruments works in a slightly different way, but the technology allows you to use them to create music that actually sounds good. Have

TIP

The GarageBand app is really big, about 369 MB, so it won't download over 3G due to the data cap. Instead, download over Wi-Fi or to the computer (and then sync to the iPad).

Figure 16-9
To use the Smart Drum instrument, just place the pieces where you want them. Voila! You're off and running.

I mentioned that it even allows the musically challenged to make music that sounds good?

- **Smart Drums** allows you to play the drums well … without actually having any rhythm. Just position the drums on the smart pad. Your placement controls the volume and the complexity of the rhythm. Experiment by moving the drums around, or tap on the dice in the lower left corner to get a random setup. You can also change the type of drums you are playing by tapping on the drum kit on the left. Garage-Band has six different drum kits: three traditional and three drum machines.

- **Smart Bass** is comprised of four different basses from which you can choose. Play your bass by chords or by notes. And if you need some help, just turn on Autoplay.

- **Smart Keyboard** offers four different choices for your keyboarding needs. Choose a Grand Piano or a Classic Rock Organ, Electric Piano or Smooth Clav. And turn on Autoplay to let the app help you out. Each of the instruments has different controls. For example, you can control the rotation of the horn; you can adjust the Classic Rock Organ from slow to fast; or turn on Sustain. You can also control the Auto Wah and Phaser in the Smooth Clav.

- **Smart Guitar:** If you've ever wanted to play an Acoustic Guitar or maybe a Hard Rock Guitar (which looks suspiciously like a Gibson), you can live the dream here! Strum the cords up and down, or just tap a chord to play each one separately. Or, you can turn on Autoplay and pick a cord; the app will handle the rest. My favorite part of using this app is watching the strings bend as they play … just like a real guitar.

Figure 16-10
To play the touch drum instrument, just tap.

Touch Instruments

There is another set of instruments in GarageBand, and it's the Touch Instruments. They're aimed for people with a bit of musical talent.

The two touch instruments included are drums and keyboards. You can play these instruments by tapping on the iPad screen. The app knows if you're tapping hard or softly, and the instruments respond accordingly. The touch instruments have the same controls as the smart instruments—just no auto mode.

The really fun part is using the touch drums. You're playing a virtual drum kit. Tapping on the edge of the drum makes a very different sound than banging in the middle. It's just like a real drum kit … but way less expensive and much smaller!

Playing the touch keyboards is like having eight different keyboards, including the Grand Piano and Classic Rock Organ as well as a Whirly and Heavy Metal Organ. When you pick the organ, you can control the draw bars … just like you would on a real organ.

Figure 16-11

This guitar amp has the help tags turned on and a stomp box controller activated.

Others Tools

There are three more ways to create music in the GarageBand app. The first is for those out there who actually play guitar.

* **Guitar Amp** allows you to plug in your real electric guitar to the iPad. You'll need an adaptor. Check out the Apogee JAM Guitar Input ($99.00), which has a ¼-inch input for a guitar or bass and a control knob for easily managing the input. And once the guitar is plugged in, you can use eight different combinations in each of four categories. For each choice, there are eight different amps. That's a lot of musical options! You

can also add up to four stomp boxes to make your own custom pedal board. Just tap on the pedal icon on the top right, and then add, remove or adjust the pedals to your liking. Tune your guitar by tapping on the tuning fork. Get that axe in tune!

* Use the **Audio Recorder** to record vocals or other sounds into GarageBand. Choose between the built-in microphone or an external microphone. Just watch the meter and make sure it doesn't go into the red too much. If it does, your sound will likely be distorted on the recording.

* The **Sampler** allows you to record a sound and then play it back using the onscreen keyboard. The GarageBand app comes with some samples built-in, but it's easy to create your own. Just tap on the New Sample button and then tap the Start button. Record the sound, and then tap the Stop button. Your sample is now ready to be used.

Create a Recording

Playing a tune or just playing around is one thing, but GarageBand allows you to do much more. It's an eight track-recording studio. Follow these directions to get a good idea of how to create a song with this cool app.

1. Open GarageBand and pick an instrument—any instrument.

2. Tap the My Songs button on the top left of the screen.

3. A screen will appear. This is where the songs you create are stored. If you have no songs, then the following message will appear: "No songs exist in the My Songs browser. Tap here to start a new song."

4. Tap on the message to return to the instrument browser.

5. Pick any instrument to start playing.

6. Tap on the puzzle piece icon at the top left part of the screen. This allows you to adjust the song section length. I like to set the section length to Automatic so that the length is not limited to eight bars (the default).

7. Next, tap on the Instrument Settings icon. (It looks like a set of three sliders.)

8. Here, depending on the instrument you're using, you can adjust the track volume, the track panning, echo level and reverb level as well as the quantization. You can merge recordings and control the master effects here, too. The Master Effects controls the Echo and Reverb for the whole track. (Depending on which instrument is used, options may vary.)

9. Set the song settings by tapping on the wrench icon on the top right. This opens the Song Settings menu, giving you control over the Metronome, Count In and Sound. You can also set the tempo and the key here.

10. Now you're ready to play. So tap the Record button and go for it.

11. Tap the Stop button when you're done laying down a track.

12. Listen to the track by tapping the Play button in the top middle of the screen.

13. You can also look at the track in the mixing board view, accessed via the icon on the top of the screen that looks like a set of parallel horizontal lines. Find your newly recorded track. More on mixing a little later.

14. Tap on the Instrument button to get back to the instrument view. This is the button next to the track view.

15. You can now lay down another track using the same instrument or any of the others.

16. To create a new track, switch to another instrument, check your settings, tap Record and start playing. You'll hear your previously recorded tracks playing as you lay down your new track.

17. You can have a total of eight tracks.

18. When you're done recording your masterpiece, just tap on the My Songs button.

19. Your song will be saved and accessed from the My Songs menu.

TIP

Note that you can access the Help menu from the Song Settings menu, which is very useful for learning about all the bells and whistles of this app.

Edit a Recording

Edit your song using the mixing controls. From the My Songs menu, tap on the song you want to edit. If it's in the instrument view, tap on the track view to see the individual tracks in your song.

Swipe your finger from left to right on the left part of the screen to open the track controls. For each of the tracks, you can mute the whole track or send that track to the headphone jack. You can also control the volume of each track to get a better mix. Double tap on the track itself to Cut, Copy, Delete, Loop or Skip the track.

Adjust the placement of the clip and the start and stop points by using the handles on each end of the selected clip. If you have less than eight clips, you can use the (+) sign on the bottom to add another track.

When you're done editing, just tap on the My Songs button to save your song and get back to the My Songs page. Once there and with a song selected, you can now change the name of your song by tapping once on the name and entering a new one.

Figure 16-12
Take a peek at track editing on GarageBand with the help tags turned on.

Export the song by either sending it to iTunes or e-mailing it. If there are songs in iTunes, you can import them into the app. There aren't too many options here for formatting the songs though.

Right now, when you e-mail the song, it's in the .m4a (MPEG-4) format. When you export to iTunes, you can either export in the iTunes AAC format or in the native GarageBand format, which allows you to edit the GarageBand songs that were created on the iPad with the Garage Band application available for the Mac. Just tap on the (+) sign to start a new song or duplicate the current song. You can also delete the song if it doesn't meet your standards. (I have deleted a lot of songs.)

For $4.99, this app is one of the most polished pieces of programming that I've ever used, and I recommend it highly if you play music or don't play music or want to give the kids something to do. And definitely get it if you have dreams of creating the ultimate rock song! (I'm just kidding about the last part … kinda.)

djay ($19.99)

Did you ever want to be a DJ and try your hand at mixing songs? Well, this app lets you do it as if you really have two turntables. Between GarageBand and the djay app, I've been having a great time creating weird music on my iPad for weeks now. Yes, I'm driving my wife crazy.

The layout of the djay app is two turntables with mixing controls spread around the screen. Each of the turntables has a button that will open any of the songs on the iPad. This means that I can mix Billy Idol and Steel Pulse or The Barenaked Ladies with Bruce Hornsby. It's no wonder I'm driving people

Figure 16-13
This djay layout shows two turntables and the mixing controls.

Figure 16-14
The djay app can record your output. Just tap the Record button.

nuts with this app. But while it might seem like a toy, this is a really powerful program. Not only can you mix the tunes, you can *record* your mixes.

Here are some tips for getting the most out of the djay app.

- You can preview the next song using headphones, but you need a 3.5mm stereo to mono split adaptor. To get the right parts, go to **http://www.algoriddim.com/ support/djay-ipad#faq156** and follow the recommendations. With the right equipment, you can cue songs through the headphones and send the main output to speakers. The master output goes to the left channel, while the cue output goes to the right channel.

- With a tap of the Record button, you can record the output of your mixes. Tap it again to stop recording. The recordings are available in the Apps tab under file sharing as .aif files when you attach the iPad to iTunes.

- Tap on the gear icon (located under the Record button) to bring up the main djay

settings. This is where you can control the Master Volume and turn Split Output on or off. There is also a settings menu here that lets you fine tune the following:

- **Transitions:** You can adjust the style of the transition from Standard to Backspin, Brake, Reverse and Random. You can also set the duration from 0 seconds to 30 seconds. You can turn the Auto-Sync BPM (beats per minute) on or off.

- **Speed Slider:** Adjust the Range to 8%, 10%, 25%, 50% or 75%. You can invert the Speed Slider and turn Fine Adjust on and off here, too.

- **Song Loading:** From here, set the song to play immediately, jump to a queue point or reset the EQ when a song loads.

- **Vinyl:** The turns the artwork on or off and turns the Show Tape Marker on/off.

- **Library:** This allows you to turn on a full-screen view of your song library instead of a small pop-up window.

After you've loaded a couple of songs, press the Play buttons to get the turntables spinning. Tap the Play buttons again to stop them

Use the controls on either side of the turntables to adjust the beats per minute, which allows you to speed up or slow down the music to keep the songs matched.

Individual volume controls for the turntables are on the top right and top left. Across the bottom is the cue point settings, which allow you to loop and jump to a certain point on any song. Then there is the mixing slider, which controls what turntable is being used. And right above that is the Automix, which allows you to leave the iPad in charge of your music. (This works really well.)

Now go ahead and start playing some music. Then just use your finger on the turntable to scratch and mix as you would with real vinyl!

This is just a small sampling of the apps that can turn a boring afternoon into an enjoyable time with your iPad. Often, I'd rather do something creative than mindlessly play the latest game. So pick a category that appeals to you and look through the apps available on the iPad. You'll likely find a free version or at least a lite version of most apps to check them out. Spend some time to enjoy your iPad in a new way.

17

Sports

The Skim

The iPad is a real treat for all types of sports fans. The device allows you to follow live sporting events, find and watch highlights, and track all the sporting news you can imagine.

All the major sporting leagues have realized that their fans are using the iPad to follow along, so individual sports-related apps have started to proliferate the App Store. These include apps by Major League Baseball, the National Basketball Association and the National Hockey League. Right now, there is no National Football League app, but I hope there'll be one before the 2011 season kicks off. If not, there are alternatives covered in this chapter.

There are also apps that allow you to follow sports in general. And the best of these is offered by a leader in sports news: Entertainment Sports Programming Network ... better known as ESPN.

ESPN SCORECENTER XL ($FREE)
The one sports app that you'll definitely want to get is the ESPN Score-Center XL iPad app. It's free, and it has all the latest sports news, including scores, highlight clips and commentary. Best of all, you can get info about your favorite teams without having to wait. You can even have the app send push notifications to you. Set up these notifications in the Settings app anytime you want.

Figure 17-1
The ESPN ScoreCenter app offers tons of information on the front page.

Set Up Your Teams

The ESPN ScoreCenter app makes it really easy to follow your teams—no matter what sport. Actually, this is only true if the team plays baseball, basketball, cricket, football, ice hockey, rugby or soccer. But setting up teams to follow is really simple:

1. Open the ScoreCenter app.

2. Tap the MyTeams button (top).

3. Tap Add a Team.

4. Tap the sport your team plays.

5. Tap the league in which the team plays.

6. Tap on your team.

7. You'll be asked if you want to add alerts for this team. Tap yes or no.

8. Now pick the Alert Type Preferences, if available:

    • Game Start on/off

    • Each Scoring Play on/off

    • Each Quarter and Final on/off

    • Final on/off

9. Tap Done on the top of the Alert Details window.

10. You can now add another team if you want.

Choose Your Sports

You can also add sports to follow. Right next to the myTeams buttons is a mySports button that allows you to add a sport. There is a wide range of sports to choose from, including lacrosse, combat sports, tennis and even water polo. Once you've added a sport, the Settings window will open to give you access to the Settings menu. It looks just like a little gear next to the mySports button. Menu options are described below.

• **Sign into myESPN** is where you sign in so that your data is synced to myESPN. If you don't have an ESPN account, you can create one here. And because ESPN knows that we might forget our passwords, they even have an *I forgot my password* button.

• **mySports** reveals a list of sports you've listed under mySports and allows you to delete a sport or add new ones.

• **myTeams** shows the teams you follow and allows you to edit the list.

• **myAlerts** is where you can set up and edit your myTeams alerts.

• If you turn on Show myTeams first, the app will … yep, show information on your teams before general sports news, and automatically turn off the next button: *Show Top Events first.*

• Setting **Show Top Events first** to yes will automatically turn off the previous button, *Show myTeams first,* and you'll get the top sports news before information on your teams.

• Use **Send Feedback** to tell ESPN what you think of this app. The developers even give you a phone number to reach them—something I don't see much anymore.

Figure 17-2
Tapping on myTeams gives you the latest news and scores for the teams you follow.

- It's really great that ESPN includes **Terms of Use**, but it's impossible to read the information due to the formatting of the app. Hopefully this will be fixed at some point in the future.

- The **Privacy Policy** suffers from the same problem as the *Terms of Use*. It's impossible to actually read the policy. Let's hope this will be fixed in a future edition of this app.

Now that the app is set up, let's find out what the app actually does.

Enjoy the App
The ESPN app is divided into sections:
- Controls (across the top of the screen)
- Scores
- News and Video
- News Steamer (across the bottom)

Using the controls, you can change between the Top Events for Today, myTeams and myS-ports. One thing I find really slick about this app is that the videos play right in the app. At the tap of a button, the video can

fill the screen. Tapping on any of the scores will change the main window and give you Recaps, Play by Play and even the full box Scores for a game.

Every sports fan should grab this app, because it's good and it's free … and, in my book, that is a winning combination.

MLB AT BAT 11 FOR THE iPAD ($14.99)
If you are a baseball fan, then this is the app for you. The only downside is that it's $14.99 and only good for one season. So you basically have to pay $15 per season to get baseball news on your iPad. And if you want it on your iPhone as well, you'll need to buy a separate app that costs another $14.99.

The first thing you'll notice when you start this app is that you have to agree to the Terms and Conditions. But since you've already purchased the app, there really is no point in not accepting them. I actually read them, and they cover the basics. But since they're

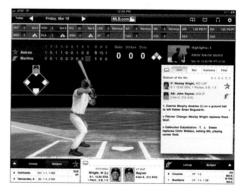

Figure 17-3
The interface of MLB at Bat 11 for the iPad is really nice. It even switches the batters stance for left- and right-hand batters.

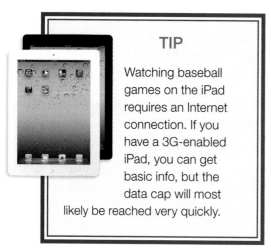

TIP

Watching baseball games on the iPad requires an Internet connection. If you have a 3G-enabled iPad, you can get basic info, but the data cap will most likely be reached very quickly.

available when you first run the app, I suggest you read them as well. This is a very well-made app with more information than I could ever use, but I'm a casual baseball fan—not a diehard.

One feature that I find to be a real winner here is the ability to watch baseball right on the iPad. The app will need to check your location and make sure that you're not in a blocked-out area, but what a great idea for the fan on the road!

If you're a baseball fan and want full coverage of all the games ... and don't mind the price, this app really has one of the slickest interfaces I've seen.

On a side note, the MLB has made a lot of old games available in the iTunes Store. You can watch your favorite games for past seasons on your iPad; and, if you're a serious fan, you can download the Games of the Year for a whole season. For example, the MLB Games of the Year for 2009 includes 63 games for $125.37. This might be a great way to pass the time between seasons.

Figure 17-4

Highlights from past seasons are available in the iTunes Store on the iPad

NBA GAME TIME COURTSIDE ($FREE)

For basketball fans, the NBA created this free app that allows you to watch video highlights. It also gives you a live court view, updated standings and player performance information.

The NBA Game Time Courtside app has a great layout, showing the whole court with the players' positions and scoring in a really intuitive way. What I really like is the ability to go back after a game to these how the game was played. The app provides scores for the whole game at a glance, but it can be broken down into quarters. You can also get a graphical review of where shots were taken and a really nice breakdown of where points were scored.

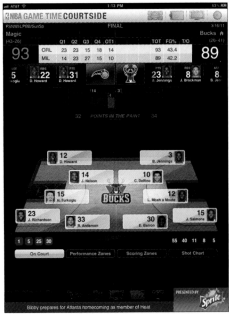

Figure 17-5

The opening screen of the NBA app shows the games that are scheduled for today.

THE NFL

There is no NFL app, but there are two other apps that can provide your football fix. As well, some teams are starting to make apps for the iPhone … and hopefully the iPad in the future.

Sunday Ticket (from DirecTV) ($FREE) This app allows you to catch every NFL game no matter where you are—even if it's nowhere near a TV. This sounds great, right? Well, there are some restrictions. Actually there are quite a few restrictions.

The first is that some NFL games are blacked out, and what you can and cannot see is based on your billing zip code. Also, Sunday night, Monday, Thursday and Saturday games are not part of the plan and will not be streamed. And I'm sorry to those readers who

Figure 17-6

The NBA Game Time Courtside interface shows not only the players and positions, but also percentages for where points were scored.

are located outside of the United States: This app won't work for you.

But here is the biggest drawback: You have to have DirecTV setup to use this app, and you have to pay for the NFL Sunday Ticket package, which costs approximately $300. Plus, you have to pay an extra $50 for the ability to watch games on the iPad. Yup, that's approximately $350 you'll need to pay for the ability to watch football on the iPad.

Of course, if you already pay for the DirecTV football package, then this might be a great option, especially if you're not going to be able to watch some of the games on your home TV. But this isn't necessarily a great app for every football fan.

CBS Sports Pro Football ($FREE)

I started using this app last year when I realized that the NFL website was not showing scores on my iPad. The website uses Flash components for the score section of the website, and the iPad cannot access Flash content.

This app is the perfect way to keep up with all the scores, plays and games as they happen. Now, while this doesn't have some of the bells and whistles or live video streaming that some other sports apps have, it does have a ton of information that's updated quickly ... and it's free.

Oh, and keep in mind that you can enter your CBSSports.com username and password to access your Fantasy Football teams. We'll cover some apps for fantasy leagues in a minute; here's the first.

To set up a fantasy team, go to CBSSports.com (via Safari on your iPad) and sign up for an account. Once you've signed up, you can

Figure 17-7
This CBS Sports Pro Football interface shows the game between New Orleans and Baltimore. New Orleans lost this one.

track your team through the season. The CBS Sports Pro Football app needs an Internet connection to run. It seems to run slower when connected via 3G than Wi-Fi; and there's a fee to use the 3G, so that part of the app isn't free.

NHL GAMECENTER 2010 ($FREE / $9.99)

The National Hockey League has two apps available for the iPad: a free version and a paid one. The free version gives you scores, stats, photos, schedules, standings, news, player profiles, the Ice Tracker, and play-by-play info.

But if you want more, and don't mind spending the $9.99, then you can get the premium version of the app. The upgrade provides the features of the free version as well as in-game video highlights and live game radio, which allows you to listen to the game. And since is the iPad 2 is multitasking-enabled, you can listen to the game while using the iPad to check your e-mail or browse the Internet.

Figure 17-8
The NHL GameCenter main page offers lots of information at the tap of a finger.

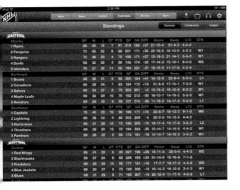

Figure 17-9
The NHL GameCenter 2010 app makes it really easy for hockey fans to get the latest scores and standings.

Both apps allow you to upgrade to the LIVE version, which is only available as an in-app purchase. It's $69.99 in the premium app and $79.99 in the free app. The live version allows you to receive live game video.

The NHL app is well-designed. The main buttons across the top of the screen give you quick access to the Main Page, News, Scores, Standings, Allstar News and More. When you press the More button, you can access

info on Teams, Players, Winter Classic and Heritage Classic.

Next to this menu bar are four more controls. The one that looks like a filmstrip allows you to show or hide the current schedule and scores. The next button looks just like a small television, and next to that is a headphone button. This is where you can purchase or log into GameCenter Live. The last icon is a small gear that gives you access to the Options menu. Basically, this is the place for the Terms of Service and the FAQ. Not too many options to address there.

FANTASY SPORTS LEAGUES

A huge number of sports fans participate in fantasy leagues. They pick players from a variety of teams to create their version of an ideal team, as much as possible. Then, they compete against other teams. This is a lot of work for participants, but the iPad can make it easier to create a team and keep track of it over a full season.

As I'm writing this, the 2010 NFL season is over, and the only football news is what's happening in the dispute between owners and players. But that doesn't mean the fantasy football players out there shouldn't be preparing for the 2011 season.

Fantasy Football Cheatsheet '10 ($1.99)

To get going, the first app to check out is the Fantasy Football Cheatsheet. Right now, the app features the 2010 season; but it's been around since 2008, so I believe a new version will be released in plenty of time for your 2011 draft.

This app gives you a ton of information, and it does so really fast. It offers recommendations on which players you should start and who's injured. And it tries to give good advice for

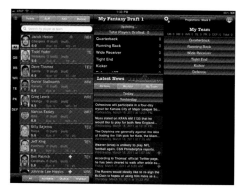

Figure 17-7
The front page of Fantasy Football
Cheatsheet '10 is packed with
information.

the whole season. For the extreme player out there, this app even allows you to create picks for multiple drafts and follow your team(s) with its dedicated My Team view.

The Fantasy Football Cheatsheet app is designed for both the iPad and iPhone, and it sells for a whopping $1.99. I know some fantasy football players, and they spend a lot of time working on their teams … and strategizing drafts and trades. So if a $1.99 app can help with all that, then I'm thinking it's a small price to pay.

Fantasy Baseball Monster '11 HD

This app started out on the iPhone, but there is an iPad version now that takes advantage of the bigger screen. It allows you to manage your Yahoo! and ESPN fantasy baseball teams in one place. You can quickly edit your lineups, trade players, and even read and post to message boards through the app.

The first time you run the Fantasy Baseball Monster '11 HD app, you'll be asked to enter your login information for your Yahoo! and ESPN accounts. So before you purchase the

app, you might want to set up those accounts.

Other Fantasy Options

There are apps available for fantasy hockey and fantasy basketball that are created by the same company that makes the Fantasy Baseball Monster app: Bignoggins Productions LLC. These apps come in a FREE LITE version as well as a $2.99 full version.

There is also a $4.99 app called Fantasy Monster Pro HD, which allows you to control your Yahoo! and ESPN fantasy leagues for football, baseball, basketball and hockey. So if you play all the fantasy sports leagues, then this is a great app for you to consolidate your work.

OTHER SPORTS APPS

There are a crazy number of sports-related apps available for the iPad. They range from Bowling Rules—which gives you the rules for the PBA, NCAA and USBC bowling leagues—to the very cool Coach WhiteBoard and Coach WhiteBoard Pro—which allow basketball coaches to use the iPad as a coaching aid. A nice collection of college sports apps created by SilverTree Technology are also available; they cover everything from SEC baseball to Pac 10 football, and they come in two flavors: a Lite (free) version and a $.99 version. There are even apps for the Cricket World Cup and for the English Premier League. If you're into sports, then the iPad absolutely has you covered. Game on …

Education

The Skim

A Learning Device • Free Tools • Preschool • Elementary School
Junior High • High School • College

When the iPad came out, many people looked at it and thought of the educational capabilities it offered. Is this crazy? Can the iPad be used as an educational tool? Apple believes that it can.

Is this practical? Can teachers and students use the iPad for educational purposes, or is it just a big toy? Well, I believe wholeheartedly that the iPad can be an invaluable tool for high school and college education, and it can be used to enhance education at all levels.

This chapter covers a wide variety of apps that apply to the learning needs of different ages and educational levels. After digging deeper into how the iPad is being used as a learning device and peeking at some free educational tools, we'll look at programs available for young kids and work our way up to college-level students.

The use of these age-based categories though should not imply that the apps have to stay in a certain group. For example, the Chem Equations app can be used in junior high or college, and the TED app is great for everyone, except perhaps young kids. This type of organization is just a guide for those who might especially benefit from the various apps that we'll explore.

DONATE YOUR iPAD

If you're one of those folks who bought a new iPad 2 and are wondering what to do with your original iPad, Apple has a suggestion: Donate the iPad to the Teach for America's iPads for Classrooms program. The Teach for America organization will take the donated iPad and make sure it ends up with a teacher in a low-income community. For more information on Teach for America, check out its website, **http://www.teachforamerica.org.**

A LEARNING DEVICE

Technology has been used by students for a long time. Anyone remember those black and white screens of the Commodore in computer lab? Well, ever since there have been computers and laptops, students have been using them. So what makes the iPad especially good for students? How does it beat the traditional laptop? Here are some thoughts:

- Size/ Portability: The iPad's size makes it easy to use in the classroom, since it's really the size of a textbook—a very thin textbook. It's easy to take notes on the iPad and carry it around.

- Internet Access: The iPad can use Wi-Fi to connect to the Internet. And if you have a 3G model, you can connect to the Internet anywhere there's a cell signal. This means that an iPad user can connect to the Internet just about anywhere at any time. This is something that a laptop just can't do without a slew of extras.

- Battery Life: The battery life on this machine is great. An iPad can last a full day on a single charge, so students don't need to sit near an outlet or drag around a bag of cables.

- Accessibility: The accessibility features of the iPad were covered in Chapter 1, and these options make the iPad usable … right out of the box … by students with disabilities.

Validating the high educational functionality of the iPad is covered in recent news, which reported that schools are starting to use the iPad seriously in the classroom. For example, the University of Notre Dame is doing a study on how e-readers will be integrated into the classroom. A project management class will be the first to go without paper textbooks and use only the iPad. There are also pilot programs to use the iPad in classrooms for deaf and hearing-impaired students, and schools like Roslyn High School on Long Island handed out iPads to 47 students and teachers to see if the iPad could replace the traditional textbooks.

Not all of the studies showing eBook textbooks have gotten the best results. For starters, many of the students were in the habit of actually writing in textbooks, marking passages and bookmarking the physical book—things that are not so easy to do on the electronic versions. But as these studies continue and changes are made, it's lear to me that electronic eBook readers and ablet computers will gradually become part of the education process.

FREE TOOLS

was always the type of student who learned better if I spent some time rewriting my notes after class. Even now, when I go to a photography workshop or Photoshop training, I come home and type up my notes. I then convert my notes to PDFs and sync them to my iPad so they're accessible in iBooks. It's a great way to keep track of notes and PDFs for a class.

The iPad comes equipped with other tools, too, that can help students better manage information and time.

iPad Calendar

Using the iPad Calendar to keep track of assignments and due dates works great, especially when you set alarms. With this help, you never have to worry about missing a due date or turning in an assignment late … as long as you actually do the work.

Dropbox

Use Dropbox to make sure that you never leave that important file on the wrong computer. Since you can access your Dropbox anywhere there's a computer (by going to www.dropbox.com), you don't even need your iPad around to access your files. But the combination of the iPad/ Dropbox/ and Internet connection means that you can never say you left the file in the wrong place. See Chapter 13 for details on using Dropbox.

iTunes U Store

There is one more built-in educational tool that you should take some time to explore, and that is the iTunes U Store. This is the free educational part of the iTunes Store. To access it on the iPad, just tap on iTunes. Then tap on the iTunes U button that's located on the bottom of the screen. There's a huge amount of information here and it is all free.

iTunes U content ranges from lectures by MIT professors on the Fundamentals of Aerospace Engineering to the Georgia Department of Education videos on learning

TESTING WITH THE iPAD

Companies are beginning to see the advantages of using the iPad in educational settings. One of the leaders in this field is Lan-School Technologies. This company has announced a new version of the LanSchool iPad application, which allows teachers to create tests on their computers and to even send out those tests to student iPads. Students can answer the questions on their iPad and the answers will be shown in real time on the teacher's device. The test questions can be true/ false, multiple choice or short answer, and they can include graphics. School is changing. For more on this, check out **www.lanschool.com.**

math. I am partial to the MoMA (The Museum of Modern Art) section, which gives overviews of the current exhibitions and has MoMA Audio for all age groups that describe the artists and works of art.

PRESCHOOL

I'm always amazed at how quickly and adeptly my nephew's fingers fly across the iPad screen … and how intuitive he finds the touch screen controls. I mean, he's only five. Indeed, it turns out that kids find the iPad really easy to use. So why not put that to good use?

ABBY MONKEY - Animal Games for Kids ($FREE/ $1.99)

App developer CFC s.r.o has twenty different apps available for the iPad. I explored the free and paid versions of the ABBY MONKEY – Animal Games for Kids. And my biggest complaint with both versions is that the opening screen shows eight very colorful buttons for eight other apps, making it very easy for parents to see what's available … but also making it much too easy for kids to see what else they want—instead of encouraging them to enjoy the app they just got.

And by tapping on any of these buttons, the app closes in order to open the App Store … conveniently right to the page that allows you to purchase the other apps. Great marketing, I guess, but this gets very annoying when your kid keeps pressing the wrong button.

On the free version, there is also a very annoying Buy Full Version button on the bottom of each page. The graphics are great and the ideas behind the games are fun … that is, the *game* is fun. The free version only has one of the games. You have to buy the full version to get all four. The full version of the app is $1.99, so if your child seems to like the

Figure 18-1
The opening screen of the ABBY MONKEY - Animal Games for Kids app allows you to easily go get more apps by the developer.

Figure 18-2
The games use bright colors and big graphics … perfect for small hands.

free version, then (s)he'll probably like the paid version.

I should make it clear here that the free version is more like a trial … to see if you want to spend the $1.99 for the full version. For this I applaud the developer. Too many times, a purchased app goes unused because it isn't what you really wanted. But you have no way to know this until you've paid for the app.

The opening screen of the ABBY MONKEY Animal Games for Kids app allows you to easily go get more apps by the developer.

The four games that come in the full version of the software are:

Matching Pictures

Bingo!

Animatch

Find Me

Each one works to improve animal vocabulary. Most of the games encourage kids to match animal graphics with their names.

ELEMENTARY SCHOOL

Math is tough, at least it is for me; but I learned early on that if I wanted to get that degree in computer science, I was going to have to learn and use math … a lot. Wish I had some of these tools available when I was trying to understand math facts.

MathBoard ($FREE/ $4.99)

MathBoard offers math quizzes to help kids practice math. The app makes it easy to practice and to learn. And it's designed for all ages … from kindergarten though elementary school.

Try this app for free by downloading the MathBoard Addition app, which gives you just the addition section of the app for free. If you like it, then you can spend the whopping $4.99 for the full version. Kidding aside, I know that $4.99 doesn't seem like much, but every purchase counts in today's economy, so being able to try before you buy is a great way to show your customers a little respect … and convey confidence in product performance.

The full version of the MathBoard app covers addition, subtraction, multiplication and division as well as squares, cubes and square roots.

Figure 18-3
Here is the MathBoard opening page. I love how it looks like an old-fashioned black board. The screen is easy to read and tapping Play will take you right into a math quiz.

When you open the app, it's divided into four sections.

• On the left is the results column.

• On the right is the main quiz screen.

• At the bottom left is the history area.

• On the bottom right are settings.

The Settings area is divided into the following choices:

• **Operator Types** allows you to pick which operators (addition, subtraction, multiplication, division, squares, cubes or square roots) are used in the quiz.

273

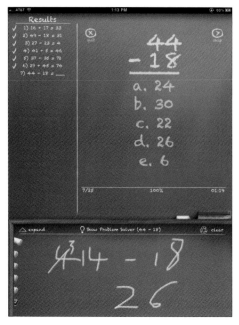

Figure 18-4

The MathBoard quiz page has a scratch area on the bottom to show your work.

- Tap **Problems** to decide what type of questions are presented and how many. You can choose to get multiple choice or fill-in-the-blank questions.
- **Number Range** allows you to choose the minimum and maximum numbers—from -9999 to 9999—that are used in the problems. You can also select a required number that will be in all the questions (in case the student is having a problem with the number 3, for instance).
- **Digit Limit** lets you to set the minimum and maximum upper digits that are used in division, so that the answer is challenging enough but doesn't go on forever.
- Tap **Time** to set the quiz as a time-elapsed quiz or a time-allowed quiz.

- **Extras:** Here are the addition, subtraction and multiplication tables as well as the problem solvers for addition, subtraction, multiplication and division.
- **More from Pala Software** connects you to more offerings by this app's developers.

When you start the quiz, the screen changes. The top half shows the quiz results and the question, while the bottom half is a scratch area where you can show your work. Just use your finger to write in the area. It works great

JUNIOR HIGH

When I was in junior high, Pluto was still a planet. And now there are some great apps for those interested in our solar system. I explored one that costs $13.99 and another that's free.

Solar System for iPad ($13.99)

When this app opens, all the planets, moons and other astral bodies that are explained in this app are visible. Just click on any one of them to get started. That will open a page with information about the selected object.

From here, use the navigation controls across the bottom to check out the data about that object. You can also:

- View a gallery of images of the object.
- Slide the rocket ship across a distance chart to pick another object.
- Tap on a button to go to the previous page
- Tap Home to get back to the opening screen.
- Tap the Back button to return to the page you were on previously.
- Tap the Next button to bring up more pages about the current object.

When you're looking at the main page of items in our galaxy, notice the Orrery button.

Figure 18-5
On the opening page to the Solar System app, tap on any of the pictures to access that solar body's page.

Figure 18-6
The information page for Planet Earth shows its position in the solar system. The app navigation tools are positioned across the bottom of the screen with the main space devoted to information about the planet.

This shows the motion of the planets in relation to each other, and you can control the speed. Keep in mind that the developers of the app took some liberties with the size and speed of the planets to make it possible to actually see them all. You can also access this feature right on the Home page of the app by tapping on the Orrery button (top right).

The view from the main page keeps the sun in the middle of the screen and has the planets rotating around it. Tap on any of the planets to focus, and use the iOS pinch-to-zoom functions to zoom in and out of the screen.

The same people who developed the Elements app that I cover in the High School section (next) created this app. The company does a great job on these apps. And while this one is smaller than the Elements app, it is still a hefty 843 MB, so there is no way you can download it over 3G. You'll need to access the Internet via Wi-Fi to download this app.

NASA HD App ($FREE)
This app, created by NASA, is free. It includes basic information about our solar

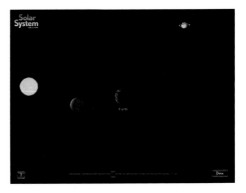

Figure 18-7
The Orrery view shows Earth in the center of the screen.

system and has some of the best photographs, which come from NASA's extensive collection.

The collection of photographs is located under the Tab NASA IOTD, which … unless you already know what it stands for … can be a little confusing. NASA IOTD stands for the NASA Image Of The Day. It's the bottom left

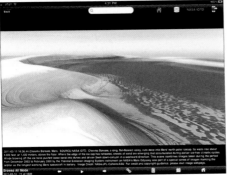

Figure 18-8
The NASA app homepage shows the NASA IOTD and APOD buttons as well as one of the NASA IOTD pages.

button on the front page of the app. If only for these images, I think everyone should take a look at this app.

Right next to the NASA IOTD button is the APOD button—Astronomy Pic of the Day. Another great collection of images … all for free.

HIGH SCHOOL

One of the hardest subjects for me in high school was chemistry. I wish I could blame it on the teachers or outdated textbooks or poor lab equipment, but none of that is true. I just had a really hard time understanding chemistry, and I wish I would have had access

to these apps. They would have made life easier for the high school me, and there's a chance I would've been more interested in the subject and paid more attention. Oh well. Take a look at these cool apps …

The Elements: A Visual Exploration ($13.99)
This app makes the Periodic Table of Elements come alive. It has one drawback; it's huge. At 1.71GB, this app can really take a chunk out of the space on your iPad, especially if you have the 16GB version.

When you open this app, you are presented with the Periodic Table. Just tap on an element to bring up its first page. Here, you get the basic information about the element. Tap on the WolframAlpha link to bring up even more data on the element in question, including current prices if the element price is tracked, like Gold or Platinum. Or get more information on the second page of the element. This is accessed by tapping the Next button on the bottom right of the screen.

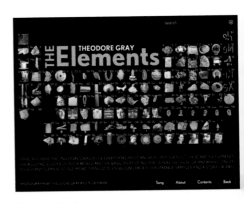

Figure 18-9
In the Periodic Table as shown in the Elements app, each of the element icons is actually moving, which is obviously impossible to show in a still image.

The second page shows a description of the element and images of the element being used. This is where the creators of the app get really fancy. You can rotate any of the images on the page, or double tap on the image to open it full screen. When the image is open full screen, you can rotate it around with a finger and view the object in 3D.

There are two ways to do this: The first involves a special pair of glasses that cost $4.99 plus shipping and handling. The second method is to cross your eyes and look without the glasses. But not everyone can view the 3D objects the second way; I know I can't.

Switch between the two methods by pressing the LR button (which splits the view and puts the image for the left side on the left side and the images for the right side on the right), or you can press the RL button (which switches the position of the two images). The LR setting is meant to used with the glasses, while the RL setting is for those who can see the 3D effect without the glasses.

To order the glasses, tap on the (?) button, which opens the Help screen and allows you to order. If you're a teacher, you can also purchase learning aids though the iPad app here.

Chemical Equation Toolbox ($1.99)
This app is really useful for those students who need to work with chemical equations. It can be used by college students as well. The Chemical Equation Toolbox app allows you to enter chemical equations and see if they are balanced.

One really useful feature is that you can bring up a traditional keyboard as well as a Periodic Table keyboard.

If you need to work with chemical equations, check out this app. It's not expensive and has

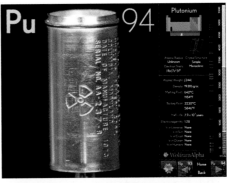

Figure 18-9
The first page shows the element information, and the second page shows the uses. Each of the images depicting uses for the element can be made full screen and viewed in 3D.

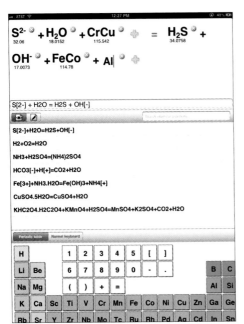

Figure 18-11
You can enter chemicals directly into equations from the Periodic Table in this app.

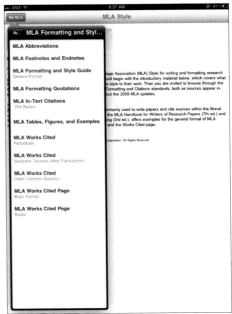

Figure 18-12
MLA information is easy to find using a drop-down menu.

a really intuitive chemical-entry interface. The only thing I find odd is the use of a floppy disc icon as the Save button. Does anyone actually use 3.5 floppy discs anymore?

COLLEGE

Going off to college is a big deal, and anything that can make it easier is a good thing, right? Let's see how the iPad can help.

One of the best uses of the iPad is as an eTextbook reader. It's so much easier to run or bike across campus when carrying a single tablet device with textbooks loaded onto it than a big backpack with all those books weighing it down. Even better, the apps mentioned here allow you to get information on writing papers, renting your eTextbooks and accessing your class information right

from the iPad.

So if you're a student reading this, these are the arguments you need to make to get the iPad for school. Or even better, ask your parents to get you a new iPad 2 so you can video conference using FaceTime with them when they start missing you.

My MLA ($1.99)
This app is a guidebook for students who have to write research papers using the MLA (Modern Language Association) style. The MLA style is used most commonly when writing papers in the liberal arts and humanities. This app offers a complete guide to using the MLA style, including examples of the general format, in-text citations, endnotes/ footnotes and the Works Cited page. My MLA has a ton of information, but

Figure 18-13
This CourseSmart bookshelf shows the textbooks in the library.

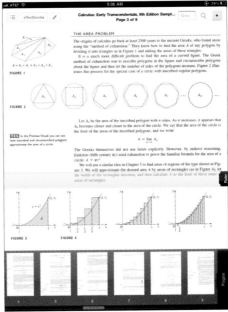

Figure 18-14
The ruler lets you easily keep your place on the page.

The layout is very simple, allowing you to find what you need easily.

There is basically a one-button navigation (top left of the page). You just navigate through the menus until you find the information you need. It's that simple. And having this guide handy can really help any student who has MLA-style papers to write.

eTextbooks by CourseSmart ($FREE)

I was introduced to this app when I was waiting in line to buy the iPad 2. I had a discussion with the guy standing next to me, and it turned out he was a student using the iPad and the eTextbooks app from CourseSmart for his textbook needs.

The idea behind the service is great. You rent electronic versions of your textbooks and then you can access them on your iPad … or your iPhone or computer. When you load the app onto your iPad, walk through a demonstration that shows you what your textbooks will look like.

The main hub of the app is the bookshelf, which stores your textbooks. Tap a book to open it and, wham, the textbook is in front of you. There's one great feature that can really help when reading an eTextbook, and that is the ruler. Activate it with a button on the left side of the page. When you tap it, a transparent ruler appears across the page. Move it up and down as you read to keep you place. Double tap the ruler to make it go away.

Navigation in CourseSmart is also really easy. Just swipe your finger to turn the page or use the Pages tab on the bottom left. A single tap opens a thumbnail view of the pages; swipe through to find the page you need. Or use the Apple pinch-to-zoom gestures to zoom in and out of a page. This is really helpful for those late-night cram sessions, when the text seems to get smaller as the hours pass. This app also

lets you highlight, annotate and share blocks of information. And you can create notes easily with a tap on the Notes button (top right).

Purchase any Online eTextbook through your iPad from the CourseSmart app. Just:

1. Open the CourseSmart app.
2. Sign in to your account.
3. Tap the Shop button that's located in the upper right corner.
4. Search for your eTextbook by entering the ISBN, book title or author's name. Then tap the Search button.
5. Look through the results and tap on the title you want to buy.
6. Tap the Buy Online Subscription button.
7. Enter your billing information and tap Charge Credit Card.
8. You can only rent one eTextbook at a time. So if you need multiple books, you'll have to repeat this process for each one. You can have multiple books on the iPad; you just have to get them one at a time.

Here is the biggest negative of the program … and a very important piece of information: You have to be connected to the Internet for this service to work. That means, you have to be on a Wi-Fi network or attached by 3G to even view an eTextbook.

CourseSmart has announced that the company is working on an offline reader, but it is not available as I write this. So make sure that you have a 3G-enabled iPad with a data plan in place or that there is Wi-Fi where you plan on using this app.

Blackboard Mobile Learn ($FREE)
Many schools use the Blackboard service to either teach entire classes online or as a course management system. And this app is only useful if your school uses it. So the first thing to do when exploring this app is to find out if it's used at your school. Do this by going to the technology department at your school and asking. Or just download the free app and search for your institution. (The second way is much easier.)

When you run the app for the first time, it will ask for the name of your school, so it can start setting up Blackboard for you. When your school appears on the screen, just tap to select it. The Login screen opens. This is where you need to enter your username and password, which should have been supplied by your school. If you don't have one, check with the technology department.

Once in, you can turn on the Remember Me function—a decent idea if you are the only person using your iPad. But if you want to make sure that your roommate or friend can't check out your work and grades, then keep this turned off.

The layout of the app tries to use all the screen real estate of the iPad, and it does a good job. When you log in, a list of the classes you're taking (that are Blackboard-enabled) appears on the left. Tap on the class to open it, and the class menu will appear on a blackboard. Tap any of the choices to open them; the navigation is very intuitive.

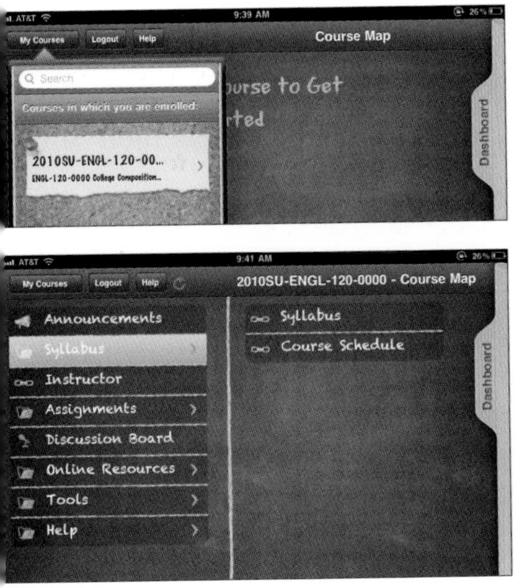

Figure 18-15
The classes in which you're currently enrolled appear on the left. Tap on the class to bring up its information.

> ## TIP
>
> 
>
> If your school uses the no-cost version of the Blackboard Mobile Learn for higher education in the US, Puerto Rico and US Virgin Islands, then you cannot use 3G to access the app—only Wi-Fi.

Blackboard does a great job with this app, allowing students to access their classes from the iPad. It also works for instructors. Log in as an instructor to access all the classes you might be taking and those you are teaching. You can even add and edit content right on the iPad. This makes class management from your iPad convenient and easy.

TED ($FREE)

This is the iPad app for the very popular series of talks put on by TED (Technology, Entertainment, Design) that takes place around the world. The basic idea of this app is to give iPad users access to, as the TED website states, "Riveting talks by remarkable people, free to the world."

The talks are usually not very long, but this program really does feature some of the best presenters in the world talking about subjects that they find to be important. Talks cover a wide range of subjects. For example, you'll find Mark Bezos' speech, "A life lesson from a volunteer firefighter" as well as Madeline Albright's "On being a woman and a diplomat."

The app allows you to save any of the talks for offline viewing. Just tap on the Save Talk button, and the talk will be saved to your iPad for viewing later. Just remember that each saved talk takes up space on your iPad.

I hope that you'll download this app and listen to some of these talks. They really are great.

INDEX